Funding Urban Services

After teaching economics for some years at the Australian National University and publishing *Economic Policy and the Size of Cities*, Max Neutze was appointed the foundation head of the Urban Research Unit in the same university, the first such research group in Australia. A leading urban economist with an international reputation, he has published on housing, urban land, transport and other services, and urban planning. An engagement with policy questions is one of the features of his research and writing. He has been a member of a number of government review and advisory committees.

Max Neutze's publications include *The Suburban Apartment Boom* (on the United States), and two books, *Urban Development in Australia* and *Australian Urban Policy*, which became standard references in the field. Following his recent retirement he is now Emeritus Professor and Visiting Fellow in the Urban Research Program, Australian National University.

# Funding Urban Services

## *Options for physical infrastructure*

Max Neutze

ALLEN & UNWIN

First published in 1997 by
Allen & Unwin
9 Atchison Street
St Leonards NSW 2065
Australia
Phone: (61 2) 9901 4088
Fax: (61 2) 9906 2218
E-mail: frontdesk@allen-unwin.com.au
URL: http://www.allen-unwin.com.au

National Library of Australia
Cataloguing-in-Publication entry:

Neutze, Max.
    Funding urban services: options for physical
    infrastructure.

    Bibliography.
    Includes index.

    ISBN 1 86448 418 7.

    1. Infrastructure (Economics)—Australia. 2. Infrastructure
    (Economics)—Australia—Finance. 3. Urban economics. I. Title.

338.4330994

Set in 10/12 pt Times Roman by DOCUPRO, Sydney
Printed by South Wind Productions, Singapore
10 9 8 7 6 5 4 3 2 1

# Contents

# Acknowledgments

This book has evolved over much of my professional life, starting with a seminar in Oxford convened by the late Denys Munby and including Christopher Foster and Peter Wiles. In recent years I have learnt a great deal from Patrick Troy whose knowledge of the engineering of these services nicely complemented my economics. Timothy Hau, Department of Economics, University of Hong Kong, supplied information about recent developments in proposals to introduce electronic road pricing in that city. James Bond carried out a literature search on estimates of demand elasticities, the results of which are used in Chapter 4. I was helped also by reading the draft manuscript of Stephen Merrett's 1997 book *Introduction to the economics of water resources: an international perspective*, UCL Press, London.

# 1 Introduction: Why study urban physical infrastructure?

In developed and highly urbanised countries the provision of roads and public transport, water, sewerage and drainage, communications and energy, both to and within cities, absorbs a considerable proportion of the total funds available for investment. It is difficult to measure the precise proportion because little of the information about investment identifies whether it is located in urban or rural areas. In this respect estimates made for Australia give a good indication of the situation in other Western countries. In the years 1970–71 to 1973–74, 49 per cent of total gross fixed capital formation occurred in cities, and of that some 18.6 per cent was in physical infrastructure, so that it accounted for just over 9 per cent of all investment (Neutze 1978). More recent estimates are less comprehensive but on the information available it is likely that the proportions have fallen to some extent.

The Industry Commission (1994a, Table A3.5) estimated that 40 per cent of total road expenditure in 1991–92 occurred in urban areas, and of the $2.1 billion of total road expenditure in urban areas, $1.2 billion was investment. The Commission's estimates of investment in urban rail systems in the same year (Table B1.3) show that it accounted for 58 per cent of the Australian total. Using a different measure, information on the value of water and sewerage assets in 1989–90 (Industry Commission 1992, Table D.1) shows that 54 per cent were used for the provision of services in metropolitan areas, a further 34 per cent for services in smaller centres and for water supply in rural areas, and the remainder for irrigation. No similar figures are readily available for gas, electricity or for communications but the great majority of the consumption of each of these services occurs in urban areas.

Physical infrastructure accounts for an even higher proportion of public investment. In 1991–92, 55 per cent of gross fixed capital formation by state and local governments was in water, sewerage and drainage, fuel and energy, and road and rail transport. In the same year, 65 per cent of total gross fixed capital formation by all governments combined was on the above services, together with communication and other forms of transport. Of this total, two-thirds was spent by state, territory and local governments and one-third by the Commonwealth, mainly on air transport and communications. The other major items of public capital expenditure are schools, colleges and universities, hospitals, housing and community services and recreational and cultural facilities. Most of this expenditure is on social infrastructure, which is not covered in this study.

Investment in physical infrastructure is a very important commitment for all levels of government, and a particularly important commitment for state and local governments. When state and local governments are short of funds it is generally politically easier for them to reduce (defer) capital expenditure than current expenditure. Because physical infrastructure accounts for such a large proportion of their capital expenditure they have little option but to reduce their expenditure on it, and many of those cuts fall in urban areas.

Why is the provision of these services a collective responsibility? In sparsely settled rural areas it is possible for individual families to draw their water from the nearest creek, to sink a well or build a dam and to dispose of their wastes in a sump. If the conditions are favourable and the holdings large enough, the neighbours will not be affected. It may be efficient also for the family to generate its own electric power. But when the family wants to communicate with others or to travel somewhere else it is almost certain they will use public roads or railways and post and telephone services that will carry the vehicles and messages of other families as well as their own. If they are close enough to urban areas to use the much cheaper electricity available from large generators, they will do so through mains that supply their neighbours also.

In urban areas there are even greater economic advantages in using networks that supply the transport and communication requirements of many members of the community. For water and sewerage, the reasons for collective rather than individual provision are different: as the density of settlement increases, the waste from one family is likely to foul the water supply of other families downstream in the drainage catchment. Collective provision of water and of water-borne sewerage in urban areas was developed first as a public health measure and to reduce the nuisance resulting from individual means of disposing of noxious wastes.

Individual provision of water in cities involves collecting rainwater from roofs or sinking individual wells where groundwater conditions are suitable. Rainwater tanks can be a significant source of supply where rainfall is high and reliable enough, despite the fact that the cost of tanks is relatively high. In most urban areas tanks need to be supplemented by collective supply, especially in high density residential areas, and such a source of supply is inadequate for many industrial and commercial activities. Except in cities where the supply of high quality groundwater is very large, individual wells are unlikely to provide an adequate supply for all users, and without charges related to the volume of withdrawals they can result in inefficient use of a valuable collective resource and depletion of stocks. Notwithstanding the limitations of private provision of water, there are good economic and environmental reasons for greater reliance on it than has occurred in recent years.

Wastes that are currently disposed of through urban sewerage systems are of two main kinds. 'Sullage' is the term generally used for the 'grey water' that results from washing clothes, dishes and human bodies. It contains soap and detergents and small amounts of non-infectious and inoffensive wastes. Where soil conditions are suitable it can be used for irrigation of lawns and gardens, but this is possible only where there are suitable areas of lawns and gardens and where storage is possible prior to its use. The second kind is human excreta which is both offensive and often infectious. Composting toilets capable of converting these wastes into harmless and inoffensive materials suitable for use as fertiliser are being developed. Both of these individual means of dealing with wastes require gardens and lawns close to where they are being generated, which is rarely the case in high density residential or commercial and industrial areas. Until these innovative means of individual waste disposal are adopted more widely, cities will continue to rely mainly on collective provision of water-borne sewerage systems.

There are other services for which the investment in infrastructure is much smaller but which provide networks of services. The classic example is the postal service which is a collective way of transferring documents and parcels that is much more efficient, if slower, than sending them individually. Individuals can compost or burn the solid waste they generate but for many kinds of solid wastes neither is practicable. Furthermore, burning is often banned for environmental reasons and composting is possible only where there is adequate space. Whether they are to be dumped or recycled, solid wastes have to be collected and that is more efficiently done collectively. It is much cheaper for households and other small producers of solid wastes to have their garbage collected by the same truck that collects the garbage of their neighbours.

The third service of this kind is public transport. Public roads and pathways are required for any movement of goods and people by land. Some of the movements of people are more efficiently undertaken in vehicles that carry large numbers: that is by public transport.

## Environmental and health issues

There is a two-way interaction between the provision of infrastructure services on the one hand and health and the quality of the environment on the other. In one direction, many of these services were first introduced to protect and improve environmental quality and health. This is most obviously the case for sewerage and solid waste disposal, the purpose of which is to reduce the nuisance and the public health risks that result from the unregulated individual disposal of different kinds of wastes. It is also true of the provision of a supply of potable water, which was needed to ensure that water was safe to drink. An adequate supply of water was necessary also for the water-borne sewerage systems that were introduced late in the nineteenth century. Drainage was needed to cope with water which fell in such quantities during heavy rainstorms that it could not be absorbed into the ground. As cities developed, increasing areas were covered by roads, roofs and other impervious surfaces and the proportion of rainfall that ran off, the speed at which it ran off and the flooding that resulted all increased. Better roads were needed to deal with the congestion caused first by slow horse-drawn vehicles and later by motor vehicles. Electricity and gas supplies were introduced in part to reduce the pollution in urban areas from coal and wood fires and steam trains.

But few of these services are able to fully eliminate the environmental damage and health problems they were designed to deal with, and a number of them bring new kinds of environmental degradation and health risks. For example, before sewage reaches treatment facilities some of it leaks out into urban watercourses. During periods of heavy rain rainwater leaks into the sewers, causing them to overflow into drains and creeks. Even with secondary treatment of sewage, a large volume of nutrients, mainly phosphates and nitrates, is discharged in the treated effluent into natural water bodies. The resulting growth of algae reduces the level of oxygen and causes algal blooms which kill fish and make the water toxic and dangerous to swimmers. With only primary treatment the discharges can contain offensive material and may also contain dangerous pathogens. Sewerage systems move most of the sewage out of urban areas, though sometimes only to their ocean borders, and they remove most of the harmful and offensive material before it is discharged into the environment. As cities grow the absolute volume of sewage increases, so that ever higher standards of transmission and treatment are required to limit danger to health and damage to the environment.

Stormwater drains have traditionally been designed to move water as quickly as possible from residential and commercial areas towards natural watercourses and the coast. Because the water runs off and moves more quickly than it did prior to urban development, the intensity of the flooding downstream from a given intensity of rainfall is increased, and if the downstream parts of the drainage basins are also within the urban area, drainage systems transfer the problem and make flooding in low-lying areas greater.

The provision of piped water supplies collected in bushland or rural areas and from underground aquifers, and their treatment to kill any pathogens, has removed many of the traditional sources of water-borne diseases. But it has introduced new diseases resulting from the proliferation of pathogens, some of which are resistant to most methods of water treatment, in reservoirs and water mains. Furthermore, the chlorination of water itself, especially in the presence of organic matter, is suspected of releasing carcinogenic products into the water supply. The collection and storage of water in dams for urban use floods river valleys and reduces water-flows downstream. When the water is used for irrigation in urban or rural areas it washes nutrients into the drains and thence into natural watercourses.

The impact of urban transport on the environment is profound; most notably the use of motor vehicles in urban areas produces air pollution, reducing amenity, causing respiratory problems and lead poisoning. All forms of transport that rely directly or indirectly on the burning of fossil fuel increase the volume of carbon dioxide in the air and contribute to global warming through the greenhouse effect. Transport is also one of the main sources of noise nuisance in urban areas, and road accidents are one of the major causes of injuries and premature death.

The use of electricity creates greenhouse gases in the locations where it is generated, and the use of gas produces them where the gas is burnt, often within urban areas, but since the greenhouse effect is global rather than local, location does not matter. Solid waste collection and disposal moves large volumes of waste from within the urban area to landfill sites, usually on the outskirts of urban areas, where it reduces local amenity and, unless well managed, can cause water pollution. Telecommunication, with its unsightly poles and wires, has its own impact on the environment. Users of the new mobile phone technology also receive low level electromagnetic radiation. The only effect of the postal system is its modest contribution to the volume of traffic in urban areas.

Until relatively recently the environmental effects of the use of urban infrastructure services have been regarded as of secondary importance, but they have now become of greater concern to most people. New priorities have been established which see more resources being put into reducing the environmental impact of infrastructure, for example through improved sewage treatment, the phasing out of lead in petrol and the introduction of vehicle emission controls. New technologies are being introduced that collect stormwater and treat sewage near their origin and thus reduce the need for drains and sewers, and permit the stormwater and the treated effluent from sewage treatment to be reused locally. These new technologies in turn suggest that new locally oriented institutions might be needed to provide infrastructure services to meet demands in sections of large metropolitan areas leading to much less reliance on massive city-wide networks.

The amount of pollution produced by infrastructure services varies with the extent to which the services are used. New funding mechanisms that rely more on user charges to discourage excessive use of the services also reduce the damage their use inflicts on the environment. These funding mechanisms have environmental as well as economic advantages.

## Infrastructure and land-use planning

The costs of providing infrastructure and the revenue that it will yield vary with the location of the development it serves. For example, it is more expensive to provide roads and hydraulic services in rocky areas and hilly topography, and it is almost always more costly to provide services in places that are remote from existing service networks. In addition, the ability of suppliers to predict when and where their infrastructure will be needed has an important influence on their ability to plan efficiently, to achieve a high level of use of its capacity and thereby to reduce the cost per unit of service provided. Land-use planning can assist in both of these respects. Land-use plans take account of the costs of servicing development in different locations along with the demand for development in different locations. If planning and control are effective, that is, if changes in land use follow the plans, they increase the efficiency of infrastructure services in two ways. First, they limit development in locations which are expensive to service and second, they increase the predictability of the location and sequencing of development.

Similarly the implementation of land-use plans can be greatly strengthened if suppliers of services use them as the basis for their demand projections and investment programs. Thus the availability of road access encourages development, and access to both water and sewerage are necessary for development. Lack of access to these services similarly reinforces land-use planning decisions that an area should be withheld from development either permanently or for a period. Given the responsibility of governments for both the provision of most infrastructure and land-use planning, it is somewhat surprising that they have not required that land-use and servicing plans be developed together and that they be implemented in such a way as to complement one another in the interests of improving amenity and the environment and of efficiency in the use of resources.

There are several reasons why this has not occurred in the past, and why it has begun to occur to a greater extent in recent years. First, most of the public authorities responsible for the provision of infrastructure were established long before the Australian states began to take land-use planning seriously after World War II. The service authorities were well established and powerful bureaucratic organisations responsible to senior ministers long before the

7

planning authorities were created, usually under junior ministers. Second, the providers of infrastructure were large spenders on capital items and, in order to avoid political interference in their day-to-day operations, had a tradition of some independence of the elected government. Planning, however, despite its professional basis, inevitably made some people more and others less wealthy and therefore was an intensely political activity that an elected government could ignore only at its peril.

Third, a number of service authorities had a degree of financial independence of the governments to which they were responsible. For example, a large proportion of the road funds of both local councils and state road authorities came from Commonwealth-levied petrol taxes as earmarked funds rather than from the council's or the state's budget or state loans. Electricity authorities were able to raise much of the investment funds they needed from their own revenue because of the buoyant demand for electricity. Telephones, airports and postal services were provided by the Commonwealth government, which was neither responsible for land-use planning nor subject to state and local planning controls.

Water and sewerage authorities, however, relied mainly on property rates for their current revenue and funded most of their investment through long-term loans amortised from rate revenue. As a result they were less independent of state governments because they had to rely heavily on getting a share of the borrowing rights allocated to each state by the (Commonwealth–State) Loan Council. Also, the level of water and sewerage rates, which are taxes related to some degree to ability to pay rather than a price for a service, were more of a political issue than the price of electricity or of telephone calls.

For reasons described in the next section, the investment funds available to service authorities have fallen significantly since the early 1980s. As a result their ability to provide services for new areas of urban development has been severely limited and they have been forced to seek ways of reducing the demands for new services and alternative ways of obtaining investment funds. One way to economise on investment funds was to ensure that land was released for development in a sequence which allowed the service authorities to plan efficient staging of their investments. This required a greater emphasis on timing as part of land-use planning than had previously been the case. Each of the planning authorities in the state capitals developed land-release programs which projected which areas would be released each, say five-year, period. An important consideration in deciding on the release programs is the cost of the infrastructure necessary to provide services to the release areas (NCPA 1993a). It was possible to use land-use controls also to restrict development to locations that can be serviced at minimal cost. This has increasingly been occurring in both the long and the short term. Land that is expensive to service will not be included in the release areas, and of the land included in those areas, that which can be serviced at minimal cost will be released first. An example of the first is land in the Hawkesbury catchment in Sydney which would require very costly investment in the control of surface run-off to avoid unacceptable reduction in the water quality in the river. An example of the second is the choice of areas for immediate development in the eastern suburbs of Melbourne where there are major roads and trunk sewers available with the capacity to take the extra load the new development would impose.

## Periodic crises in adequacy of supply

As urban settlements grow and as standards of living and expectations of amenity and environmental quality increase, the supply of infrastructure services increases to meet those expectations, but supply seldom increases steadily in proportion to demand. Rather, supply increases in spurts interspersed by periods during which the quality of services gradually declines until there is a crisis of sufficient magnitude to stimulate the government to remedy the situation. To some degree these periodic crises are a reflection of cycles that occur in government expenditure as politicians and voters swing between being preoccupied in one period with the inefficiency of the public sector and in another period with the need to improve the quality of the environment and the amenity of the cities in which people live. The problem was well captured by John Kenneth Galbraith's phrase, 'private affluence and public squalor', coined in the post World War II period following the years of neglect of public investment during the depression of the 1930s and diversion of public funds to the war effort. The period of the long boom which followed saw many of these inadequacies in public investment overcome.

To some extent also the 'spurt effect' reflects swings between periods of rapid economic growth when it is relatively easy for governments to raise revenue and times of recession when there is strong resistance to taxation. Periods of rapid population growth, however, put greater demands on infrastructure. It was the post-war growth in Australia's population due to immigration and the baby boom, following low investment since the 1920s, which put a severe strain on public investment in the 1950s and led to the introduction of requirements that developers pay the cost of providing infrastructure needed to serve new developments.

There is, however, another reason for periodic crises. A high proportion of the cost of providing most physical infrastructure services is the cost of providing and maintaining the capital assets required. Investment in capital assets takes two main forms. The most obvious is the additional capacity needed to serve new demand. In the case of infrastructure services this new demand often takes the form of new urban development which needs new investment to connect it to the existing networks. In most countries this investment is now the responsibility of developers of the new property and the assets are transferred free of charge to the authority responsible for provision of the services.

The other form of addition to capacity is in the headworks, hydraulic and energy supply mains, arterial roads and public transport. The following two chapters describe in some detail the effect of increases in demand on the quality of service provided by infrastructure of given capacity. The decline in the quality of service occurs first in places where there are bottlenecks and at periods of peak demand. As demand grows throughout the system these episodic, sometimes sporadic, problems are frequently tolerated for long periods while more urgent needs for investment are met. There is a general lack of awareness of the limits to capacity within the established networks, except in the case of arterial roads and freeways where congestion makes road users very conscious of it. The advocates of urban infill and consolidation frequently make the assumption that there is adequate capacity in hydraulic services to cater for any increase in demand that will result. It is only when a crisis occurs, when the sewers or treatment facilities overflow and seriously pollute local streams, where water pressure is insufficient to fight a fire, where power cuts or restrictions on water supply are required or when congestion on a major road reaches an intolerable level that governments find the pressure to devote a large amount of resources to investment in these services irresistible.

While investment in increasing the capacity of the existing networks is easy to defer for a short time when demands for government funds are high relative to their supply, many forms of expenditure on maintenance and replacement of existing assets can be deferred almost indefinitely. Underspending on maintenance of durable assets is not limited to urban infrastructure; it is pervasive among owners of public buildings. It is generally more urgent to provide some new facility than to adequately maintain the assets that are already in place, and nobody erects plaques to a minister who initiates a program of spending on deferred maintenance. The users who depend on the availability of the new facility are a concentrated pressure group; those who might be affected by the decline in the quality of service from existing facilities are dispersed. Especially where the facilities are underground and their deterioration is unobservable until a breakdown occurs, the only pressure for more maintenance comes from the engineers and managers to whom it is obvious that expenditure on maintenance and replacement will bring a very good return: a stitch in time saves nine. Only when roads become impassable because of deterioration or are blocked by collapsed sewers, when water mains burst, roads and houses are flooded during rainstorms, is there support for a program of maintenance and replacement.

Changes in many countries can be illustrated by those that have occurred in Australia where there has been a gradual decline in the proportion of Gross Domestic Product accounted for by Government Gross Fixed Capital Expenditure since the 1970s and a sharp decline since the mid 1980s. The percentage, which had been between 7 and 9 per cent almost every year from 1949–50 to 1986–87 fell to around 5 per cent in 1992–93. Some of the fall occurred in electricity where there was excessive investment in the early 1980s in anticipation of a resources boom which did not eventuate, but from a longer-term perspective that over-investment simply disguised, for a period, the general decline since the late 1970s in the proportion of the country's resources that were being put into capital expenditure on infrastructure. Apart from electricity, the declines occurred mainly in roads, water, sewerage and drainage.

This long-term decline occurred for several reasons. The first was the end of the long boom and the onset of recession in the economy, with unemployment rising from around 2 per cent of the workforce in the early 1970s to 8 to 10 per cent in the early 1990s. The rate of growth of output slowed considerably, so that it became less easy for governments to fund the new capital expenditure from economic growth, especially when it had to pay unemployment benefits to an increasing proportion of the workforce. To make matters worse consumption continued to rise, a good deal of it being satisfied by imports. Export income was adversely affected by a decline in the price of Australia's exports relative to its imports. As a result, Australia had to borrow from other countries to pay for some of its imports. The opening of the Australian economy and financial system to international competition made it impossible to deal with these problems by restricting imports as had occurred in earlier years. The only way to restrain the demand for imports was to reduce demand in general.[1] The ways to do this were to use monetary policy—increasing interest rates—or fiscal policy—raising taxes or reducing public expenditure—either of which would increase unemployment.

Increased taxes would at least have had the advantage of providing the government with more revenue, which might have reduced the expenditure constraints and permitted more to be spent on infrastructure. But the microeconomic reform programs of governments in recent years have stressed the need to open all sectors of the economy to competition, which is easiest to achieve if as many functions as possible are carried out in the private sector. This policy is based on the belief that because private firms compete for resources and for custom, and if they do not succeed will go out of business, they are more efficient users of resources than governments or government business enterprises (Industry Commission 1989). Under this reform program increases in taxes, including property rates to fund water and sewerage services, were out of favour for two reasons: first, because they make markets less efficient by reducing incentives and making prices higher than resource costs; and second, because higher taxes permit higher government expenditure which is regarded as inefficient if not unproductive. Government expenditure on infrastructure was especially unpopular among the reformers because the services that result are often provided at zero price, or at prices less than their full resource costs. As a result there is excessive demand and to meet it the infrastructure authorities are believed to over-invest.[2] Because these beliefs were driving the policy agenda, despite the increased burden of paying unemployment benefits (personal benefit payments increased from 10 to 11 per cent of GDP between 1984–85 and 1991–92) the proportion of GDP levied in taxes fell slightly (from 30.7 to 30.2 per cent between 1984–85 and 1991–92).

With revenues growing very slowly and expenditures on the unemployed growing more quickly, the Commonwealth cut its payments to the states (from 9.1 to 7.7 per cent of GDP). Faced with a severe reduction in revenue but with growing demands for funds for education, health and the other services for which it is responsible, the states looked to other sources for revenue, including their business enterprises. The states required their business enterprises to provide a dividend on the net value of their assets, even though the great majority of these had been provided by users of the services rather than the state governments. In effect this resulted in a tax on the use of the services. Public authorities providing infrastructure, in accord with prudent management practice, frequently put much of their provisions for depreciation into sinking funds that were set aside for the future renewals of their assets when they reached the ends of their lives. These funds were raided by the state governments. In effect this amounted to a tax on future consumers of these services who will have to pay more than their share of the cost of replacing assets. In addition, both state and Commonwealth business enterprises that own assets have been seen as sources of additional funds to reduce budget deficits or to avoid raising taxes by selling off assets that were paid for over the years by users of their services. Finally, these enterprises have been forced to defer maintenance, further reducing the value of assets owned by governments.

Each of these activities has been justified politically as being needed to reduce government deficits. But selling off assets to pay for current expenditure is only a short-term measure and makes the community as represented by its government poorer. This can be disguised in the short term only because governments do not produce balance sheets. If they did, it would be clear that these sales are neutral with respect to public wealth under the following condition: if the revenue from the sale was used to pay off public debt and the savings in interest cost that resulted equalled the expected flow of net returns from the enterprise. If, as recent research by John Quiggin (1994) suggests, the saving in interest that occurred has generally been smaller, the sale made the government and its citizens poorer. Even when they are neutral overall, they lead to a redistribution of wealth between generations and between regions. These issues are discussed in more detail in Chapter 9.

**Policy options**

Four broad kinds of policies have been proposed, and to varying degrees adopted, to deal with the problems discussed above. The first is to change the institutional framework within which infrastructure services are provided. The most commonly recommended change is some form of privatisation, a term used to describe a range of measures, some of which are alternatives and others complementary. The second is to change the form or the structure of urban areas in such a way that it is less costly to provide them with infrastructure services, and the cities are more environmentally sustainable. The most commonly recommended change in form is consolidation. The third is to introduce new kinds of technology in order to reduce both the cost of infrastructure services and the environmental impact of the city on the natural environment. The fourth is to change the way in which infrastructure services are funded. The proposed change here is to place less reliance on property taxes, fuel taxes and developer charges, and more on user charges.

This book argues that privatisation has little to contribute to dealing with the problems that have been identified. It concentrates on alternative funding mechanism and argues for greater reliance on user charges. A recent book by Patrick Troy (1996) deals, inter alia, with changes in the form of urban areas in the context of a critique of urban policy in Australia. It argues that consolidation is unlikely to result in the large savings in infrastructure costs which are often claimed for it, and that new technologies have the potential both to save cost and to reduce the damage to the environment.

*Privatisation*

Steps were taken to limit direct government control over the provision of some infrastructure services, soon after they became government responsibilities, by creating statutory authorities at arm's length from the government to ensure that ministers did not become involved in the day-to-day operations. The objectives were to avoid political involvement in their detailed operation and to ensure that sound business principles were followed. These relatively independent authorities were expected to operate much like a private company. A different kind of private sector involvement was introduced in the late 1950s and early 1960s when developers became responsible for the reticulation of infrastructure within their subdivisions. This was later extended to include a contribution to the off-site infrastructure costs that were incurred to serve the demands resulting from a subdivision.

Although these authorities began their operations using contractors for construction, once they developed their capacity to directly supervise works they began to rely on large day labour forces in which there was a daily contract with individual workers. This had the great advantage that there was a high degree of flexibility in their levels of employment but the blue-collar workers had no security, even when they worked for the authority over many years. Since World War II there has been a decline in the use of day labour and an increase in the use of private firms as contractors for some of the design and most if not all of the construction work. In the last decade contracting out has extended beyond construction to include operation of some facilities such as water purification and treatment plants and sections of freeways. In other cases the operation of existing assets has been contracted out to the private sector. If the public authority pays the private firm a fee for operating the facility, these contractual arrangements can be considered in principle as an extension of construction contracts, though they introduce new questions relating to the sharing of risks because of the time over which they operate.

The degree of privatisation and the nature of the risks to be shared increase in scope when the private operator receives its revenue directly from the public through the sale of the service. Finally, privatisation reaches its greatest level when the investment decisions and some of the risks that accompany them are made by the private firm. This may result from the sale of a whole operation to a private firm, for example, sale of the Hunter District Water Board, or sale of part of an operation, for example, the water retailing operations of a section of Melbourne Water or sale of part of the generating capacity of the State Electricity Commission of Victoria. As discussed in Chapter 9, these transfers raise major questions in relation to who bears the risks and the need for regulation of a private firm operating in a situation in which a monopoly is sanctioned by government.

*User charges*

The funding of different elements of urban infrastructure has relied on very different kinds of mechanisms. Electricity, gas, telephones, public transport and postal services have relied heavily on user charges based on the extent of use of the service. The first three have used fixed access charges also, and public transport has received significant subsidies from government to cover its deficits. Loans amortised from operating revenue, but guaranteed by the parent government, have been the source of finance for investment. Water, sewerage and drainage and garbage services have traditionally been funded from property taxes (rates) with government guaranteed loans used for capital expenditure. In the late 1950s and early 1960s a significant amount of the cost of capital expenditure on hydraulic services began to be funded through developers, either by way of cash contributions or assets constructed by developers and transferred free of charge to the authority responsible for provision of the services. In the past decade there has been an increase in the use of charges per unit of water used. Local roads were funded from local rates until the introduction of developer requirements and developer charges, which relieved local councils of a significant proportion of that cost. Since the 1920s arterial roads and more recently urban freeways have been funded primarily from a tax on motor fuels.

One of the disadvantages of reliance on taxes of different kinds to fund the provision of urban infrastructure is that users are encouraged to use the service without considering the cost of providing it and without considering the effect on the environment. It is argued in following chapters that charges that vary with the extent of use of a service are the most desirable source of funds and that such charges should replace most other kinds of funding, including access charges and property rates, and should replace also part of the revenue currently being collected through developers. It would be necessary still to finance capital expenditure from loans which would be amortised from the revenue from user charges. It is suggested also that developers continue to be responsible for the cost of reticulation of services within their subdivisions and for connecting them to existing networks.

This book shows that there are many similarities between conditions of supply and demand in the various urban infrastructure services it covers. Its recommendations for greater reliance on user charges simply argue that the methods of funding of gas, electricity and telephones can and should be extended to the funding of roads, water, sewerage, drainage and garbage.

# 2 The nature of physical infrastructure services

## Physical and social infrastructure

Infrastructure may be defined as 'the network of services in a society which are essential for its cohesion and for the efficient functioning of the economy' (*Penguin and Macquarie Dictionary of Economics and Finance* 1988). According to Katz (1982) the term was introduced in the early 1950s. It has been much used in development economics to mean 'social overhead capital', which may be divided into economic overhead capital such as much of transport, energy and telecommunications which provides services to industry, and social capital such as education, police and health services which provides services to people. Frequently the same services are used by both. Grant (1982) records that the term first entered the planner's vocabulary:

> in the narrower sense as describing physical services upon which new development is dependent, such as roads and streets, drains and sewers and water supply. But it has been given an extended meaning in more recent years as including the whole range of services and facilities affected by new development, such as education, health care, social services, recreational facilities and other amenities.

There are several different senses in which infrastructure services can be seen as being 'public' rather than 'private':

1  They are normally provided by governments (education, health, open space, public transport and roads); or
2  They are 'public utilities' which means that all properties in a particular area are normally supplied by the same network

(telephones, electricity, water, sewerage or gas). Public utilities also have an obligation to supply services to all users within the service area who want them.

Most public utilities also are either provided by government or, where provided by the private sector, are subject to regulation. The distinction between physical and social infrastructure throws some light on the nature of these services. Physical (or economic) infrastructure is sometimes defined as providing services to property while social infrastructure provides services to people. It is more accurate to say that physical infrastructure services are provided to occupants of property at the property they occupy, while social infrastructure services are provided at particular locations to which users are expected to travel. A little more broadly, physical infrastructure services are provided where people live and work or provide links between places where people work, live and carry out other social, economic and cultural activities. On that definition this book will be dealing with physical and not with social infrastructure. The services included are water supply, sewerage, stormwater drainage, solid waste disposal, roads, public transport, electricity, gas and telecommunications.

Physical infrastructure produces services rather than goods, and services are distinguished by the fact that they have to be consumed where they are produced. Water, for example, can be thought of as a commodity or a good which has only a small value or, on occasions such as rainstorms or floods, a negative value. Water supply, however, is a service which involves delivering potable water to particular locations at particular pressure. Sewage is a commodity with a decided negative value but sewerage services collect sewage from particular locations and dispose of it in ways that cause little damage to people and the natural environment. Transport is a service that moves goods and people from particular origins to particular destinations over particular routes. Similarly electricity and gas supplies deliver energy to particular locations and telephone services permit messages to be transmitted between particular pairs of locations, or sometimes multiple locations. All of these services have other important characteristics, but location is one that must be taken into account in studying their supply and demand, the appropriate institutions for providing them, and how they should be funded.

Physical infrastructure conjures up the image of something like a road, pipe or wire in, on or above the ground. Perhaps the most useful criterion for judging the·extent to which a service is provided through physical infrastructure is the proportion of the costs that are used to provide a physical network of this kind, though garbage removal, postal services and bus public transport have nothing more physical than a network of routes on the public road system. Ownership of the networks is increasingly separated from ownership of the services provided through the networks, a separation that has always existed with roads. Services become less dependent on infrastructure the less they rely on fixed networks; for example, it is arguable that taxi services rely on the road network, but not to any extent on their own networks. Telephone services, which have been firmly based on a network of copper wires and more recently optical fibres, are breaking free by the use of mobile phones, satellites and 'wireless' communications. They may in the future cease to rely on a physical network.

The boundary between physical infrastructure and other kinds of services is not entirely clear and it changes over time. For example, taxis provide public transport, though not over a fixed network of routes, and local open space provides services to people in the locality where they live, but does not involve a network. They are not considered here because neither involves a network. Most if not all infrastructure services are provided by public enterprises in at least some Western countries.

Social infrastructure services are provided by government (though rarely only by government) mainly because it is believed they should be available irrespective of ability to pay, or because they provide public goods or merit goods. Services provided by physical infrastructure, on the other hand, are provided by the public sector or by regulated private firms, because of the inefficiency or instability of competitive private provision. For this reason they are often known as natural monopolies. Since physical infrastructure services are provided publicly for efficiency rather than equity reasons, equity considerations are less important in considering how they should be funded than is the case with social infrastructure services. The relative merits of alternative charging mechanisms are discussed in Chapter 6.

## Particular features of physical infrastructure services

Physical infrastructure services have a number of features that distinguish them from other industries and that influence the choice of method of funding.

## Location specificity

Like all services they are consumed at the same place as they are produced: they cannot be transported but are provided at a location or over a particular route. From the users' point of view services provided at different locations or over different routes are different products, and may not even be close substitutes.

## Networks

Each has a network which is used for moving energy, materials, information, goods or people. The relative importance of the network in the total cost of providing different physical infrastructure services varies considerably. Thus the cost of producing and transporting electricity and gas to a city is large relative to the cost of distributing it within the city. For example, in 1991–92, 70 per cent of the expenditure of the electricity segment of ACT Electricity and Water, which buys all its electricity from outside the ACT, was spent on purchase, and only 30 per cent on distribution within Canberra and administration. Expressed another way, in 1991–92 62.4 cents revenue was collected per dollar of value of electricity network assets. By comparison, because the network costs of water supply and sewerage are a much higher proportion of the total cost of supplying those services, it collected only 7.6 cents per dollar value of the water supply network assets and 10.1 cents per dollar value of sewerage network assets.

## Natural monopolies

Physical infrastructure providers are natural monopolies because of economies of scale in their networks. As a result it is generally cheaper for a single network to provide services to all consumers located close to one another, and it is often cheaper for one network to provide services to all consumers in larger areas.

These economies are of two kinds. The first applies especially to those links in the various networks that have the lowest capacity, generally those closest to consumers. They are present, but less important, in the links with higher capacity. Economies of scale in pipes and wires mean that the capacity increases more rapidly than the cost. For example, the cost of a pipe increases roughly in proportion to the radius but its capacity increases in proportion to the cross-sectional area, which rises with the radius squared. Scale economies arise in the provision of roads because each property uses its access road for only a tiny fraction of the time it is available, and all of the users combined do not use nearly the full capacity of the minimum-width safe road. As a result it is less expensive to have the residents in a street served by the same water, sewer, gas and electricity main and the same access road and to have excess rain go into the same drain. Economies of scale in the provision of public transport arise mainly in the costs borne by users rather than in the costs to providers (Mohring 1972). The greater the number of riders who use public transport in a particular corridor, the greater the (temporal) frequency of services that can be provided, and the greater the (spatial) density of routes that can be serviced. As a result the distance users have to walk from their homes or workplaces to public transport and the time they have to wait will be shorter.

Similarly there are economies resulting from the same garbage truck collecting the garbage from all houses in a street, and from a single bus collecting all the passengers who want to travel on a particular route at a particular time. Because the same economies occur in links with larger capacity and because of the advantage of being able to travel readily from any place to any other place without changing the network, there are economies from having single networks serving larger areas. In some networks, however, these economies disappear above a certain level of capacity, for example, enough passengers on a route to fill large buses providing a high frequency service or enough users of a road to fill it to capacity at peak periods.

The second kind of economy results from the fact that it may be cheaper to serve different kinds of users using a single network. For example, residential demand for water is heaviest outside working hours and commercial demand heaviest during working hours. If both kinds of users are served by the same network they make better use of capacity than if they were served by separate networks.

These two kinds of economies comprise a much more restricted reason than is usually given for natural monopolies. In particular they do not imply that there are decreasing costs in the supply of any of these services to a large urban area as the urban area grows. The economies from connectedness of a network that make it easier to travel throughout a city if the roads all connect and public transport services are coordinated tend to make them natural monopolies. But, for reasons given in Chapter 3, there are also diseconomies in very large networks and it is arguable that many infrastructure services experience increasing costs as the city they are serving grows and their outputs expand with it.

Networks of different kinds have different cost characteristics from individual links in the network. For example, there may be economies of scale in a road link because capacity rises more rapidly than road width and because shoulders and median strips are a fixed cost. Nevertheless the network may suffer increasing costs as the density of traffic increases because delays at intersections become longer. On the other hand, it may be very costly to expand an existing road but much less expensive to expand network capacity by building a new road nearby to relieve congestion on the existing road.

These reasons for natural monopoly do not apply to social infrastructure. Hence there are few if any cost penalties from private schools and hospitals competing with one another and with their public counterparts, but competitive *distributors* of water, gas or electricity offering services to customers living in the same locality are very rare (though there may be competitive *producers* using the same distribution network). British experience with deregulation (Chapter 9) shows that it is uncommon for there to be competitive bus services on routes with a high density of demand, but it may not be inefficient (Industry Commission 1994a). The introduction of competition in telecommunications is partly based on communication other than through a physical network and partly on competitive transmission facilities over high volume routes and sharing the use of networks over lower volume routes. Traditional arguments about economies of scale have been used to justify having single authorities responsible for each of these services throughout a metropolitan area, and in some cases throughout a state. The conclusions are often correct but for different reasons.

*Privileges and obligations*

For reasons outlined above, providers of infrastructure services often are granted a monopoly over the provision of services within a service area or at least along a bus or garbage collection route. In return, like public carriers in the transport industry, they are obliged to meet all demands from within that area.

In the nineteenth century water services were first provided in cities by private firms in an unregulated market. One result was that there were indeed multiple mains in individual streets and the streets were frequently dug up to repair, replace or lay new mains.

In times of water shortage, companies would discontinue supply to low income suburbs because it was more profitable to supply to higher income areas. In order to be equitable and to avoid complex cost calculations, supply authorities often levy the same annual charge or the same level of property taxes on each class of property, or the same price per unit of service, to consumers throughout their supply area. When costs vary greatly between parts of a service area, it is arguable that the resulting cross-subsidies are not equitable, and can result in demands for services from potential customers who can be serviced only at a loss. These equity issues are discussed in Chapter 6.

*Capital intensity*

Most, but not all, physical infrastructure services are capital intensive in that the capital cost of capacity is a high proportion of the total cost of the service. The extreme case of this is probably water supply. It is possible to conceive of a city whose water supply system consisted of dams which collected water which did not need to be treated, service reservoirs and distribution mains all fed by gravity. The only costs of operation would be maintaining the capital assets and charging the customers. Much the same could be true of a modern telephone system, though it does require modest amounts of electricity and most modern telephone systems are involved in providing value-added services. Capital intensity has important implications for calculation of the marginal cost of some of these services. Once installed, capacity costs are sunk so that there is very little variation in cost with the volume of water provided or the number of telephone calls made as long as there is adequate capacity. These implications are taken up in Chapter 3. For other services such as thermal electricity, garbage collection and public transport, purchase of fuel or labour costs are relatively more important and hence the variable costs are a higher proportion of total costs.

*Durability, specialisation and immobility*

Many of the assets that provide physical infrastructure are durable, specialised and immobile. Because of this, it is more efficient for the same assets to be used to provide services in a particular location over a long period of time. A decision to build a dam or install a water main in a particular location provides the capacity to supply that service for many years. Products supplied during each year of its life are in technical terms joint products.

Because of these features also, to a greater extent than for most assets, investment in urban infrastructure is irreversible. One result of the fact that the assets cannot easily be sold or used for other purposes is that the markets for these services are generally not fully contestable (see Chapter 3): because so much of the cost of providing the service is the cost of assets which, once installed, cannot be sold for any other use, an existing supplier would be prepared to reduce prices to a very low level to keep its market. As a result, in the absence of regulation, it is not easy for a competitive supplier to enter the market. This reinforces the strength of the natural monopolies.

Because of the immobility of the assets, investment planning for physical infrastructure requires assessment not only of the volume of future demand for the services involved, but also of its location. That is why investment in urban infrastructure services is more efficient with effective land-use planning. In return, land-use planning becomes more effective when it is used in the planning of infrastructure investment and is supported by appropriate charging for infrastructure services. This could, of course, be seen as an unholy alliance, limiting the opportunities of private investors. These two aspects encapsulate the trade-off between predictability and flexibility, one of the major themes of urban policy. These issues are pursued in Chapter 10.

Because of these features of infrastructure networks, pricing and investment decisions concern the best use of existing capacity as well as how much and when to add to capacity (see Chapters 6 and 7). When demand on a link in a network increases to near capacity the quality of service falls, or the cost per unit of the service of a given quality rises. Many networks must be analysed as a whole rather than as separate links because some links are substitutes. Other parts of the network are complementary: increasing loads in one link result in increasing loads on others. For networks as a whole, capacity to provide the service is determined first by coverage—the area over which it is available and the intensity of coverage of users within its service area, and second by bottlenecks—limits to the ability of sections of the network to meet the demands placed on it. Correspondingly, investment decisions concern extension of the network and relief of bottlenecks. Increases in demand relative to capacity for the network as a whole cause the same increase in costs or degradation in service as occurs on individual links, though the degradation in service occurs first in parts of the network where capacity is limited relative to demand.

Publicly owned durable infrastructure capital sunk in the ground adds to the value of property in the area served. Whether those assets are funded through long-term loans amortised by charges on beneficiaries, or through capital charges levied as a condition of approval of land development, affects the distribution of the cost burden between different generations of owners and occupants of property. It can affect also decisions about the timing of development and therefore the supply of developed sites. This issue is discussed in Chapter 6.

*Costs of adding to network capacity in established urban areas*

It is generally more expensive to add to the capacity of an established urban network than to provide greater capacity at the time of initial development, that is, the marginal cost of capacity is higher in the short than in the long run. The reasons are: first, economies of scale and the significant cost of installation mean that it is much cheaper to provide one pipe of capacity $2x$ than two pipes of capacity $x;$ second, the existence of physical infrastructure itself increases the value of property and hence the cost of acquiring additional land for roads, especially where there are established buildings; third, the existence of roads, pipes and wires makes the laying of additional roads, pipes and wires in established urban areas more costly; and fourth, adding to capacity causes disruption to services in established areas. These arguments apply with particular force to adding to road capacity unless sufficient right of way for the expansion has been reserved.

Because it is cheap, it is frequently efficient to provide spare capacity, or in the case of roads additional right of way, at the time of initial development even if there is only a low probability that the demand increase it is designed to meet will appear in the near future. For these reasons, the fact that there may be long-run economies of scale in planning for a higher level of use does not necessarily imply that the cost of adding to capacity within an established area will be less than the average cost of the existing system. This 'planning' long run for adding to infrastructure capacity occurs only when a city is being built or rebuilt on a clear site.

That option is very rarely available to established cities so that nearly all analyses of costs of adding to capacity relate to some kind of short run.

*Lumpiness in capacity*

'Lumpiness in capacity' means that it is more efficient to add to capacity in relatively large lumps than in marginal increments, as assumed in most of the models used in economic theory. Lumpiness is a feature of the headworks of some services, especially dams used to harvest and store water: it generally pays to build a dam to its full height at one time rather than adding to its height every few years. Lumpiness occurs also in high capacity links in networks where increased capacity may require replacing a pipe with a larger one or duplication. It is relatively important also in relieving bottle-necks in tree-type networks such as sewerage and drainage.

It is less of a problem in true networks such as water supply, gas, telecommunications and roads in which individual links are substitutes for others. Adding to the capacity of one link relieves the pressure on substitute links. It is less of a problem also in services such as bus public transport and garbage collection where the cost of an additional vehicle and crew in large cities is small relative to the overall capacity. The implications of lumpiness for costs are explored further in Chapter 3.

*Multiple products*

Just as services delivered at different times and to different places may be thought of as different, though often joint, products, so are the different services produced by a single infrastructure system. Because of economies of scope (jointness in production) it is often more efficient for the same assets to be used to provide a range of different services. For example, the same roads provide both access to properties abutting them and routes for through traffic, and provide also the somewhat different services needed by cars, buses, trucks and bicycles. Water mains provide both volume for regular consumption, and access to water at pressure and at a high rate of flow for firefighting.

Frequently these different services place different demands on the network and headworks, and therefore their costs are different. For example, buses and trucks are relatively few, but since they are heavy they need strong (thick) roads, while cars are relatively light, but since there are large numbers of them they need wide roads. Normal residential and industrial use of water requires a large volume at steady flow and modest pressure but firefighting requires little water but needs a high rate of flow at high pressure for short, unpredictable periods at unpredictable locations. In Chapters 6 and 7 it is argued that these different products can, and in some cases should, be charged for in different ways.

*Externalities and public goods*

Where one: it is possible for more people to consume a good or service without any additional cost either to producers or to existing users, and two: it is not possible efficiently to exclude those who do not pay from using the good or service, the products are known by economists as public goods. The services produced by physical infrastructure are rarely public goods, though an uncongested access road may be a local public good for the owners of the properties to which it provides access.

The historic origin of arterial roads and freeways was as 'public rights of way' and, because of the difficulty of charging directly for their use, they are regarded as public. But they are not public goods in the technical sense defined above. Once traffic reaches a level where there is some congestion, additional users can only be accommodated either by slowing down existing users or by investing in additional capacity. Some services, however, have 'public good' components. For example, the public health benefits from having a potable water supply and from adequate collection and treatment of sewage flow to the community as a whole, and it is not possible to exclude anyone from receiving those benefits. At the margin, however, it may not be public health benefits that determine the extent and therefore the costs of these services. There are, nevertheless, obvious health and environmental benefits (externalities) to the whole community from each property being adequately sewered and having its garbage removed.

As well as these positive externalities there are also substantial negative externalities from the use of all of the main elements of physical infrastructure. The drowning of river valleys and reduction in the flow of rivers which results from the provision of water supply, air pollution from transport, water pollution and flooding from stormwater and sewage effluent, and emission of greenhouse gases from the burning of fossil fuels are matters that need to be taken into account in decisions about pricing and the mode of provision of these services. These issues are the subject of Chapters 6 and 7.

### Long-term consumption decisions

The demand for physical infrastructure services is greatly influenced by decisions about location and investment that are taken infrequently. Decisions about where to live and work affect the location of demand for all services and the volume of demand, especially for travel. Decisions about purchase of housing and consumer durables, landscaping and lifestyle have a major long-term effect on the demand for hydraulic services, energy and travel. Chapter 4 discusses these aspects in more detail.

## Reasons for government involvement

Why are issues about the funding of these services questions of public policy? Why are they provided by governments or by heavily regulated private firms rather than simply being left to the competitive market? There are many services that are cheaper to provide for many users than for individual users to provide for themselves, for example, cinemas, retailing and banking. None of these is seen as a government responsibility. The answers to these questions derive in part from the features discussed in this and the previous chapter, and they underlie much of the discussion of appropriate charging regimes in later chapters. There are five main reasons for public involvement in individual services; commonly more than one of these reasons is relevant and the relative importance of the different reasons varies between services. Each of these is discussed in some detail with respect to energy and water and sewerage in Ernst (1994, Ch. 2).

- They provide essential services
- The services are natural monopolies
- They require compulsory access to land
- They produce public goods and externalities
- Their provision impacts on equity and the rights of citizens

The first reason is suggested by the term *essential services,* which was used in the past to describe urban infrastructure (e.g. Mathews 1967). These services were regarded as essential for people to live in urban areas—essential for the health and wellbeing both of the individual residents and to protect the health and amenity of residents as a group. (Not all, however, have always been provided to everyone living in Australian urban areas; at various times there have been significant unsewered residential areas.) Part of their essential nature is reflected in the economic concept of elasticity of demand: the amount of these services people use is not much affected by their cost to the user. Another part of their nature is reflected in the moral view that these services should be available to all citizens at a reasonable cost. A third is that they are needed to deal with the externalities of urban living: to protect the urban environment and the amenity of other people living in a city, including future generations, as well as to satisfy the needs of direct consumers. Because of these features, the government has the responsibility to ensure that they are provided, whether or not it provides them itself.

The second reason is that these services are *natural monopolies,* a concept which is described and defined in some detail in the following chapter. Essentially this means that it is more expensive to give individual consumers a choice of suppliers than to have a single monopoly supplier responsible for supplying all consumers in a particular area. This can be illustrated in the case of water supply. The cost of giving consumers a choice is having a number of parallel water mains installed in each street. Multiple trunk and reticulation mains throughout a city adds greatly to the total cost of the service. Competition between suppliers results in higher cost, so generally there is only a single supplier. It is also more efficient to provide a public transport system in which services that feed passengers from one route or service to another can be coordinated[1], and a road system in which users can move freely between all roads.

As a result of the absence of competition and the fact that all users need these services for their own use, any private provider could make a large profit at the expense of consumers by charging high prices. Citizens generally are not prepared to trust their provision entirely to a private firm over which they have no control through their elected representatives. If not publicly provided the services are regulated.

This is the main, though not the only reason that most physical infrastructure services—water, sewerage, drainage, roads, public transport, electricity, gas, telephones and garbage collection—are provided by governments, or by regulated private monopolies. For other services, including ports and airports, the economies of scale occur in the terminal facilities themselves. A feature of all of these services is that capital costs account for a high proportion of their total costs.

The third reason is that most of these services require the right to *compulsorily* acquire land for transport routes or the right to access to land for installing pipes or wires above or below the ground, in order to provide their networks, often to each individual property. Only governments have the power of compulsory purchase or access, and the roadways which provide the most convenient routes for many of the networks are government owned and controlled.

Fourth, services that produce *externalities* have effects, either beneficial or damaging and sometimes both, on people other than the users of the services. Those services that provide *public goods* produce only externalities. Public goods have to be provided for the community as a whole because it is impossible or too costly to charge users for them or, to express it in another way, to exclude those who do not pay from some or all of the benefits. The classic example is defence. Among urban services police, fire services, the courts and public open space are to a considerable extent public goods. These services are not provided through costly networks and are not included in this book. Competitive markets do not produce public goods because private producers could not cover their costs, and they produce too little or too much of services with favourable and unfavourable externalities respectively.

As pointed out in the previous chapter, some physical infrastructure services produce significant favourable and unfavourable externalities. Only governments can take account of the collective costs and benefits of provision of those services. The alternatives are for them to provide the services themselves or to regulate private providers.

The fifth reason relates to *equity and the rights of citizens*. Some services, primarily social infrastructure services such as education, health and welfare, are provided, at least at a basic level, to all citizens as a matter of right, irrespective of their ability to pay the cost of provision. Collectively, we are not willing to leave the distribution of the benefits of these services among citizens solely to the private market. One of our objectives, then, is redistribution in kind between the rich and the poor. Provision of social infrastructure services is seldom a public monopoly; all that is necessary is for governments to ensure that they are provided at low or zero cost to those who cannot afford the market price.

Equity can be defined as equality of opportunity (education) or of outcome (health). The importance of the equity objective and of citizens' rights varies among these services: it is very important for infant health, mental health, primary and secondary education, but less important for tertiary education and elective surgery. Equity is an important consideration in the provision of a range of services to small towns and remote locations, public transport for school children and provision of public transport outside peak hours for the benefit of people without access to cars, and lower charges to pensioners for a range of services. Although equity is not the primary objective of governments in providing physical infrastructure services it is *an* important objective, especially in the case of public transport, and is considered in determining the way in which all such services should be funded.

For these reasons governments have the right to provide these services, need to exercise their powers to provide the necessary land and access, and have the responsibility to ensure that they are provided at an acceptable quality and at a reasonable cost to all citizens. There are two ways in which the government can fulfil its responsibilities. The first is that it can itself supply them, either directly or through a statutory authority which it creates for the purpose; the second is to delegate its responsibility and the necessary powers to provide the service to a private firm, subject to conditions about the quality of supply and the level of charges to ensure that it does not exploit its monopoly position or damage the environment. Under the second option, conditions need to be varied from time to time and compliance with them needs to be monitored: the behaviour of the firm must be controlled by regulation since it cannot be controlled by competition. The choice between these alternatives is discussed further in Chapter 9.

Whether supply is by government or by a regulated private firm, the government will be held responsible if consumers believe that prices are too high, the quality of the service too low or the environment is not satisfactorily protected. The government is the owner of the right to supply these services, and the responsibility for ensuring that they are supplied in a satisfactory manner inevitably rests with the government. Privatisation under these circumstances has a quite limited meaning, as will be explained in more detail in Chapter 9. It essentially involves a contract in which certain rights are transferred to a private firm in return for certain under-takings. Given these non-transferable responsibilities of govern-ment, in the long term many of the risks involved in their supply continue to be borne by the government.

# 3 Costs of infrastructure services

It is intuitively appealing that charges for a service should reflect the cost of providing it. To be a little more precise, the price of a unit of a service should equal the cost of increasing the output of the service by one unit: its marginal cost. This is the principle of marginal cost pricing. Such charges seem to be equitable and, as will be demonstrated in Chapter 6, they also encourage the use of an appropriate amount of the service. To design a charging system that meets this criterion, we need to know what influences costs, how to measure the cost and level of use of the service and how much revenue such a charging system will produce. This chapter examines aspects of costs that need to be understood in designing an appropriate charging system.

The determinants of the cost of infrastructure services reflect their unusual characteristics described in Chapter 2 (pages 20–28). In the first part of this chapter we assume that the volume of use of a service is the only relevant measure of output. We examine how costs vary as the volume of use changes, first on the assumption that the capacity of the infrastructure is fixed (short-run costs) and then on the assumption that capacity can be varied as volume of output varies. The latter costs are known as long-run costs because it takes some time to carry out the investment needed to vary capacity.

Long-run average costs may fall with increases in output, reflecting economies of scale, or rise, reflecting diseconomies of scale. Where there are economies of scale, the cost of an additional unit is lower than the average cost of the earlier units of output produced, that is, marginal cost is below average cost. A price that is set equal to marginal cost will, then, not produce enough revenue to cover total costs. Conversely, if there are diseconomies of scale such a price will yield a surplus.

The later part of the chapter looks at the complications introduced by the fact that urban physical infrastructure produces, at the same time and using the same resources (i.e. jointly), different dimensions of services, and the same services at different times and in different locations. It considers the determinants of environmental (external) as well as financial (internal) costs and includes both volume of use of the service and other influences on cost such as the location and the time distribution of use. A final and minor determinant of costs of those services that are charged to individual customers, the cost of measuring the use by each customer and the administrative costs of charging for that use, are fixed costs per customer and do not vary with any measure of output. They are not explicitly discussed further in this chapter, though they are a minor factor tending to reduce unit costs as demand per consumer increases.

Throughout this book the different services provided through urban physical infrastructure are discussed within the same framework as far as possible. There is, however, one major difference in the cost structure between providers of transport infrastructure and providers of infrastructure services to individual properties. The costs of road transport services are shared between the provider of the roads and road users who provide their own vehicles and pay their operating costs and bear the time costs of the people and goods being transported. This occurs rarely with other services.[1] It is this division of cost responsibility which produces the externality that one road user imposes on another and the consequent inefficiency in the volume of use of roads. Under congested conditions, average costs, which are experienced by individual users, are lower than marginal costs to users as a group. This is less of a problem for public transport that has its own right of way and provides its own vehicles because both the costs of right of way and the vehicle operating costs (but not the travellers' time costs) are borne by the provider. Road-based public transport suffers from and causes the same congestion as private road use. As well, additional passengers increase the journey time of all passengers as a result of the time taken in boarding and leaving a bus or tram.

A somewhat similar phenomenon occurs with the telephone system where the time of users is required to make calls. When the system becomes congested the probability of making a successful connection falls, resulting in marginal costs above average costs. Consumers buy other services at their property boundary and all of the costs of operating the networks and delivering the services are paid by the operating authorities. The costs of congestion in those networks, except for external environmental costs, are all borne by the operators, who can make their decisions about capacity in the light of those costs.

A second feature distinguishing transport is that roads especially are major users of land. Indeed many other services can be cheaply provided underground or overhead. As a result, the cost of providing roads is much more sensitive than the cost of other services to land value, and therefore is higher in the inner areas of cities.

## EFFECT OF OUTPUT ON COSTS

### Capacity is fixed

In this section we assume that volume of output is the only product. It was pointed out in Chapter 2 that capacity costs are a high proportion of the total costs of many forms of infrastructure and that adding to it is often very expensive. It is not surprising then that capacity is a more binding constraint on the output of many infrastructure services, and a more costly constraint to relieve, than it is in most other industries. This is especially true of network services such as water, sewerage, drainage, roads, railways, energy and telecommunications, but less true of bus services and garbage collection.

While there is spare capacity, the variable cost per unit of output is likely to remain relatively stable with growth in demand. Since increased output spreads the fixed costs of capacity over more units of output, average costs decline. But as the level of demand for a service approaches capacity, the average variable costs of the service rise; at some stage this increase exceeds the fall in average fixed cost so that total average cost per unit of output increases. The increase in variable cost as capacity is approached can be a cost to users or to providers or both. Some cost increases occur on the supply side, for example, the use of pumps for a greater proportion of the time can increase the amount of water or gas that can be supplied through pipes of given size. Greater use of traffic police at intersections can increase their capacity, and employing additional bus drivers can make more intensive use of the existing stock of buses.

Non-price user costs (shortened term: 'user costs') increase as demand is increasingly constricted by limited capacity. These cost increases are very evident in the case of roads where, as capacity is approached, congestion results in slower trips, higher vehicle operating costs, more collisions, more air pollution and, if heavy vehicles are involved, greater damage to the road surface. Examples for other services are increases in the probability of an unsuccessful telephone call; reduced water pressure at higher elevations or gas pressure at the end of the line; power cuts; water restrictions in periods of low rainfall; sewers and sewage treatment facilities leaking and overflowing during rainstorms; flooding during rainstorms; having to stand on buses or trains; being unable to get onto the preferred bus or train service; and the services not arriving on time. The severity of these effects of supply constraints vary from the mild effects on most users of reducing water pressure to the dramatic, in some cases dangerous, effects of electricity cuts.

Because of the relatively unpredictable nature of demand for almost all of these services, when demand approaches capacity there is an increased risk of being unable to meet demand rather than a particular occasion when, as in the case of storable commodities such as wheat, the warehouses become empty. Because of the dispersed locations to which they are delivered, demand will exceed capacity in some locations before it does in others.

As capacity is approached, various measures can be taken to extend output without major capital expenditure. For example, the volume of traffic flow on a main road can be increased by traffic management measures such as limiting left and right turns during peak hours, extending the phases during which traffic lights permit traffic to flow on the major route by limiting interruptions to permit cross traffic, limiting entry of vehicles to congested routes at peak hours, and linking the phasing of series of lights on the main route to speed up the passage of platoons of traffic. Some part of the costs of such measures is of course borne by the users who experience longer delays in crossing the main route or have to take less direct routes to their destinations because of their inability to make desired turns. All of this reminds us that it is necessary to consider the costs of all users and the capacity of the network as a whole to accommodate desired trips. There are similar opportunities in hydraulic services and gas. More fluids can be transmitted through pipelines by booster pumping to increase the pressure, but this increases energy costs and is limited by the strength of the pipes.

As capacity becomes more fully used, the cost of meeting increased demand rises more steeply until eventually the only way to provide an additional unit of volume to one user is to deprive an existing user of that unit; thus the short-run marginal cost of the service becomes its opportunity cost: the value of the service to users whose supply is withdrawn. As more vehicles try to use a road, the volume of traffic flowing past a point per hour increases up to a certain level as speed falls, but beyond that level the fall in speed offsets the increased density of vehicles on the road and the volume declines. At some stage it becomes cheaper to increase capacity than to extract more output from the existing capacity.

**Capacity is variable**

The long-run cost of providing a service is the lowest cost of providing a particular level of the output when capacity can be varied so that it is at its optimal level for any given output. The question to be asked here is what happens to cost levels if the scale of the whole operation changes? Are there economies or diseconomies of scale: are long-run marginal costs greater or smaller than long-run average costs?

Before examining this question it is useful to look at the relationship between short- and long-run marginal costs. This is an important issue for pricing. If demand increases beyond that for which the existing level of capacity was designed, there are (obviously) two alternative ways in which it can be met. One is by increasing capacity, the cost of which is the long-run marginal cost. The other is by meeting the increase in demand by using the existing capacity more intensively in one of the ways described above, the cost of which is the short-run marginal cost. Since the optimal level of capacity is designed to minimise the cost of providing a given output, short- and long-run marginal costs must be the same when capacity is at its optimal level. If they are not equal, costs can be reduced by increasing or reducing capacity, in which case (by definition) it is not at an optimal level.

Another way to make the same point is to consider the two alternative ways of increasing output mentioned above. If it is cheaper to increase capacity to meet an increase in demand, that is what the operator should do. If it is cheaper to use the existing capacity more intensively, that is the optimal course of action. The objective should be to have a level of capacity at which the cost of the two alternatives is the same. The important conclusion is that when capacity is optimal, short- and long-run marginal costs are equal.

The definition of long-run costs requires somewhat closer examination for urban infrastructure services. The true long-run cost is really a planning cost: what would be the cost, including capacity cost, of providing a particular volume of services for a newly developed city or a suburb of a given size, in a given location and with given demand characteristics? In a normal industrial situation the long term is defined as the period long enough for the level of capacity to be varied. For some infrastructure assets, including most headworks such as dams, electricity generating stations, and water and sewerage treatment facilities, the same kind of definition can be used, though since the assets involved are specialised, immobile and have a very long life it takes a long time to reduce capacity.

For the networks of pipes, wires and roads that comprise a large part of the capacity of urban infrastructure, however, the planning long-run marginal cost, defined as the cost of increasing capacity at the time an urban area is first developed, is generally lower than the cost of supplementing capacity *at any later stage*, for two reasons. First, the provision of these services itself increases the value of any land which is needed for supplementing their capacity. This applies especially to roads and is known in the literature as 'the increasing supply cost of land' (Small et al. 1989, p. 101). Second, once a city is established it is more expensive to install pipes and wires and to widen roads because of the cost of digging up existing roads and other public and private structures and the disruption this causes.

To handle this problem it is useful to distinguish planning long-run costs from quasi long-run costs, the latter including the cost of expanding the capacity of infrastructure in an established urban area. If capacity is extended to cater for demand from an extension of the urban area on a green-fields site, the two costs will be different only to the extent that serving the new suburb requires increased trunk, main or arterial road capacity within established parts of the city. If, however, the population growth occurs within the established areas of the city the cost is likely to be different: it may be higher or lower. It is the quasi long-run cost as defined here that is important in thinking about charges for urban infrastructure services. The planning long-run costs as defined in textbooks can be achieved only when new settlements are built on green fields; they can never be achieved in the expansion of established urban areas. The analysis of returns to scale also needs to take account of the distinction between planning long-run and quasi long-run costs.

It follows from this argument that the cost of replacement of network capacity in established areas may be very high, especially in the case of hydraulic services which are installed underground and which are essential for the continued operation, and indeed occupation, of a city. In some cases it may be necessary to install completely new sewers while the old ones are still functioning. Few cities in the Western world have faced this problem in a serious way. The water supply and sewerage systems were installed late last century and had a design life of about 100 years. To date it has been possible to extend their lives by relining and other expedients, but sewer collapses show that this is unlikely to be the best strategy in the very long term.

One of the important characteristics of services that are provided through networks is that some parts of the network are generally operating much closer to capacity than others. This is reflected in the common use of the term 'bottleneck' for those sections which are a constraint on ability to meet demand. Increase in the capacity of an existing network commonly takes the form of relieving bottlenecks, which may involve increasing the capacity of the section of road or hydraulic main concerned, or of providing additional capacity on an alternative route or relief main. Large lumps of capacity are common, but if they are provided to relieve bottlenecks they may be fully used relatively quickly as flows transfer from other routes, pipes or wires. For this reason lumpiness is a less serious problem in making investment decisions in networks than appears to be the case if they are analysed section by section.

One of the generally accepted characteristics of many of the utility-type services provided by urban infrastructure is that there are economies of scale in their production. As a result, long-run costs are believed to decline with increases in output, and competition between a number of suppliers is inefficient and unstable. Hence they are known as 'natural monopolies'. To examine whether or not there are genuine economies of scale it is useful to consider headworks and network costs separately.

## Headworks costs

These costs, which include water harvesting, storage and treatment, sewage treatment and disposal of the treated effluent, garbage disposal, and the production of electricity and gas, are not essentially different from the costs of large industrial and mining operations. The average construction and operating cost of headworks per unit of output commonly falls as the scale of operation increases, up to some particular level of production. Beyond that it is roughly constant.

Such constant returns to scale beyond some level of output will occur, however, only if all of the inputs are available at constant cost as output grows. There is one scarce input into the headworks of these services, the land and natural resources close to the city, which generally increases in cost as a city expands. This occurs for two reasons. First, good dam sites close to the city are scarce and as a city's demand for water increases it is necessary to harvest water from more costly or more remote sites. The water may be more costly because the dams are more expensive per unit of yield, because it must be transported further or with more need for pumping, or because its opportunity cost is greater because there are other valuable uses of water, whether for irrigation, recreation or environmental purposes. Similarly, it may be necessary to draw from more costly or remote sources of natural gas, coal or sites for hydroelectric generation of electricity, though lower transport costs in these cases reduces the impact of remoteness on delivered cost.

Second, the capacity of the natural environment in and close to a city to absorb wastes is limited. As a city grows, it is necessary either to treat water-borne city wastes to a higher standard of purity or to pipe the effluent further from the city for discharge into the environment. This reason for increasing costs applies to sanitary sewage, the pollutants carried in stormwater, and to solid waste which often has to be transported further from the city as nearby landfill sites are exhausted.

One way to think about these costs is as a royalty or resource rent to be paid for using resources which are scarce and have alternative uses. The long-run marginal cost of supplying water to a city is the cost of providing water from the cheapest source that has not yet been tapped. Since the sources that have been tapped are presumably less expensive, the water authority should pay a rent to the owner (the state government in Australia) for the right to draw water from these lower cost sites. A similar argument applies to the long-run marginal cost of disposing of solid waste or of water-borne wastes. These factors, causing increasing cost of services with city growth, in some circumstances will be large enough to offset the economies of scale in the storage and treatment of water and wastes. Where they are sufficiently large, the average headworks cost per unit of service will increase as the city grows.

Technological change is another factor affecting the cost of headworks as a city expands. A rapidly growing city can take advantage of the new and more efficient technologies embedded in capital assets more rapidly than a city which is growing slowly or declining, which must wait for the replacement of the assets in which the old technology is embedded. In a growing city, the older headworks capacity for services such as electricity and water supply is used only in periods of peak demand, or as emergency capacity for periods of drought or in the event of a breakdown. Differences in the technology which is appropriate at different scales of output is one of the reasons for economies of scale. For example, technological improvements in high voltage transmission of electricity have permitted cities to reap economies of scale from large-scale generation on the coalfields.

Lumpiness in additions to capacity is a separate, but related, characteristic which affects the cost of expansion. It is often cheaper per unit of capacity to install or add a large amount of capacity than a small amount, though the optimum size of increment also depends on the cost of investing in capacity before it is needed. At any given percentage rate of growth, demand for a service in a large city will grow by larger absolute amounts each year, so that a large city will be better able to take advantage of installing larger lumps of capacity at lower cost. Lumpiness in headworks capacity occurs most obviously in the provision of water supply dams, and it has implications for investment and pricing which are discussed in later chapters.

In summary, the average cost of headworks capacity per unit of output will tend to fall with urban growth up to the point where the city is large enough to use the capacity of the most efficient plant, and beyond that if it is growing quickly enough to make use of lumps of additions to capacity of an efficient size, and to quickly make use of new technologies. The average cost will tend to increase because of the limited capacity of the local environment for harvesting and storing water and for coping with wastes. At some scale it would be expected that economies of scale would be more than offset by increasing costs.

*Network costs*

True (planning) economies of scale occur in the parts of the networks which carry a low volume in almost all of the services being discussed. They occur not only because the capacity of pipes and wires to carry fluids and energy increases in proportion to the square of the radius while costs increase in proportion to the radius, but also because of the relatively high capacity of the minimum width needed for safety on access roads and of a single track railway and of a water main that provides for firefighting. They are most marked in the elements of the network where the volumes of flow are at their lowest, which is in access roads and reticulation of other services within residential subdivisions.

Since there is very little congestion on access roads and the cost of providing such space varies little with the capacity provided, local access roads effectively produce local public goods for the properties to which they provide access. Like other public goods, they should be funded by some kind of tax on the beneficiaries that is unrelated to their use. Because of the much lower cost of installation at initial development than at any later date, and the low cost of providing a safe margin in capacity, it is usual for water, sewer, gas and electricity mains within subdivisions also to have sufficient capacity to meet significant increases in demand from within the subdivision. For them too, the marginal cost of providing for additional demand is small and they should be funded from a charge that is unrelated to use. These cost conditions are a major part of the reason for services within subdivisions to be funded from development charges, a matter taken up in more detail in Chapters 5–7.

Elements in the networks that carry progressively larger volumes experience less marked scale economies. The margin between the planning long-run marginal costs of meeting increased demand and the long-run average cost becomes smaller. More important, the quasi long-run marginal costs rise to approach quasi long-run average cost, and when the volume of flow approaches capacity they exceed it. As a result, when demand grows beyond the design capacity of a network, the cost of providing for additional demand will increase.

Analyses of the cost characteristics of a network that deal with it section by section, distinguishing those lightly used sections in which there are large scale economies from those heavily used sections where there are diseconomies of scale, have limited value. It is better to recognise that all users of these services use the different parts of the networks that have differing capacities and carry very different volumes. Although the lightly used sections account for most of the length, the heavily used sections, almost by definition, account for most of the volume. Considering any network as a whole, it seems likely that economies of scale may be pervasive, though at very different levels, when considering planning long-run costs. But when capacity is expanded to cater for growth in demand in an established city, what we have defined as quasi long-run costs are likely to show increasing costs in some areas and decreasing costs in others. The overall effect of growth on cost can be determined only by detailed studies of individual cities, and indeed by detailed studies of individual proposals for growth in particular locations.

From the point of view of charging, there are two criteria for choosing whether to analyse costs at a network level rather than section by section. The first is whether decisions of users have a major influence on the extent to which they use different sections. The second is whether different kinds or levels of charges are needed in different sections to achieve charging objectives. These questions are taken up in Chapter 5.

From the point of view of investment policy, a network approach requires a focus on bottlenecks. These can be defined as those sections of the network where the demand is highest relative to capacity. These are evident in the case of roads in congestion on links in the network, and delays or accidents at intersections. In the case of hydraulic services they are evident in loss of water pressure in high altitude localities, and leakage or overflow of sewers in wet weather. The proposition that there are not necessarily economies of scale with city growth can be illustrated with respect to water supply and roads.

*Water supply*

The situation is very similar for water, sewerage, gas and electricity. Let us distinguish four different sources of expansion of demand. Unambiguous scale economies occur in only the first of the four cases.

1   Water supply is being planned for two different forms of development on a stand-alone 1000 hectare site. In one form the demand for water will be 50 per cent greater than in the other. Because the cost of pipes increases roughly in proportion to their length and diameter but their capacity increases in proportion to their diameter to the power of about 2.6 (because the cross-sectional area increases as the square of the diameter, and because friction between the water and the pipe decreases with size), it will cost less per kilolitre to transport water to, and to distribute it within, the development where the demand per hectare is greater.[2]

2   Water supply is being planned for two stand-alone developments, one of 1000 and one of 1500 hectares, and the expected demand is proportional to the area. In this case we cannot be sure whether the cost per kilolitre will be higher or lower in the larger development. If the source of water is a remote catchment rather than underground aquifers, there will be economies in transporting the larger volume of water from the catchment to the larger development, but the additional 500 ha may be closer to or further from the source, and the pipes within the larger development will be longer as well as some of them being of larger diameter. Average cost in total may be lower or higher in the larger development.

3   The demand for water within an established urban area increases by 50 per cent as a result of changes in land use or increased density of use. There is likely to be spare capacity in some but not all of the mains and pumps bringing water to and distributing it within the area. Usually some will be bottlenecks. Increasing the capacity of mains in established areas requires replacing old mains with larger ones, or laying additional parallel mains, both of which can be very expensive for reasons given previously. Whether the marginal cost per kilolitre delivered will be above or below the average cost of supplying the original area can be determined only by examining individual cases. There may be spare capacity as a result of the fall in population which frequently occurs as a suburb ages, but other land use changes and greater use of water per head could result in increased demand. This is the quasi long-run equivalent of the genuinely long-run cost as defined in case 1.

4  An additional 500 hectares is opened for development adjacent to an established, similar, 1000 hectare subdivision. The cost of supplying water to the second area depends on whether sufficient capacity was allowed in the bulk mains for the expected additional demand. If so, it will be very similar to case 2 as long as the time between the two stages is relatively short. There is no general presumption that the cost of supplying water to such a development will be above or below the cost of providing it to the first 1000 hectare development. This may be seen as the short-run equivalent of the long-run costs in case 2. If the further development was not foreseen, it is more likely that the additional cost of supplying the extension will be higher than of supplying the initial development, for the same reason that the quasi long-run marginal costs of case 3 are higher than the planning long-run marginal costs of case 1.

Cases 3 and especially, 4, describe the ways in which most of the growth in demand for water in an established city occurs. As the city becomes larger spatially from type 4 growth, the supply lines within the built-up area become longer and it becomes more likely that the marginal cost of increasing the distribution capacity to meet additional demand will be above average cost. Within established areas, investment in urban infrastructure services is primarily a matter of relieving bottlenecks.

*Roads*

In contrast to 'pipe-and-wire' services, there is as yet no agreement on whether or not there are economies of scale in the provision of arterial roads and freeways in urban areas. There are economies of scale with increases in the width of individual sections of roads: two lanes in one direction can carry more than twice as much traffic at a given speed (cost to users) as one lane. Beyond a four-lane road, capacity is close to proportional to the number of lanes, though the median strip, emergency stopping lanes and the buffer strip between the edge of a freeway and the edge of the right of way are 'overheads', which need only be provided once no matter how many lanes there are on a freeway. In urban areas, however, intersections are important components of costs of provision of roads, and of delays and hence user costs. For example, the land occupied by an intersection increases as the product of the width of the two roads (the square if the two roads are of the same width). Intersection costs may take the form of land and construction costs of grade-separated intersections or of user costs of delays at intersections. In addition, the above arguments with respect to the network costs of pipe and wire services apply to the road network. Users generally have more discretion about what sections of the road network they use than they do about which section of the water or sewerage networks they use. Choices about where to shop, work, and carry out leisure activities as well as choices about where to live and work affect which parts of the road network are used. The use of roads is less self-optimising in the short term than the use of water and electricity networks because individual drivers have to find the quickest routes. In the long term, however, they may be more self-optimising in that individuals may change their trip destinations to avoid congested roads but cannot even see where there are bottlenecks in other services.

It has been common to assess whether roads have increasing or decreasing cost by comparing the costs of road links which carry a varying (weighted) number of vehicles in a given time. Taking a network perspective which includes the cost of intersections, a more appropriate unit is the (weighted) number of vehicles that can get through a road network from some distribution of origins to some distribution of destinations in a given time. In either case it needs to be recognised that the cost of road transport is shared between providers (pavement, right of way, maintenance, control, administration) and users (vehicle operating costs, time of occupants, risk of accidents) of roads; the costs to both need to be included.

The two best estimates of variations in cost with volume along an urban freeway link are that average costs are either 1.03 (Keeler & Small 1977) or 1.19 (Kraus 1981) times marginal costs per unit of flow along a highway, representing modest economies of scale. The first is statistically not significantly different from constant returns to scale and the second not much higher. Both are based on cross-sectional data and provide estimates of planning long-run costs of roads of different capacity.

These assessments of scale economies assume that flow along a road is the correct measure of output. Just as pipe and wire services produce *access to* water, electricity, etc, roads produce *access between* different parts of an urban area, which is much more difficult to measure than flow along a road. Mohring (1976, pp. 144–5) considers the situation in which the capacity of a freeway grid is doubled by converting it from a two mile grid to a one mile grid.

Increasing capacity in this way increases the number of intersections between freeways as the square of the density of the grid. In urban areas the cost of construction of freeway intersections is quite high relative to the cost of the freeway. For arterial roads the equivalent cost of intersections is mostly the cost of delays. In either situation, consideration of the road system as a network reduces the economies of scale relative to consideration of route capacity alone. At the same time as there are constant or increasing returns to scale on individual links there may be diseconomies of scale in the network. Intersection costs have no equivalent in most of the other networks, though there are some parallels in switching in telecommunications.

As cities grow spatially, rather than through increasing density, journeys to provide access from all parts of the city to the employment and other opportunities it provides tend to become longer (Neutze 1965). Among other effects, this increases the density of traffic in many areas and results in the network effects noted above. At the same time, however, employers and providers of services decentralise to suburban areas, and drivers and travellers trade off the cost of long journeys against the greater range of opportunities that are accessible by making long journeys, and make most of their journeys to places close to where they live or work. As a result, journeys do not lengthen to the extent implied by the spatial growth. In recent years, there is some evidence that while the average length of journeys to work in the CBDs of Sydney and Melbourne have lengthened, the average lengths of other journeys have become shorter (Troy 1996, p. 117).

If the volume of traffic increases within an existing urban area, unless the growth has been anticipated and space reserved for road widening, the cost of increasing capacity (quasi long-run) is likely to be a good deal higher than the planning long-run cost of providing wider rights of way at the time of original construction. The two alternative ways in which capacity and speed of flow can be increased are to widen existing roads or to build new roads to take some of the pressure off existing through roads. The advantage of the latter is that, because frontages of arterial roads (but not freeways) attract high density activities, the cost of the land needed to widen them is generally high. The cost of widening freeways depends more on the availability of space and the cost of lengthening overhead bridges. Alternative routes are often a cheaper option, whether they involve widening minor roads or new routes through land that is not intensively used.

Because land in urban areas becomes more valuable as a result of the provision of roads and other urban services, the quasi long-run cost of increasing capacity in either of the above ways is higher than the planning long-run cost. That difference may be near zero if sufficiently wide rights of way are provided when the road is initially built, but those reservations have costs if the expected growth in traffic is uncertain. In any event it seldom occurs. The quasi long-run cost is relevant for pricing, and provides relevant information about scale economies. Given the very modest planning economies of scale with increasing flow found by Keeler and Small (1977) and Kraus (1981) it seems certain that when the increasing cost of land is taken into account there are decreasing quasi long-run returns to scale.

## COSTS WITH MULTIPLE PRODUCTS

As argued in Chapter 2, most infrastructure services provide more than one product. From the point of view of producers a product is different from another if the two are not close substitutes. If providing other products in addition to volume adds significantly to total cost, funding methods need to be adapted accordingly. The following are examples of what is meant by different products.

*Roads*

In the recent literature on the economics of roads it is recognised (especially in Small et al. 1989) that arterial roads produce two distinct products: durability (or strength) to carry heavy vehicles which is almost entirely used by trucks and buses, and capacity to carry a large number of vehicles which requires wide roads and which is predominantly used by cars. The road system includes also local roads in both rural and urban areas whose major function is to provide vehicular access to properties. There is seldom a clear distinction between access roads and through roads though, at the extreme, rural lanes and urban cul-de-sacs provide only access and freeways provide only for through traffic. All other roads provide, in varying proportions, for both access and through traffic.

To use conventional economic terminology, access, durability and capacity are joint products of most roads, and of the road network as a whole. This does nòt imply that they are produced in the same proportion for all roads or all networks. It simply means that in many situations it is more efficient to have roads that provide two or all three products than separate roads providing for each. To use more recent terminology, there are frequently economies of scope from providing roads that produce two or three of the products. Small et al., however, argue that there are diseconomies of scope in providing for heavy vehicles and cars on the same roads because this means that all roads have to be thick enough (and have overhead bridges with enough clearance) to carry trucks and buses. If trucks were not permitted on some freeways, as on some American parkways, the pavements could be much thinner. This view is most relevant for roads which mainly provide for through traffic. For example, a road between an industrial or wholesaling area and a port or airport might be for heavy vehicles only and some roads between residential areas and recreation or employment areas could be for light vehicles only. This view is less relevant for the majority of roads for which the provision of access is a major function, thus in general access roads need to be thick enough to carry heavy vehicles without being damaged.

Measurement of the durability and capacity provided by roads and assessment of their costs is not in principle difficult. Measurement of the amount of access they provide, and the cost of providing more access, is more difficult. One measure of access is the density of roads (excluding limited access roads) in an area: kilometres of road per square kilometre. On this measure the cost of providing greater access is the cost of greater road length. Providing access from through roads results in economies of scope, especially during periods when through traffic does not use the whole capacity. There are likely to be diseconomies of scope when through traffic is close to capacity: vehicles entering or leaving the flow of traffic, and vehicles parking on the roadside while their occupants visit a property, reduce the road's capacity to carry through traffic. We might estimate these costs by measuring their effect on the capacity of the roads to carry through traffic.

As detailed by Small et al., the short-run marginal cost of durability is the additional cost of repair and resurfacing resulting from the passage of a truck or bus along a road. This cost is generally recognised as increasing with the cube or fourth power of the weight per axle of the loaded vehicle. The long-run cost is the cost of providing thicker pavements. The short-run marginal cost of capacity is the additional cost to other users of the congestion caused by the addition of a vehicle to the flow of traffic on a route. As described above, that cost increases with the volume of traffic relative to the capacity of the route, and therefore varies with the time of day. The long-run cost is the cost of providing additional capacity by relieving bottlenecks. The marginal cost of access has two elements:

1 On roads which carry enough through traffic to cause significant congestion, the short-run marginal cost of access is the increased congestion cost from additional vehicles leaving or entering the road between intersections. Its long-run marginal cost is the cost of providing an additional lane for turning traffic in bottlenecks. Where access involves the provision of parking on the roadside, the short-run cost is the effect of parking on congestion costs, and its long-run cost is the cost of land and the capital needed to provide the space.

2 On uncongested roads, the short-run marginal cost of providing access to an additional property is small and may be zero. If the roads are primarily provided for access purposes, their long-run cost must be considered a collective cost to all the property owners to whom access is provided. The cost is the total rental value of the land, capital cost of construction and maintenance cost of the road. If they are primarily through roads, the long-run cost of provision of access will be very small also. If they have mixed purposes, the division of land and capital costs between the two functions is essentially arbitrary.

To anticipate Chapter 7, since vehicular access to a property and parking space adjacent to a property are 'rights' attaching to property fronting a road, it is appropriate that their cost should be recovered as a charge on the property to which they give access. It follows that optimal charges for durability and capacity need not pay the total cost of the road system.

*Other services*

In similar fashion, a water supply system provides a volume of water, access to a supply of water for individual properties and water at high pressure for firefighting. A sewerage system provides access to a network of pipes that can transport wastes from individual properties to treatment and disposal facilities and the capacity to treat those wastes. It has also the capacity to transport and treat those 'trade wastes' which cannot more efficiently be treated at source. Garbage services provide collection from individual properties, transport to the disposal facility and disposal. Public transport provides for peak-hour travel mainly between suburbs and the CBD and a few other major employment centres, travel to and from school, and off-peak services mainly for people without access to cars. The marginal cost of providing each of these products is in principle measurable.

*Location*

The services provided at different locations are different products: much of the capacity used to supply water, sewerage and electricity to one part of a city cannot be used to supply them to another part; and the transport facilities that provide access between particular pairs of locations are of less use, sometimes of no use, in providing them between other pairs of locations.

*Time*

Services delivered at different times are different products from a cost point of view for a somewhat different reason. While the capacity used to provide electricity in the early hours of the morning is also used to provide it in the evening peak (the two are joint products), since all available capacity is used in periods of peak demand, it is not possible to produce more in the evening peak by reducing output in the early hours of the morning.

These examples provide a framework for general consideration of the different products provided by infrastructure services. Each infrastructure service can be seen as delivering three broad kinds of products.

First, access to the service requires a network which usually links individual properties with a source of the service or with each other, but in the case of public transport, links points serving localities rather than individual properties. Access always requires a network of pipes, wires, roads, rails, bus routes or garbage collection routes. The denser the network and the greater the area over which the network extends, the greater the level of access provided. Thus the cost of providing more access is primarily the cost of providing it to more locations, which requires a greater length of pipes, wires, roads, railways and routes.

Access provides the option for the service to be used, no matter if, or how much of, it is used. It has a cost which is independent of the volume of use. If volume is considered as the sole measure of output, the provision of access appears as an overhead cost. The fact that dimensions of services other than volume are often ignored is responsible for the frequently-expressed view that there are economies of scale in the provision of infrastructure services, especially for services such as water and sewerage where access costs are a high proportion of the total cost.

Access can have a different meaning in relation to public transport. There access has something in common with quality of service. Access improves with the spatial density of public transport routes and with the frequency of services along such routes. Greater access reduces both walking time and waiting time.

Second, volume of use is the conventional 'product' of infrastructure services. Producing a given volume of a service requires that the headworks have the capacity to cope with the volume of demand and that the roads, pipes, wires, etc. have the capacity to provide the volume of the service that is demanded at each location. In addition, it requires expenditure on the operating costs of the services: fuel for energy supply and transport, including costs of pumping water and sewage, chemicals for treating water and sewage, and the time of vehicle drivers and passengers.

For most purposes it is important to distinguish the volume of service as a different product according to where it is provided. Both operating costs and capacity costs vary between locations, and a significant part of the capacity needed to provide the service in one location will not be useful in supplying it in another.

For some purposes it is useful also to subdivide the volume of service into different products depending on when it is produced. The time distribution has a major impact on the capacity costs of both headworks and networks, especially for services which are expensive or impossible to store (water, gas, goods transport, telecommunication, passenger transport). In general the level of capacity is determined by the peak level of demand, reduced to the extent that it is efficient to store the product to meet some part of that demand.

Third, quality dimensions include the ability of roads with thick pavements to carry heavy loads, and the ability to draw water at a particular rate and a particular pressure for firefighting, which varies with the size of and pressure in mains. Each of these dimensions has a significant influence on costs. The right to discharge particular trade wastes into sewers affects the cost of providing and maintaining sewers and the cost of treating the effluent. The voltage at which electricity is supplied is inversely related to cost per unit of energy because while it is cheaper to transmit at high voltages it is costly for the supplier to transform high voltage to lower voltage. The frequency of public transport services outside peak hours is a quality of service independent of volume of use, and is costly to provide. The frequency of garbage collections, the quality of water delivered and the comfort of travel on public transport are additional quality dimensions. Reliability is an important dimension of all of the services concerned since reducing the probability of services being unable to meet demand in peak periods or failure of a component of the service requires reserve capacity in headworks and major components of networks. Reliability falls as demand for the service approaches the capacity of the headworks and networks to deliver it.

**Economies and diseconomies of joint production**

While the different 'products' provided by each service are not substitutes from the point of view of producers, they are generally produced together because that is cheaper than producing them separately. Like the classic economics textbook example of wool and mutton, they are joint products. The extent of jointness is sometimes known as the economies of scope, $S_c$, and defined as the proportionate savings in costs from producing the products together compared with producing them separately (Bailey & Friedlander 1982):

$$S_c = [C(Y_1, 0) + C(0, Y_2) - C(Y_1, Y_2)]/C(Y_1, Y_2) \text{ } (equation \text{ } 1)$$

where: C is the cost of production, and
$Y_1$ and $Y_2$ are the amounts produced of products 1 and 2

$C(Y_1, 0) + C(0, Y_2)$ is the cost of producing the two services separately and $C(Y_1, Y_2)$ the cost of producing them together, so that $S_c$ is simply the proportionate increase in cost from producing them separately rather than together. If there are diseconomies of scope, $S_c$ is negative. The level of economies of scope varies greatly between different infrastructure services and the different products each produces. Providing access and volume of a particular service to a particular property are joint products, though they could be separated to some degree if there was greater scope for services to be provided by individual households for their own use. For example, much of the water required for use within a house could be collected from its roof, but access to a public supply might still be demanded for firefighting and for periods of low rainfall. Households which have rainwater tanks would then have a demand for access but a smaller demand for volume. Similarly, with some landscaping, much of the stormwater falling on a property could be stored or allowed to soak into the ground on a residential lot, but access to the stormwater drains would still be required to cope with the overflow during heavy and prolonged rainstorms. Again, the use of composting toilets could eliminate the need for access to sewerage for dealing with personal waste, and grey water could mostly be used for irrigation, but in periods of high rainfall it might be necessary to have a sewer connection to dispose of grey water which cannot be absorbed into a residential lot. In each case, the capacity of the dams, water mains, drains, sewers and treatment facilities could be somewhat lower, but the cost of providing access would be much the same.

While there are large economies of scope in using the same network for delivering services to adjacent properties, the economies are smaller when considering different sections of a large metropolitan area. There have been and are different distributors of electricity, gas and water to different parts of a number of Australian cities. Despite the fact that there are economies from being able to share reserves, and from having easy and transparent connections between parts of the network serving different parts of a city, there is no evidence that the cost of such arrangements is markedly higher than if there was a single distributor. Similarly, the provision of local roads in metropolitan areas by a number of local councils and of major roads by state authorities has not resulted in obvious cost penalties. There are economies of scope in all the properties within a catchment being provided with both sanitary and stormwater drainage by a single authority, but there are also advantages in having separate services for subcatchments and for dealing with environmental problems within smaller areas, as is argued in Chapter 11. Much stormwater drainage in metropolitan areas is the responsibility of municipalities, which seldom correspond with catchments.

Different products should be provided by a single supplier when there are economies of scope (joint products) because it is more efficient to produce them together than separately; hence the argument for hydraulic services to be provided by authorities whose service areas correspond with catchments. Changes in technology or in demands may reduce the jointness so that it becomes efficient to produce them separately. Small et al. (1989), for example, argue that there are diseconomies of scope in providing for heavy vehicles and light vehicles on all roads. Their reason is that the great majority of road space is required for cars and light vans, and roads for them could be made much thinner at considerable cost saving if heavy vehicles were confined to specially constructed roads with thick pavements. In addition car-only roads would have a higher capacity where there is only limited grade separation because the slow acceleration of heavy vehicles slows down other vehicles.

There is a cost in such a separation of functions which was not considered by Small and his colleagues. To get access to properties for collection and delivery, heavy vehicles need to be able to use most roads, otherwise costly transhipment is required between long distance heavy and lighter vehicles. Additionally, relatively heavy garbage trucks are regular users of residential streets. Even if heavy vehicles were permitted to use 'thin' roads for access purposes only, the length of trips by heavy vehicles would be increased significantly. Nevertheless there are advantages, not least in improved safety, in prohibiting heavy vehicles from using residential streets except for access; this can often be achieved by designing residential subdivisions so that they do not provide convenient through routes. The costs and benefits of urban freeways which carry light vehicles only are worth investigating.

A similar case can be made for other services. Thus it may be worth providing a separate sewer for some kinds of trade wastes, especially if separation permitted cheaper treatment. The fact that local sewage treatment and local storage of stormwater can provide water more cheaply than tapping additional fresh potable supplies makes it attractive to provide dual distribution systems, with the lower quality water being used for irrigation, and possibly for toilet-flushing and firefighting. Whether or not it is economic to do so depends in part on whether a resource rent is charged for extracting fresh water to reflect the environmental costs of the extraction and other opportunity costs.

One implication of the multi-product view of these services for economies of scale has been considered already: if services are seen as simply producing volume, the costs of providing access are overheads, and economies of scale will be exaggerated. For a single-product firm, economies of scale can be measured as the ratio of average to marginal cost of production. The average cost of one product in a multiple-product firm is not easily defined. In their survey article on multi-product industries, Bailey and Friedlander (1982) derive an equivalent to economies of scale for one product of a two-product firm ($S_1$) as the ratio of average incremental costs (AIC) to marginal cost (MC), where the AIC of product 1 is defined as the increase in the firm's total cost because it produces product 1 as well as product 2, per unit of product 1:

$$AIC_1(Y) = [C(Y_1, Y_2) - C(0, Y_2)]/Y_1 \qquad (equation\ 2)$$

and the economy of scale in the production of product 1 is:

$$S_1 = AIC_1(Y)/MC_1 \qquad (equation\ 3)$$

Multi-product economies of scale ($S_m$) are then the average of the economies of scale of the two products, weighted roughly by the share of each product in the marginal cost of total production and amplified according to economies of scope:

$$S_m = [wS_1 + (1 - w)S_2]/(1 - S_c) \qquad (equation\ 4)$$

$$Where\ w = Y_1MC_1/[Y_1MC_1 + Y_2MC_2] \qquad (equation\ 5)$$

If $Y_1$ was assumed to be the only output, single-product economies of scale ($S_s$) would have been:

$$S_s = [C(Y_1, Y_2)/Y_1]/MC_1 \qquad (equation\ 6)$$

The calculation of multi-product economies of scale in equation 4 recognises that average costs need to be calculated by dividing the total cost in some way by the output of the two commodities, rather than by attributing all costs to one product. The equation effectively compares the weighted average of average costs with the weighted (using the same weights) average of the marginal costs. In general, then, the multi-product economies of scale will be lower than the single-product economies of scale of equation 6. The difference will depend on the relative cost, and the economies of scale in production, of the product ($Y_2$), the marginal cost of which is ignored in equation 6. In addition, other things being equal, the larger the economies of scope the larger the multi-product economies of scale. Economies of scope are included in equation 4 to take account of the relative cost of producing the products together compared with producing them separately.

The effects of including access as a second product rather than assuming volume is the only product can be illustrated for water supply and roads. The cost of providing access to water, relative to the cost of producing volume, can be thought of as the cost of the whole of the distribution system relative to the cost of delivering treated water to one point in a city: the cost of retailing relative to the cost of wholesaling.[3] The cost of providing access roads relative to providing volume is much more difficult to define since so many roads provide both. A minimum cost of access might be the cost of local roads relative to the cost of arterial roads. Over 90 per cent of the number of kilometres of urban roads are local roads, though they are less costly per kilometre. For both water supply and roads, the cost of providing access is large relative to the cost of providing volume. In general there seem likely to be few economies of scale in providing access in either case, if access is measured as the number of properties connected per km. As a result the use of equation 6 rather than the correct equation 4, for either water supply or urban roads, is likely to over-estimate economies of scale.

Another way to argue that multiple-product economies of scale are likely to be smaller than the single-product measure is that the multi-product measure considers additional costs—the cost of the capacity needed to provide users with access or some other product such as reliability—as variable rather than fixed costs. Such a change in perspective reduces economies of scale in production unless:

• The economies of scale in the additional product are larger than in the provision of volume; or
• The additional product accounts for little of the cost of production.

There are economies of scope between services delivered at different times of the day, the week and the year wherever sunk capital costs are a major cost of providing the service and where it is impossible or very costly to store it from one period to another. Indeed such economies over time extend to much longer time periods because of the durability, specialisation and immobility of the capital invested in providing capacity for those services which have physical headworks or networks. For these services an investment decision today must take account of the expected demand and its location for many years into the future. (This does not apply to bus services or garbage collection.)

Considering peak and off-peak outputs as different products adds little to the conventional theory of peak period pricing. In that theory it is recognised that the marginal cost of meeting peak demands includes the marginal cost of adding to capacity as well as the marginal variable costs that must be met in off-peak periods. Off-peak periods, when capacity is not a constraint at all, can be ignored in deciding on optimal capacity.

## OTHER FACTORS AFFECTING COSTS

### Predictability and projections of future demand

The jointness of supply (economies of scope) over longer periods has important implications for the efficiency of investment decisions. The first is that good decisions require accurate estimates of future demands for the various products and their distribution over time and space. All investment decisions are based on projections of future demand, but this is particularly true for investments in physical infrastructure assets because of their longevity, immobility and specialisation. Because of these characteristics, the cost of providing services is very sensitive to the predictability of demand. If predictions are wrong, the provider will either have surplus capacity which cannot be used for any other purpose, or will have to either add to or replace pipes or wires with others of larger capacity long before the old ones have worn out. Because capacity is used fully only during peak periods, it is especially important to have accurate forecasts of peak period demand.

Just as the provision of services in peak and off-peak periods are joint products because they use the same capacity, so are the provision of services in successive periods over many years. In estimating future demand, monopoly infrastructure authorities have the advantage that they do not need to be concerned about their share of the local market, though there is competition between authorities responsible for services such as public transport and roads, gas and electricity. The major factors affecting demand over time are changes in the population and its distribution in an urban area, in the level and kinds of economic activity and the technologies used, and in the method of charging and level of charges for use of the service.

Service authorities face two problems, however. First, because of the durability of much infrastructure, they need very long-term projections of demand over periods during which technologies used in the provision and the use of their service are likely to change. Second, substantial parts of their durable networks are designed to meet demand in particular locations so that the location as well as the quantity of demand needs to be projected. Third, they need to predict peak period demand in each location.

It is not surprising that authorities responsible for providing road and rail transport, water, sewerage, drainage and telephones have put large resources into predicting the location of future growth in demand. They have a large stake in the success of the efforts of planning authorities to implement land-use plans that define the locations in which urban growth is to take place and where particular land uses are to be located.

One way to reduce uncertainty about the location of future demand is for the service authorities, in conjunction with the land-use planning authorities, to plan a sequence of developments and to base their investments on that sequence. Any development that is proposed out of sequence would be charged the additional cost of servicing the site out of sequence.

In some circumstances it is more efficient for increases in demand in a metropolitan area to be concentrated in limited parts of urban areas. Under these circumstances demand will grow more rapidly in the selected areas so that the capacity of the infrastructure will rapidly be used. The disadvantage is that as new residential areas age their population and their demand for services sometimes fall, so that capacity exceeds demand.

Given uncertainty of supply and/or demand, the amount of capacity needed, and hence the cost of providing the service, will be higher the greater the planned security of supply, especially when capacity is lumpy, or when the time required to plan and construct additional capacity is long relative to likely periods of shortage. Supply security can be defined as the frequency and severity of periods in which supply falls short of demand. Where variations of supply and demand (sometimes in the opposite direction, as in the case of water) are large, the cost of reducing the probability and severity of shortages can be a high proportion of total costs. The main services affected by climatic variation are water supply (droughts), sewerage and stormwater drainage (heavy rain causes overflows of sewers, bypassing of treatment facilities and flooding) and electricity and gas (temperature extremes cause high demands for heating and cooling). The costs of improved reliability are the cost of increased capacity, and greater expenditure on maintenance.

## Environmental costs

It was argued in Chapter 1 that there are both environmental costs and benefits from the provision of infrastructure services. In considering whether there are economies of scale in the provision of infrastructure services it was argued that environmental costs tend to produce diseconomies of scale with city growth. On the other hand the benefits are largely independent of city size. Environmental costs rise more rapidly than the size of a city because of the limited capacity of the environment within and around a city to provide water and energy and to absorb waste products. Among the services being considered in this book, all except telecommunications have very significant environmental costs. Overhead telephone wires cause environmental degradation, though even this disappears with undergrounding or the use of mobile phones and satellite technology. Mobile telephones produce environmental dangers for their users but not for the general community, though mobile phone towers are unsightly and produce electronic emissions.

Which of the 'products' are responsible for environmental benefits and costs? Most of the benefits are obtainable by access to the services concerned and require only a modest volume of use. For example, it is access to clean water for human consumption, and to sewerage services for the disposal of wastes, which provides most of the environmental benefits. The provision of access to some services causes environmental costs, for example roads and overhead electrical transmission and reticulation. The level of environmental costs is determined mainly, however, by the volume of use of the services. Thus it is the volume of water demanded which requires the flooding of river valleys and which eventually either increases the volume of sewage effluent, or run-off from lawns and gardens, carrying nutrients and other wastes into rivers and lakes. A greater volume of water as well as a greater volume and concentration of waste material in sewage increases the cost and difficulty of separating the wastes from the water in treatment plants. The volume of stormwater which runs off the hard surfaces in an urban area during rainstorms determines the extent of flooding. Similarly, the volume of vehicle movement and the volume of electricity and gas consumed are the main factors determining the amount of air pollution and the emission of greenhouse gases arising from transport and use of energy in a city.

**The location and nature of development**

The location of urban development affects costs in several ways. First, topography and geology: it is more costly to provide services on sites which are steep, at a high (or very low) elevation or which are rocky. Second, location: it is more costly to service locations which are some distance from established areas and the networks which serve them because of the length of the necessary connecting roads and mains. Even if it is simply a matter of development being 'out of sequence', the economies of scale in network costs require that the connections be installed with sufficient capacity to cater for the demands that will arise when the intervening areas are developed. The costs of excess capacity will be higher, the greater the volume of out-of-sequence development. Locations remote from water catchments can be serviced only by transporting water over long distances. Those remote from large water bodies into which treated effluent can be discharged require either long-distance transmission or a higher level of treatment.

The on-site cost of services depends also on the nature of development of the site. The layout of a site and the pattern of subdivision have significant impacts on service costs. It is argued in following chapters that developers should pay on-site costs because it gives them an incentive to design subdivisions that can be serviced inexpensively.

This chapter argues that it is necessary to recognise the multiplicity of products of most infrastructure services in order to understand the factors affecting costs. This does not detract from the great importance of the volume of use of each service as the major determinant of the cost of supplying it. Volume of use is the main determinant of both financial costs and environmental costs. The costs of providing access are, however, still very significant for some purposes. In subsequent chapters, the findings of this chapter will be used in discussing alternative charging mechanisms. In particular the arguments for and against separate charges for access and volume of use will be evaluated, along with the case for different levels of charges for use at different times and in different places. This chapter has argued that, despite the clear economies of scale in individual links in the networks through which they are provided, it is not clear that there are economies of scale in providing these services to growing cities. If that is true, it is quite possible that all costs could be covered by volume charges set equal to the marginal costs of supply. It does not follow, however, that volume charges alone are the best method of charging.

# 4    Demand characteristics

In subsequent chapters it will be argued that charging for the use of services according to the quantity of use can perform a valuable function in discouraging excessive use and thereby saving costs, and reducing the adverse environmental effects that result from their use. Such charges will have substantial desirable effects only if the level of charge affects the level of use significantly. If, as is often argued, prices have little effect on demand, they will have little effect also on cost or on environmental damage. In such a situation they affect the distribution of income, and indeed they could be argued to be more equitable, but have little effect on the use of resources or on the environment. Low elasticity of demand, however, has the desirable effect of permitting providers to raise additional revenue by raising the price, and makes the services a good base for indirect taxes. Where there is also a monopoly supplier (as there is for many of these services, for reasons spelled out in the previous chapter), governments need control of prices. These services provide collective as well as individual benefits. To the extent that collective benefits are important at the margin relative to user benefits, the case for charging users is weakened.

This chapter discusses the sensitivity of demand to charges which vary with those dimensions of output that the previous chapter showed to be the main determinants of cost. The most important is volume of use, but others include access, the different quality dimensions of the service, such as service reliability, the location of use, and the time distribution of use. It also discusses the difference between sensitivity of demand to the level of charges in the short and the long run, and non-price factors affecting demand. The first part of the chapter describes some general features of the demand for these services, including the significance of collective demands, and the second deals with individual services.

## CHARACTERISTICS OF THE DEMAND FOR PHYSICAL INFRASTRUCTURE SERVICES

### Non-price influences on demand

One of the remarkable features of studies of the demand for most infrastructure services is that in many cases non-price factors appear to have more influence than price. There are several reasons for this.

First, in Australia it is rare for a price, in the usual sense of the word, to be charged for the use of a number of services (sewerage, drainage, garbage, private road transport).[1] Even where a price is charged, it is frequently a component of a two-part tariff (water, electricity, telephones and gas) and the separate influence of the variable part (the price) on the demand is correspondingly reduced. Also, its effect is difficult to assess, especially if the fixed charge also varies over time and between users. Indeed there is evidence from the United States that consumers base their consumption decisions on the average price they pay for water—their total water bill divided by their total use of water—rather than on the marginal price (Martin & Wilder 1992; Foster & Beattie 1979). One reason for the limited use of prices has been that policymakers believe that demand varies little according to the level of price, but in turn the limited use of prices makes it difficult to assess whether or not that belief is correct. Public transport is the only service for which there is commonly a single charge for a particular service, but its price (fare structures) includes a fixed charge and a variable charge per unit distance so that no single price is readily observable. The use of both private and public transport involves costs to users in the form of their time and the use of roads involves vehicle operating costs, as well as the cost to providers of the services, but neither the dollar value of the time spent by users nor much of users' vehicle operating costs are readily observable. The costs of providing these services are recovered in a variety of ways; for example, road costs are recovered by a kind of two-part tariff: fixed registration and driving licence fees and a fuel tax that varies with the distance driven.

Second, most demand studies have been designed to assess the need for investment. Since much of the investment is required to provide access rather than volume of use, and to provide the service at particular locations and at times of peak demand, it is not surprising that demographic factors, the projected location of residential and commercial development and the projected time distribution of demand are commonly more useful than price as predictors of the relevant dimensions of demand.

Third, some of the demand for access to services results from legal requirements and is therefore quite insensitive to price. For example, nearly all developed urban property is required to be connected to water, sewerage and drainage and to have road access, and anti-littering laws require households and businesses to have non-recyclable garbage collected or to dispose of it themselves, usually in public depots or tips.

Fourth, because of the complexity of prices and the fact that they are often levied on measures of use that are not readily observed or controlled by users, the provision of information and education can help users to know how they can make savings by economising on their use of services. Such information is needed if prices are to have their maximum impact on the level of demand. The labelling of appliances to indicate their level of use of water or energy, advice to home owners about how to use water efficiently on lawns and gardens, advice to industrialists about how to recycle and thus reduce their discharge of trade wastes, advice about insulation and energy efficient design of buildings, and advice about (as well as provision of convenient means of) recycling of household wastes are examples of ways in which improved information can lead to demands for services falling and becoming more sensitive to price changes.

Fifth, because of the effects of the use of many infrastructure services on other people, users can be persuaded to reduce their use on the grounds of social responsibility. If they are to respond to such appeals, they need information about how they can, for example, change their behaviour in ways that will reduce damage to the environment; reduce the use of exhaustible resources; or save public funds by making it possible to defer the date at which a new water supply dam will be required. Consumers are urged to reduce their use of services not only because it will save them money directly but also because it will improve the quality of the environment, reduce the emission of air pollutants and reduce the costs of supply authorities, and thus save them money indirectly. Examples are ACT Electricity and Water's campaign based on the slogan 'Save water before it costs the earth' and Melbourne Water's 'Don't be a Wally with Water'. The responsiveness of consumers to appeals for environmental responsibility can be seen in the appearance on supermarket shelves of, for example, recycled paper products and phosphate-free detergents that are labelled as being environmentally friendly. Further evidence is the success of recycling programs in reducing the volume of garbage going into landfill.

## Public goods and collective benefits

The initial public provision of roads, water, sewerage, drainage and garbage collection and disposal was mainly aimed at producing benefits for the community as a whole rather than for individual users. That public provision achieved most of its objectives: potable drinking water and sewerage systems reduced diseases, flooding and litter were reduced, and travel became safer and more comfortable. This success facilitated forms of urban development that are highly dependent on the provision of infrastructure and its use expanded, bringing many private as well as the original collective benefits. Use of the services themselves also produces 'public bads' in the form of air, water, noise, aesthetic and land pollution. In this section we concentrate on the public benefits and collective demand for infrastructure services. To the extent that the marginal benefits from increased use are collective, individual users should not be charged and decisions about provision of the services should be taken collectively.

Until they become congested[2], roads are public goods: additional users do not reduce the level of service to existing users, and it is inefficient to attempt to ration their use by charging users. Hence roads were, and sometimes still are, known as public rights of way. Many access roads within residential subdivisions, in rural areas and in some industrial areas still have those characteristics: the demand for them is a collective demand of the owners of the properties to which they provide access. Once the volume of traffic reaches quite modest levels, however, additional vehicles on the road reduce the average speed and the use of roads becomes at the margin a private good. This difference between roads that perform different functions is important in the discussion of optimal charging regimes in later chapters.

Clean water supplies and the collection and disposal of sewage were provided initially as means of protecting public health from water-borne diseases and preventing the public nuisance that results when individuals dispose of effluent. There are, of course, also private benefits (including strictly private health benefits) to individuals and businesses. The continuing importance of the public benefits of water and sewerage services can be seen in the prevalence of diseases caused by water-borne pathogens in cities without adequate hydraulic services, and in concerns about the environmental effects of raw or partially treated sewage being discharged into the environment. The collective demand for the public health benefits and the beneficial effects on the environment of these services will be reflected only poorly in the results of studies of factors affecting individual levels of use. In this case 'the public' includes at least all the residents in an urban area.

Drainage was introduced to limit flooding, and continues to perform that function, whether it be flooding of one allotment by run-off from adjacent allotments, or flooding of low-lying land from run-off from land higher in the catchment. Drainage is not a pure public good because each household has to find some way of disposing of the rainwater that falls on their own roof. Nevertheless, because of the inefficiency (in many cases impossibility) of every owner of urban property liable to flooding negotiating with every owner of property liable to contribute to that flooding, it is commonly provided collectively. Charging the costs of drainage to the owners of property responsible for generating run-off can be seen as both equitable and, if the charges are appropriately designed and if property owners can take measures to reduce run-off, efficient in encouraging such measures.

Some of the benefits from garbage collection, and all of the benefits from its disposal accrue to the public rather than to individuals. The public benefits from collection because it reduces the extent of littering. Once an individual's garbage is collected that person has no individual interest in it, though the community has a great interest in it being disposed of in ways that do not damage the environment. The public benefits are handled partly by anti-littering laws and partly by the public provision of garbage collection and disposal.

A great public benefit from the provision of electricity, and to a lesser extent gas, in urban areas is that it has reduced greatly the pollution of air in cities from the burning of coal and other fuels.

Electrification of suburban railways and the reduction in pollution from cartage of coal within cities have had important benefits. Except where hydro or nuclear sources have replaced fossil fuels as a source of energy, there has not, of course, been a saving in the global volume of greenhouse gases emitted.

## Private goods and private benefits

In addition to the public good demand there is a very significant demand from individuals and property owners for a convenient and reliable supply of potable water, a means of conveniently disposing of wastes, a way of getting rid of excess water during storms, roads and public transport services that permit rapid and safe travel and transport of goods, and a reliable supply of electricity, gas and telephone services. Even this simple listing reflects the different dimensions of demand for most of these services, but studies of demand concentrate mainly, and sometimes exclusively, on the demand for the volume of use of the services. This section examines also other dimensions for which there is an individual demand.

## Demand for volume of use

It is almost impossible to estimate how responsive demand would be to changes in price where there is no price—no charge that varies with the volume of use—or where prices are the same over a long period and for all consumers. For many services, however, there is a user charge which varies over time and between places, and the sensitivity of the volume of demand to changes in the level of charge can be estimated. Where consumers bear a part of the variable costs of consumption because they use their own valuable time, as they do when they travel within cities, it is possible to estimate the elasticity of demand with respect to money costs and time costs. Together such estimates give some indication of the likely effect of changes in money costs.

Individual, commercial and institutional consumers make decisions that affect the volume of each service they use. Some decisions have a direct effect, but others only an indirect effect, on the volume consumed. An example of the latter is that a decision about the design and siting of a house indirectly affects the demand for energy for heating and cooling. Notwithstanding the importance of non-price determinants and the fact that many of the decisions that affect the volume of use are taken primarily for other reasons, the demand for volume of infrastructure services can be analysed in the same way as the demand for other goods and services. But because of the importance of non-price factors relative to price, it is not surprising that the demand for many such services is relatively inelastic with respect to price.

The reasons for low elasticity of demand in the short run can be explained in another way. Direct final consumption of infrastructure services by individuals and households is relatively small. With few exceptions they are used as an input into the production in the household of something else that is desired, just as they are used in firms to produce goods and services for sale. Households use them to produce satisfaction of wants (Ironmonger 1972). This is most easily seen in the case of electricity which is not consumed directly at all, except by accident, but is used to drive specialised items of equipment that produce a comfortable living or working environment, clean clothes, floors, dishes and bodies, cooked food and entertainment. It is the satisfaction of wants using electricity, rather than electricity itself, that is demanded. To use the term coined by Kelvin Lancaster (1966) for a similar concept, its ability to satisfy these wants is the 'characteristic' which is demanded. Electricity is only one input into satisfying wants such as a comfortable living and working environment. Other inputs include capital invested in buildings, heating and cooling equipment, and their maintenance.

Using another concept from demand theory, the demand for electricity is 'derived' from the demand to satisfy a range of wants. It follows from the theory of derived demand that the demand for electricity will be less sensitive to changes in the price of electricity (less price elastic) the lower the proportion of the cost of electricity in the total cost of satisfying the want or producing the demanded characteristics.

There are few alternative ways of satisfying a number of the wants that are satisfied by many infrastructure services. For example, there is no close substitute for electricity in the provision of light, and few substitutes for the many uses which rely on small electric motors such as vacuum cleaners and refrigerators, or electronic equipment such as television sets and computers. For safety reasons there is almost no substitute for electricity for driving lifts. Where there are substitutes for the use of electricity, they require investment either in different equipment or in buildings that are better insulated and designed to make use of solar heating and natural ventilation, all of which are long-term options.

These reasons for low inelasticity of demand apply with greater or lesser force to other infrastructure services. Very little water is drunk. Most is used: with land and investments in landscaping to provide a pleasant environment; with electricity and consumer durables for cleaning; or with other equipment for flushing of wastes through a sewerage system. There are no substitutes for water in most of its uses, and the alternative ways of meeting wants that water usually satisfies, for example, composting toilets and gardens that use less water, require significant capital expenditure and satisfy the wants in rather different ways. Similarly roads are used with vehicles and the time of travellers to get people to places they want to go, and goods to where they are demanded. One estimate is that petrol accounts for less than 15 per cent of the total cost of operating a vehicle; as a result the elasticity of (the derived) demand for petrol is low, especially in the short term.

*The impact of price on demand in the short and long run*

While changes in price have some immediate impact on the demand for goods and services, it takes time for the full response to occur. A long time is required before the full impact is felt of a change in cost on the demand for many urban physical infrastructure services, because demand is greatly affected by long-term decisions about where to live and work, what kind of dwelling to live in and how to landscape the allotment, and the ownership of motor vehicles and other consumer durables that are needed to use the services. Short- and long-run demand for these services have much in common with short- and long-run cost. Short-run demand is less elastic and reflects the responsiveness of the level of use to changes in the costs of satisfying wants on the assumption that the locations of home, work and school, the consumer durables available, and the landscaping of homes and public areas are all fixed. In the longer term all of these factors will themselves respond to changes in the cost of services: a sustained increase in the petrol tax and hence its price will result in people living closer to work, or working and shopping closer to home, and perhaps owning fewer cars and using more public transport. An increase in the price of water will result in some people switching to landscaping which needs less irrigation, fitting water-saving devices to showers and toilets and possibly installing rainwater tanks so that they can use the rainwater that falls on their roofs.

If the other inputs needed to use electricity are items of durable capital equipment there will have to be a large change in the price of electricity to make it worthwhile scrapping them in the short term. In the long term, however, when the capital items reach the end of their productive lives, demand will be more elastic. The near-zero observed short-term cross-elasticity of demand for gas and electricity, which are often considered as close substitutes in many areas of use (Department of Energy 1989), is because the demand for both gas and electricity is a derived demand and the equipment needed to use gas for almost any purpose cannot be adapted to the use of electricity and vice versa: an increase in the price of electricity will cause very few people whose houses are fitted only with electric stoves to switch to gas for cooking in the short term. Low cross-elasticities are found between public and private transport for similar reasons. Goodwin (1988) reports that the mean cross-elasticity from a number of studies of demand for public transport with respect to petrol price is 0.34. On the other hand, where wants can be satisfied using alternative services that require much the same capital equipment, cross-elasticities are much higher. For example, Thomas and Syme (1988) found a remarkably high cross-elasticity of demand between bore water and mains water in Perth of 3.5, even though bore water requires capital to be invested in a bore and possibly a pump.

Many studies of the elasticity of demand for urban services have assessed only short-run impacts and have found very low price elasticities. Such studies frequently include as independent explanatory variables the ownership of consumer durables such as cars and washing machines, location, and size of allotment. In the long term those variables are at least partly endogenous: all can change in response to price changes. Elasticities of demand for urban transport and electricity are usually two or three times as high in the long run as the short run (see Goodwin 1992; Voith 1991; and Dahl & Sterner 1991 for transport, and Department of Energy 1989 for electricity). Dahl and Sterner report elasticities of demand in the short run (less than a year) for petrol use in private vehicles of –0.24 to –0.31 with an average of –0.26. In the long run (ten years) the range was –0.80 to –1.01 with a mean of –0.86.

In a strict sense, long-run demand responds to expectations about future prices rather than past or current prices, but expectations are heavily influenced by past experience. Short-term variations in price due to seasonal fluctuations or variations that are used as part of a rationing scheme to cope with a temporary shortage, as in the case of water in times of drought, will produce only a short-term demand response. Because such short-term responses to changes in prices are small it is common for other rationing procedures to be used—electricity cuts and restrictions on water use—in addition to or instead of price increases, to meet short-term supply shortages.

## Demand at different locations

As pointed out in Chapter 2, infrastructure services, like other services, are consumed where they are produced. Therefore, demand is always location specific. How sensitive is demand at different locations to infrastructure prices at those locations? Because differences in prices between different parts of urban areas for most services are either zero or small relative to the other advantages and disadvantages of living or working at different locations, different prices as such seldom have a large effect on the choice of location. Those other advantages and disadvantages might themselves include differences in the level of use, and hence the cost of these services. For example, choosing to live further from work, school and shops means that trips are longer and therefore travel costs are higher; and choosing to live on sandy soils will require more water to be used for irrigation to maintain a garden.

It is common for uniform prices or charges to be levied for services such as electricity, gas, water and sewerage throughout an urban area because estimating the relative cost of supply at different locations is difficult; and because the relative cost in different locations can vary over time depending on the extent to which there is spare capacity in particular parts of the network. In addition the long-run costs of providing a number of services, for example, electricity, gas, telephones and perhaps garbage collection and disposal, seldom vary greatly between parts of a city. The previous chapter showed, however, that there are situations in which the long-run cost of providing water, sewerage and drainage and of providing roads and public transport do vary significantly with location. It has been argued (Neutze 1993; Australian Urban and Regional Development Review 1995), that charges should vary between locations in line with those cost differences.

Charges already differ with location in three respects. The first relates to public transport, in particular rail transport. The Industry Commission (1994a, p. 173) showed that the price per kilometre and the percentage of cost recovered are both lower for long than for short trips. As a result rail commuters have a greater incentive to live further from where they work than they would if they had to pay the full cost of their journeys. No estimate has been made of the locational effect of this price difference. The second applies in part at least to both public transport and roads: since the value of the time of the traveller, and the vehicle operating costs borne by the traveller, are a major part of the cost of travel, there is a direct impact on location of the user cost per kilometre. Those costs vary with the level of congestion and with differences in the value of the time of travellers. Third, the money cost of travel per unit of distance varies with location depending on the extent of congestion, although as pointed out in the previous chapter, the cost to the individual traveller varies less than it would if the cost of the congestion caused to other drivers was included in the cost of the trip.

There is a different sense in which the cost of some infrastructure services varies greatly with location. Because access to jobs, schools, shops and other amenities varies between parts of a city, the demand for travel varies. This produces the well-known impact of changes in the cost of travel on the extent of spread of cities (Mills 1972; Muth 1969). There is a good deal of evidence (Marchetti 1992) that time spent on travel remains relatively constant as cities grow: travel distances increase roughly at the same rate as average speed increases because of better roads and faster cars, buses and trains. This may be partly because income usually increases over time as travel speed increases and the demand for travel is relatively income elastic. But it may also reflect the relatively high long-run elasticity of demand for travel with respect to both user money costs and user time cost per kilometre.

Because changes in location involve high social as well as financial costs, location decisions are long-run decisions and any changes in location in response to changes in the relative price of services at different locations are likely to be slow. Aggregate changes in location are even slower than individual changes because, if a number of individuals move away from a location, the price of property there falls, which attracts some new occupants, and the extent of the fall in the level of occupancy is reduced as a result.

Most of the aggregate location responses occur through new development and redevelopment, though the rate at which buildings are allowed to deteriorate is also affected by changes in the demand for accommodation at the buildings' location.

## The time distribution of demand

The previous chapter showed the importance of the time distribution of demand as a determinant of costs. The volume of services demanded at any given price during a given period depends on seasonal and diurnal climatic differences, cultural and biological factors such as hours of work, sleep and attending school and when meals are prepared, and unpredictable events such as rainstorms, heatwaves, cold snaps and building or bush fires.

The cost of supplying the service varies markedly between peak and off-peak periods where capacity costs are a high proportion of total costs and the services are expensive or impossible to store, as is true of electricity and urban travel (and water in some areas where a higher price is charged in summer). In such situations total costs could be reduced by shifting demand from peak to off-peak periods. Such a shift in demand can be encouraged by charging higher prices during periods of peak demand, if the time distribution of demand for services is responsive to the relative level of prices in peak and off-peak periods. We know relatively little about the cross-elasticity of demand between peak and off-peak periods, or even the elasticity of demand specifically during peak and off-peak periods. Relatively small shifts in time distribution of demand can be obtained by staggering working hours or by allowing flexible working hours, but large changes in working hours or inter-seasonal shifts in demand appear to be much more difficult to achieve. Many demand peaks occur during unpredictable events such as rainstorms, wildfires or very hot or cold weather. The relatively few available studies show that, while in the short run such peaks in demand are relatively unresponsive to price, in the long term prices which reflect the higher costs of meeting peak demand reduce peaking. Even in a period as short as a year, a Canadian study found reductions in peak period consumption of electricity as high as 11 per cent following the introduction of higher prices during peak periods, though this resulted in a change from uniform prices to a price from 5 to 9 pm in winter weekdays that was 5.5 times that in summer off-peak hours (Mountain & Lawson 1992).

## Demand for access

Access is required as a condition of being able to consume a volume of network services. It must be provided to individual properties before the occupants of those properties can make use of most network services. Public transport is a partial exception: it does not provide access to individual properties but it does provide varying levels of access depending on how close rail stations and bus and tram stops are to where people live, work, shop and go to school, and how directly their routes follow the routes people want to travel. In urban areas nearly all developed property is required to have access through a connection to the sewerage, drainage, water, road and electricity networks. Thus the demand for access to these services is very inelastic with respect to the cost of providing access. There have been very few studies of the demand for access to services: it will, of course, be affected by the level of user charges as well as the level of access charges.

Physical access involves the provision of roads, pipes and wires within a locality and connecting the locality to existing networks. This is usually provided by the developer and its cost passed on to buyers of developed property. Access in terms of turning on the service, maintaining and charging for the service is frequently charged for separately, and in some cases a property owner can decline to pay this charge.

### Short- and long-run demand for access

As pointed out in the previous chapter, the cost of providing access to a locality is a substantial, collective long-run cost, but the cost of providing access to an individual property once the network has been installed in a locality is small, and relatively short term, Access can be charged for as a capital sum through development charges (roads, water, sewerage, drainage), a periodic fixed charge (gas, electricity, telephones, vehicle registration and sometimes water), a charge related to volume of use, or a combination of these. Development charges are a long-term cost to users, but the other two are short-term costs which permit users to connect, or disconnect and avoid the access charges, at short notice.

If the buyers of newly developed properties are required to pay the capital cost of providing access, properties with access are more valuable than those without. In those circumstances access costs are to a large extent capitalised into the value of properties with access. Since the demand for properties with access is sensitive to their total price, the demand for access is not completely inelastic even where access is a condition of occupation: high access costs will reduce somewhat the total demand for housing and other premises. Where the cost of access to services is a small proportion of the total cost of land and building, however, the elasticity of demand for access is likely to be low.

## Demand for access at different locations

The cost of providing access to some services varies considerably with location within an urban area. The price of access, like the price at which a volume of services is provided, can be varied spatially to reflect differences between areas in its cost, though often access charges are uniform across an urban area. When developers are required to pay for on-site reticulation, variations in the cost of reticulation—part of the cost of access—are automatically reflected in the prices of new houses at different locations. Where developers are required also to pay the cost of connecting a new subdivision to the existing network, an additional part of the cost of access which varies with location will be reflected in house prices. Access charges of this kind encourage development in locations where services can be provided at lower cost. Other access costs that vary with location, such as the higher cost of the pipes needed to carry water to suburbs remote from sources of water, or the additional cost of pumps required to provide water in elevated parts of the city, are rarely charged to developers. The traditional way to discourage development in such locations has been through land-use controls. Charges for services such as sewerage and water are, of course, frequently higher in small towns where access costs are higher.

Access charges that reflect the cost of a connection may have a significant effect on whether householders choose to connect to optional services such as telephones and gas. Like electricity, these services commonly charge a periodic fixed access fee, sometimes as a component in a declining block tariff, rather than as a capital charge on developers. It is not clear that those access charges cover the total cost of providing access or whether some access costs are covered from charges for use of the service. Unlike developer charges, none of these costs will be capitalised into the value of property.

It is possible in the future that access to some services could become optional because of acceptable alternative arrangements for water supply (rainwater tanks, re-use of grey water), sewerage (composting toilets and re-use of grey water), drainage (on-site irrigation and drainage sumps) and electricity (solar generation with battery storage). If that were to occur, demand for access would become more elastic with respect to its price.

The demand for different levels of access (quality, capacity) may be sensitive to access charges that vary with the cost; for example, the size of water, sewer, drainage and gas mains connections, the voltage and capacity of electrical connections and whether or not they are installed underground, the number of telephone lines, the width of access roads and whether or not there are footpaths.

Some decisions about access and about the capacity and quality of access provided in residential areas are taken by property developers. If there is a genuine choice about quality, and if the differences in cost are passed on to buyers of the new property in the prices of allotments, purchasers can be expected to choose between allotments according to their willingness to pay for different levels of access. But that will occur only if developers both have a choice and exercise it by providing blocks with a range of levels of service. It is common, however, for many decisions about at least the minimum quality and capacity of access to be made by the supplier of the services: the local government or other service authority.

Because the supplier is responsible for the maintenance and eventual replacement of the access facilities, it will have an incentive to require a level of durability in the service that minimises the cost of future maintenance, replacements and upgrading. As a result, developers are likely to be required to provide greater capacity and durability of access facilities than is economically optimal, and home buyers may have little choice. Without such controls on quality and capacity, however, developers would have the opposite incentive: to provide too little durability and reserve capacity. The ideal is for decisions about durability and capacity to be made and the cost to be borne by the body responsible for subsequent maintenance, replacement and upgrading. Since developers seldom stay in business for the life of infrastructure investments, the service provider commonly becomes the owner after a subdivision is completed, and is the only possible candidate for performing both functions. From this point of view, service providers should be responsible for reticulation in new subdivision. There are contrary arguments, however, and this is a matter to which we return.

## Demand for reliability

It was pointed out in the previous chapter that the cost of reducing the probability of failure of a network service to meet demand, whether as a result of extreme climatic conditions or equipment failure, increases rapidly as that probability approaches zero. It is difficult to estimate how much users are prepared to pay to reduce the probability of, for example, cuts in electricity services or water restrictions, or to have a higher proportion of buses and trains run on time.

The costs of interruption of services are very high for some users, for example, the cost of power cuts to wholesalers and retailers of perishable foods, and such users would presumably be willing to pay more for reliability. Discounts are sometimes provided to non-residential consumers who are willing to accept that supply will be interrupted up to a certain number of times per year. For most consumers, however, decisions about supply reliability have to be taken collectively through political processes, it being recognised that users such as hospitals and certain process industries for whom the costs of interruption would be very high, will get priority in times of shortage.

# DEMAND FOR INDIVIDUAL SERVICES

## Transport

The demand for urban travel is derived from the desire of people to undertake a variety of activities at different locations at particular times (Small 1992, p. 36). The demand for goods transport is similarly derived from the advantages of undertaking the production, processing, storage, retailing and consumption of goods at different locations, and in some cases to deliver them at specific times. The places and times at which we do different things can be varied, as can the mode and route by which we travel or transport goods. It is not surprising that it is difficult adequately to model the determinants of demand, and through such models to estimate the impacts of changes in the costs or price of transport on its use. Urban travel is more complex also because of multi-purpose or chained trips.

There have, however, been many studies of urban travel demand, most carried out to assist in planning facilities to meet future demand. Data from these and other studies have been used to estimate the responsiveness of demand to changes in travel costs. These studies use the volume of travel, rather than either the use of roads for access or for carrying heavy loads (e.g. tonne-kms) as the measure of quantity, and the majority are studies of the demand for commuter travel. This is an important element of urban travel for which the demand is regular, for a defined purpose and for which many of the short-term determinants, such as where people live and where they work, can be measured and are likely to remain stable for some time. It should be recognised, however, that this is far from the total picture: it ignores goods transport and is unlikely to be representative of urban travel as a whole. In the United States non-work trips are three times as numerous as work trips, they outnumber work trips even at peak periods, and they grew faster between 1977 and 1983 (Richardson & Gordon 1989). In Melbourne in 1992 work trips were only some 14 per cent of the total number of trips (Industry Commission 1994a, p. 64).

The cost of urban travel to the traveller has two main components: money costs and time costs. The money costs are quite clear to the user of public transport, but the money cost of making a particular trip by road in a privately owned vehicle is more difficult to define: it clearly includes variable costs such as fuel and maintenance costs that vary with distance travelled, and parking costs. But few demand studies include the cost of car ownership, even when estimating the demand for commuting trips, although many cars are owned specifically for commuting.

The general conclusions from these studies have been surveyed in several publications (Small 1992, pp. 5–45; Goodwin 1992; Industry Commission 1994a, Appendix B). The results of the numerous studies are quite varied but there are several conclusions on which there is a consensus.

Price elasticities of demand are relatively low: very few studies show elasticities of greater than one, and many are closer to zero (Small 1992, p. 11; Industry Commission 1994a, Appendix B). Elasticities of demand with respect to time spent in commuting are markedly higher than with respect to money costs. This results from the fact that, when time is valued at an appropriate rate, time costs are at least three times as high a proportion of total cost as money costs (Hensher 1989). Travel would be expected to be more sensitive to a given percentage change in a larger than a smaller component of total costs. Similarly, were time accorded an appropriate money value and added to money costs, the elasticity of demand with respect to total costs would be greater than with respect to either component by itself. It is, however, difficult to estimate the value of time (see below) and, since the methods of valuing it rely on demand relationships, there is a degree of circular reasoning in using those estimates to establish elasticity of demand with respect to full costs. Nevertheless it is clear that estimates of elasticity with respect to time or to money costs alone will understate the elasticity of demand with respect to the two combined.

The demand for peak period travel is less elastic than for off-peak travel, presumably because a higher proportion in the peak period is non-discretionary travel such as to work or school. There is little information about cross-elasticities of demand between periods but higher peak period public transport fares and road prices would be expected to discourage travel in peak periods, or at least lead to even more spreading of the peaks than has occurred as a result of congestion.

Cross-elasticities of demand between private and public transport appear to be much lower than own price or own travel time elasticities. This is partly because much of the travel by public transport is by people who do not have access to a car or, especially in the case of travel by train, is predominantly to the city centre where road congestion and shortages and cost of parking make it difficult for most people to travel by car.

Many studies have attempted to estimate the value of travel time. They show that the value of time spent travelling is much less than of time spent walking to or waiting for public transport. Generally they show that the value of time spent travelling increases with income, though usually less than proportionately. Most but not all estimates of the value of time spent travelling fall in the range of 30 to 60 per cent of hourly wages. In addition:

- Values are generally higher for business than commuter trips and higher for commuter trips than for non-work travel;
- Values are higher for travel by car than by public transport, perhaps because of the opportunity to read on public transport; and

• The marginal value of time increases as the time spent on a trip increases.

This is consistent with findings of travel budget studies that the time spent on commuting varies little between medium-sized and large cities (Gunn 1981). Trip scheduling is an important dimension of demand, especially for travel to work and to school, and the time of travel is sensitive to relative costs. Research on this question shows that when working hours are fixed people are reluctant to arrive at work early, and even more reluctant to arrive late (Small 1982). For this reason road improvements often result in the peak demand period being shortened, as people travel closer to their desired time, rather than resulting in a fall in peak volume/capacity ratios. For this reason also, the introduction of flexible working hours in Ottawa resulted in a fall of 50 per cent in peak volumes as people were able to vary their desired time of travel.

Peaks in demand for roads and public transport result mainly from the social objective of a relatively uniform working day and working week for most workers. This permits families to spend their leisure time together and facilitates sporting, cultural and recreational activities outside the common working hours. This uniformity has been broken down to some extent with the extension of shopping hours and the hours at which other services are available. These longer hours reduce some travel peaks as well as permitting fuller use of the fixed capital of retailing and service establishments. Higher charges for travel during peak hours may result in further differentiation of working hours and extension of service hours.

Quality of service in the field of public transport has an important impact on demand. Increases in the temporal and spatial frequency of services raise demand partly because they reduce walk/wait time and partly because they permit people to travel closer to their desired times.[3] Except for trips to or from the city centre and a few other major centres, most trips by public transport are less direct, and therefore longer, than trips between the same end points by private vehicle. As jobs and services become more dispersed within urban areas, the demand for public transport falls relative to private transport. Increases in the reliability of public transport services and in the predictability of travel times by road can be expected to affect demand, though Small (1992, p. 36) reports that no measure of reliability has achieved statistical significance in explaining travel choice. The comfort of public transport, especially the probability of getting a seat, is another important quality dimension.

Safety is a very important aspect of the quality of transport services. Accidents are recognised as an important social cost of transport in investment decision making, and many investments in urban roads are made with the objective of reducing the frequency of accidents. They are also a private cost and although it would be expected that demand would be higher the lower the perceived risk of travel, this has not been incorporated in demand models, perhaps because the perceived cost of the risk is seen to be small relative to other costs or too difficult to assess.

The demand for travel by particular modes is more elastic than for travel as a whole, though still quite inelastic: demand for travel over particular routes, or particular sections of a network is more elastic than on the network as a whole; and demand for travel during shorter periods is more elastic than during longer periods. Where there are more alternatives there is more choice and demand is more elastic.

Demand is about twice or three times as sensitive in the long term as in the short term (Lago et al. 1981; Goodwin 1992; Voith 1991). In the long term travellers can make a number of adjustments that are impossible in the short term. They can change where they work, shop, go to school, have recreation, and where they live. They can buy or sell a car to facilitate the use of an alternative mode. In the short term they can readily change only their mode and time of travel and the route they take. Summarising a large number of studies, Goodwin (1992, p. 159) concludes that a sustained real 10 per cent increase in fuel price will in the short run result in a decrease in traffic of about 1.5 per cent and a decrease in fuel consumption of about 3 per cent. In the longer run traffic would fall by 3 to 5 per cent and fuel consumption by 7 per cent or more. The difference would be due to a move to more fuel-efficient vehicles.

The demand for road access follows from a demand among households and businesses to locate on separate allotments in varied locations with separate access to the public road network. Economies can be made in the cost of public access by the use of various kinds of private access including private roads, battle-axe blocks, courts or malls. When the capital cost of providing access is included in the price of an allotment, as occurs when developers or subdividers are required to pay the cost, the higher price of property with road access will have an impact on the demand for subdivision and hence the cost of providing access.

If there were charges that reflected the thickness of pavements required for their use by heavy vehicles, it is likely that the elasticity of demand for road thickness from users of heavy vehicles would be relatively low in urban areas, for two reasons. First, there is no substitute for trucks for the transport of most freight within urban areas. Second, the optimal level of mass–distance charges which result from the use of urban roads is likely to be a small proportion of the total cost of freight transport or bus operation, and an even smaller proportion of the price of the finished products that are either being transported or made from what is being transported.

We can conclude from the above that the aggregate demand for travel in cities is affected relatively little by changes in the cost of travel, especially the money cost, though it is somewhat more responsive to changes in levels of service such as road congestion or frequency of public transport, which change its time costs. Choice of mode is not very sensitive to relative cost because it is greatly influenced by the availability of convenient public transport between the desired origin and destination, access to a car and ability to drive. In the short term choice of route between a given origin and destination, and in the long term choice of origin and destination and availability of a car, are likely to be more sensitive to cost.

It follows that varying the cost of travel by introducing charging structures that more closely reflect costs will have little effect on the aggregate volume of travel in an urban area in the short term. In the long term, however, charges that vary between modes, between routes and between peak and off-peak periods can influence the demands for living in different locations and the locations of businesses and services. They can, in short, affect the form, structure and function of urban areas and the access of their residents to jobs, services and amenities.

## Water

While the technologies of the three hydraulic services have enough in common to allow their costs to be discussed together, the demand for each of the three services is quite different. Piped water supplies were introduced to cities partly as a health measure and partly as an efficient way to provide a commodity to individual properties.

The demand is therefore both collective and individual. The individual domestic demand for water is for consumption, cleaning, carriage of wastes and irrigation and the commercial/industrial demand is mostly for cleaning, carriage of wastes, incorporation into products and cooling. In addition there is a considerable demand for irrigation of public open space within urban areas in dry climates. Estimation of demand elasticities is complicated where there are increasing block tariffs. In that situation, different consumers can face different marginal prices, and some may be uncertain of the price they are paying at the margin. Also there is some evidence that consumers take account of fixed charges and the cost of infra-marginal blocks of consumption—the average cost to them rather than cost at the margin—in deciding on levels of consumption (Martin & Wilder 1992).

Studies of the demand for water have been confined almost entirely to the demand for volume of use, and the majority of studies have focused either on residential demand where cross-sectional data were used, or aggregate demand where time series data were used. The few studies of industrial use suggest that the elasticity of demand is high (Renzetti 1992). This is surprising in that water accounts for a small proportion of production costs for most manufacturing processes. It is, however, consistent with experience in Newcastle, Australia, where the steel works greatly reduced its use of water by increasing recycling following the introduction of volume charges. It is more likely that it will be cost effective for industries to recycle water than for households to do so.

Most studies of domestic demand estimate elasticities in the range of –0.2 to –0.8, but this is a weighted average of different demands. The demand for water used inside the home for drinking, washing and toilet flushing is less elastic than the outdoors demand for irrigation, car washing and swimming pools. Since the latter demands are responsible for costly seasonal peaks in demand[4], demand is more elastic in the peak than outside the peak: perhaps five times as elastic (Lyman 1992).

As with other infrastructure services, elasticities are higher in the long run than in the short run. In the short term higher water prices may persuade people to water their gardens less and economise on water in the laundry but in the long term they may plant gardens that need less water, fit low volume shower heads and dual flush cisterns, buy more efficient washing machines and even install rainwater tanks. A study of the responsiveness of demand to price in the very short term when prices were raised to encourage conservation of water during a drought in Honolulu found elasticities up to –0.2 to –0.3 (Moncur 1987).

The evidence from cities that have introduced volume charges for water suggests that they have a significant impact on the level of use. For example, a careful analysis of the effects of the introduction of charges in Newcastle concludes that it reduced consumption by 20 to 29 per cent (Viswanath 1989). It is not possible to estimate an elasticity from these figures since the percentage increase in price (from zero) was infinite.

As with other services, factors other than price affect the demand for water in both the short and the long term. These include income, household size (water consumption is often measured per person), evaporation/transpiration rate, rainfall and income. In the long term allotment size, gardening practices and the number and water efficiency of appliances can be varied, and in the very long term the size of allotments.[5] Education has been found to be effective in reducing demand for water (Nieswiadomy 1992), partly because the ways in which behaviour patterns can be modified to reduce the use of water are not obvious to consumers, and partly because education stresses both the environmental advantages of reducing consumption and the collective financial savings from deferring future headworks if water consumption is reduced.

Although the cost of supplying water varies between peak and off-peak periods (both within a day and within a year), it is rare for its price to vary accordingly, partly because balancing storage is possible for short period fluctuations, and in many areas for seasonal fluctuations, and therefore cost variations are not as great as for electricity and roads. Nevertheless charging at higher rates during periods of peak demand is increasing in North America where peak demand is an important determinant of system costs. Similarly the cost of delivery varies between parts of a metropolitan area, but few suppliers charge a higher price even to properties at higher elevations where pumping costs are higher. Therefore we know nothing about cross-elasticity of demand between times and places. They would be expected to be very low between different seasons and locations but might be quite high for irrigation between different times of the day.

The value of access to water supply in urban areas is generally much higher than the cost of providing access to individual properties—both the cost to developers of providing a connection and the cost to suppliers of reading meters and sending accounts—and therefore demand is very inelastic. A supply of water is needed not only for consumption and washing, it is essential also for waterborne sewerage, to which nearly all urban properties are required to be connected. To the extent that the cost of access is passed on as a higher cost of housing, and the demand for separate dwellings is price elastic, the demand is likely to be somewhat responsive to costs. Access in this context includes not only the ability to draw water at a certain rate but to have access to a much greater flow and pressure from street mains in the event of a fire. It is this latter demand which determines the size of mains and water pressure in residential and most commercial areas. A study in South Carolina estimated the demand for access from delinquency rates and found that delinquency increased significantly as price increased, but was much less elastic with respect to the income of households.

With recent developments in composting toilets it is becoming increasingly possible to achieve one of the main public health objectives of urban water supply, disposal of human wastes, without the need for large volumes of water. As a result, it is likely in the future that housing will be permitted in urban areas that have neither a sewerage nor a water connection. Such houses, like many in rural areas, would rely on storage of rainwater from roof catchments and would store water that had been used for washing for irrigation. The allotments for a subdivision comprising such houses would be cheaper because of the lower capital costs of installing services, and their annual cost also would be lower because there would be no water and sewerage charges. Their fire insurance premiums, however, might be a good deal higher. The response of home buyers to the offer of such housing would provide an indication of the level of demand for access to a piped water supply (and piped water-borne sewerage). In the long term the availability of such an option would increase the elasticity of demand for both access to and volume of water.

The demand for reliability of water supply is an important, but largely unmeasured, dimension of demand. Decisions about the reliability of supply are collective decisions. Consumers can reveal their preference for reliable supply only by moving to an urban area with a more reliable supply, or by political activity. It is difficult to assess the importance of that factor among other determinants of location decisions.

## Sewerage

Like the supply of piped water, the provision of piped sewerage meets both an individual demand for cheap and easy disposal of human and industrial wastes and of water that has been used for cleaning (grey water), and a collective demand to avoid the nuisance, environmental damage and health risks that occur if such wastes are disposed of individually. Until the 1970s (and still in Perth) substantial parts of Australia's large cities were not connected to piped sewerage and relied mainly on individual methods of sewage disposal (septic tanks or nightsoil collection). Depending on soil type, septic tanks either have to be pumped out frequently, in which case they are little more than modern and hygienic versions of nineteenth century cesspits, or they cause some pollution of groundwater.

The sewage produced by industry and commercial activities varies greatly in composition and, as pointed out in the previous chapter, both the composition and the volume affect the cost of its collection and treatment. The volume of large, mostly industrial, dischargers is generally measured and volume charges are levied. Trade waste charges also reflect the amount of particular pollutants discharged. There have, however, been no assessments of the elasticity of demand for disposal of particular pollutants through the sewers. The volume of sewage discharged reflects mainly the volume of water used for particular purposes, so that the demand for volume reflects those water demands. Because of the opportunities for recycling, the demand by many large users to discharge a volume of sewage can be expected to be relatively elastic as it is for consumption of a volume of water.

The techniques currently available for measuring the volume and composition of sewage flows are too expensive to install in residential and small commercial premises. As a result, the charges paid by owners or occupants of such properties either are fixed or vary in proportion to water use. Without charges that are proportional to use, it is not possible to estimate the elasticity of demand, though it is likely to be very low, in line with the elasticity of demand for domestic internal use of water. Almost by definition, the lower the volume of domestic sewage the higher the strength, but such increases in strength do not increase treatment costs, while the reduction in volume reduces both collection and treatment costs.

In summary, given current requirements to connect to sewers, the elasticity of demand for the discharge of actual wastes from domestic and many commercial premises is likely to be very low, but the volume of water in which they are carried might be expected to respond to increases in the price of water as more water efficient cisterns, showers and washing appliances are installed, especially if water discharged into the sewers can be measured and therefore priced separately. The elasticity of demand in terms of both waste materials and volume from large commercial and industrial premises is likely to be variable and could be quite high because of the opportunities for recycling. Where both water and sewerage are funded from a charge per unit of water used, the total charge will be relatively high and the elasticity of demand also relatively high.

As in the case of roads and water supply, the demand for access to sewerage services can be expected to be very price inelastic as long as all new urban housing is required to be connected, the elasticity being reflected only in the elasticity of demand for separate housing and other premises. For reasons described in the previous section, the increasing acceptance of composting toilets may permit houses and other premises to be built without connection to either water or sewerage. That possibility would increase the elasticity of demand for access and for the use of the sewerage system.

Reliability is an important dimension of the quality of sewerage services. Whereas the consequences of inadequate capacity in water supply are felt by individual users in the form of restrictions and shortages, the consequences of inadequate capacity or other failures in the sewerage system are felt mostly by the community in the form of leaking or overflowing sewers or treatment works and consequent pollution of the environment, loss of amenity and danger to public health. The demand for a reliable service is a demand for the public goods of public health and protection of the environment, and decisions about reliability are made collectively.

**Stormwater drainage**

As for water supply and sewerage, there is an individual demand for stormwater drainage, to avoid flooding of individual properties, and a (larger) collective demand, to avoid general flooding from the run-off from individual properties, roads and other public areas, and to minimise the damage to the environment from flooding. As well as the broad collective interest in avoiding flooding, there are frequently bilateral externalities when rainwater falling on one property floods a neighbouring property. Avoiding the flooding of individual properties from the rain that falls on them is generally much less costly than avoidance of general flooding. Stormwater also carries pollutants as it washes roads, roofs and parking areas, flushes drains and carries sediment. In many cities with separate sanitary and stormwater drains, stormwater is the major source of pollution of rivers, lakes and bays.

While the demand for drainage services is mainly collective, about half of the run-off comes from privately owned land, run-off being proportional to area weighted by the fraction covered by impermeable surface. If it were possible to devise a system for charging the owners of property for the cost of dealing with the run-off from their properties, would the volume of run-off be responsive to the level of such charges?

For the individual property owner the opportunities to vary discharges are limited. The collection of rainwater from roofs into tanks for subsequent use, minimising the area covered by hard surfaces and increasing mulching will all reduce the volume and the speed with which rainfall runs off a property. Both are important determinants of flooding. Soakage pits can be provided to hold stormwater and permit it to soak into the ground. All these measures will also reduce the quantities of pollutants in stormwater.

There is more that can be done during land development to slow down and reduce the flows by increasing the opportunities for absorption. Examples are the use of broad and shallow drains that are grassed rather than concrete-lined. Open space can be used for temporary flooding and absorption of stormwater, and local holding ponds can both retard run-off and allow pollutants to settle before they reach public waterways. Charging mechanisms or regulations which give subdividers an incentive or require them to include such facilities would reduce the off-site cost of dealing with stormwater. It is becoming more common in North America for municipalities to require a stormwater plan for each site that is consistent with the plan for dealing with stormwater in the whole catchment.

There is no useful measure of demand for stormwater services in terms of average volume carried. There is a demand for access and a demand for capacity (peak demand). The capacity of a drainage system is defined in terms of reliability and is commonly measured in terms of its ability to cope with the largest flood expected with some defined frequency, for example once in 20, 50 or 100 years. The demand for reliability measured in this way depends on the damage likely to result from flooding which exceeds the capacity of the drainage system.

Much run-off during storms and much of the debris and pollutants come from public areas, especially roads and parking areas. One of the challenges for civil engineering is to design hard pavements and road drainage which permit the surface penetration of water without becoming unusable by pedestrians or vehicles in wet weather.

The demand for stormwater drainage in an urban area depends on the proportion covered by impermeable surfaces. High density development increases the cost of stormwater drainage per unit area. Whether it increases the cost per person depends on the extent to which the larger areas of permeable surfaces in low density urban areas are used to absorb and retard the run-off during rainstorms.

## Electricity and gas

Although the demand for these two sources of reticulated energy have some different features they are sufficiently similar to permit them to be discussed together. The demand for both is overwhelmingly private: lighting of streets and public areas is the main source of collective demand. Both services produce greenhouse gases, at the site of consumption of gas and at the site of generation of electricity. By far the most important dimension of both products is the volume of use. The services are funded primarily from charges according to the volume of use, though providers of both services cover some of their overheads and fixed costs per domestic consumer by charging at a higher rate for the first units used in each billing period. For example, in Canberra the first 250 megajoules of gas used per month cost domestic consumers 3.2c each, amounting to a monthly fixed charge of up to $5.80, with each additional MJ after that costing 0.88c. Similarly the first 100 kilowatt hours of electricity per month cost 11.84c per kWh, and each additional kWh 7.94c amounting to a fixed charge of up to $3.90 per month. It is unlikely that these charges are sufficient to cover the cost of meter reading and billing.

Gas and electricity compete with each other in some markets (space heating, cooking, water heating) and compete with other sources of energy in some markets (gas competes with petrol as a vehicle fuel, electricity competes with diesel to fuel trains and on-street public transport, both compete with heating oil, wood and coal for space heating). Electricity has a near monopoly in the market for lighting, air-conditioning, operation of many appliances, computers, lifts, refrigeration and small electric motors, most of which are quite small users of energy. The elasticity of demand for electricity and gas depends on the competitiveness of the sub-market and on the relative importance of the more or less competitive sub-markets in the total market. The demand for both is more elastic in the long than the short term as users are able to change their space and water heating and cooking appliances.

Studies show a range of elasticities of demand for electricity. Industrial demand is generally relatively elastic. Estimates range, however, from very low, below −0.1, to above −1.0. The higher estimates generally relate to the long-run elasticities, which are commonly at least three times short-run elasticities. They will vary also with the relative importance of electricity in total costs. Elasticities of residential demand fall in a similar range, and they too are commonly at least three times as high in the long as in the short run. Some estimates have found that demand in the long term is quite sensitive to the price of gas, reflecting the importance of the uses in which the two energy sources compete.

Because the cost of supplying electricity (and to a much lesser extent gas, because it can be stored) is higher in peak periods than in off-peak periods, it is desirable to charge more during peak periods. Peaks of demand for electricity traditionally occur in winter in cold climates for heating and in summer in hot climates for air-conditioning. This is changing in some areas due to a decline in the use of electricity for heating and the increased use of air-conditioning. There are also marked diurnal peaks in the early evening due to cooking. If some of the demand for space or water heating could be transferred to night-time hours, costs would be significantly reduced. Peak demand for gas is generally during the winter, and diurnal peaks can be accommodated relatively cheaply by balancing storage.

Differential charging during peak periods especially peak periods during a day, incurs some costs due to the more costly meters required; it is worthwhile implementing such differentials only for high volume users or where the cross-elasticity of demand is sufficiently great. That elasticity is relatively low because of the difficulty most consumers have in changing the time distribution of their use of energy. Given an appropriate means of doing this, there is evidence of a significant cross-elasticity between peak and off-peak demand for electricity for water heating and space heating (Mountain

& Lawson 1992). Electricity authorities have met this demand by offering electricity at a lower price for use in domestic water and space heaters that automatically use most of their electricity in off-peak hours. Because off-peak heating requires the installation of new equipment, demand is responsive only in the long term. An American study (Sexton et al. 1989) showed that the cross-elasticity of demand for electricity between peak and off-peak periods was significantly greater among residential consumers where monitoring devices were fitted which showed continually in digital form the rate of use of electricity and the price being charged. Those devices could show consumers how much electricity was being used by individual appliances. At $US600, however, the devices cost more than the value of the savings achieved at the time of the study.

Both electricity and gas are relatively cheap to transport within urban areas, thus the cost of supply in different parts of cities is similar and prices do not vary significantly within cities.

Climate is an important non-price factor affecting demand. Extremes of temperature increase the demand for energy for cooling and heating. The pressures on and from governments to reduce the emission of greenhouse gases in recent years and the shortage of investment funds have resulted in numerous campaigns to reduce the use of energy. As in the case of water, provision of information about the amount of energy used by different appliances allows consumers to control their use of energy more effectively.

Reliability is an important quality dimension of the supply of electricity in particular because it is needed for many essential services, as well as for refrigeration and other processes for which the interruption of supply can be very costly. In times of short-term load-shedding because of supply shortage or breakdown (for example, as a result of natural disasters), priorities for continuation of supplies are followed. For some users, such as hospitals, continuity of supply is so important that they have backup onsite supply capacity. Other heavy users who can stop operation at little cost often have supply contracts that include a discount price in return for accepting interruptable supply. Domestic consumers are assumed to be able to accept short-term interruptions at little cost.

## Postal and telephone services

The demand for services provided through postal and telephone networks is almost entirely a private demand. In recent years telephone services have broadened from the carriage of voice to the carriage of data, documents and visual images, while some of the information which was previously carried entirely through copper and then fibre optic networks is now carried either by microwave or wireless transmission via mobile telephones, lessening the dependence on physical networks. New forms of communication such as electronic mail have been developed which compete with both postal and telephone services.

The demand for transmission of private information is, however, still primarily met through physical networks and by the carriage of letters and parcels. As with other physical networks there is a demand for access to telephone services and for volume of traffic. There is a very high penetration of access to telephones in Australia, which suggests that at current access charges demand for access is inelastic. It is possible that demand for mobile telephones may be more price elastic. Bewley and Fiebig (1988) found that demand for international calls by number in Australia is relatively inelastic in the short term: for ISD, –0.6 for calls to New Zealand and –0.3 for calls to other countries. Despite the higher calling rates for mobile phones and time-related charges for local calls, their use has extended rapidly in recent years, suggesting that demand for those services may also be inelastic with respect to price.

Because the use of telephones themselves does not require ancillary equipment other than the handset, which is inexpensive for fixed phones, there is no obvious reason for the large difference between short- and long-run elasticity of demand. Nevertheless Bewley and Fiebig found a long-run elasticity of –1.6 for calls to New Zealand and Papua New Guinea and –1.9 for calls to other countries.[6] More expensive equipment is needed for mobile telephony, facsimile and data transfer transmission, however, and therefore demand will be more elastic in the long run. In the long term also, with falling charges, various means of telecommunication are likely to grow relative to other means of communication.

The cost of providing these services is lower the higher the density of traffic. This results in high costs in rural areas and low costs between centres of high density activity, both between and within urban areas. Public and private monopoly carriers that traditionally provided telephone services have been constrained not to charge full cost for the services they provide in rural areas, but with the privatisation of services and increased competition charges are likely to be more closely related to costs in the future. Generally the price of both access and calls is uniform across urban areas.

Costs vary between peak and off-peak periods because of the fixed capacity of the network. At the margin, the whole cost of capacity in the network is attributable to peak period demands. Any shifting of traffic from peak periods reduces the cost per call to the suppliers. Correspondingly, prices of calls vary between times of the day and between weekdays and the weekend, but as the peak demand is mainly caused by business traffic, the scope for shifting is limited. Cross-elasticities in this market are expected to be low, but the cross-elasticity of demand between the peak and off-peak for residential long-distance telephone calls may be relatively high.

Reliability is an important quality dimension, but is now at a sufficiently high level in most advanced countries that lack of capacity in the system is rarely a reason for being unable to make a connection. Among the non-price factors affecting demand, the most important is the secularly increasing demand for access to information. In particular the increasing sophistication and capacity of equipment used for storing and processing of data and other information and the increased capacity of new telecommunication equipment have resulted in growth in demand.

**Garbage collection and disposal**

Like sewerage and stormwater drainage, garbage services dispose of unwanted material; like sewage and stormwater, garbage causes a problem at source if there is no way of getting rid of it and a problem to other people if it is not disposed of properly. Thus there is a private and a public demand for collection of garbage and a public demand for its disposal in ways which do not cause a nuisance to others. One measure of demand, as with sewage and stormwater, is the amount of garbage produced.

The garbage produced by most large businesses is collected under contract and disposed of mostly at public landfill sites. Collection and transport costs are thus borne directly by the business that produces the garbage. Households and small businesses commonly pay for garbage services either as a special lump sum tax or as part of general local taxes. Rarely does the cost to the household vary with the volume, weight or composition of garbage collected. In a few cities, however, how much households pay for garbage collection varies with the volume. The disposal of garbage, whether at landfill sites or by incineration, is a costly operation which aims to maintain the quality of the environment by avoiding the dumping of garbage in places where it would be a public nuisance.

Partly because of the absence of a charging system for household garbage that relates to volume, much attention has been given in recent years to education as a means of limiting the demand for garbage services. This is an appropriate method of discouraging excessive use of the public facilities for disposal. It aims to take advantage of the interest of individuals in protecting the natural environment and emphasises a range of options including composting organic wastes and recycling paper, some plastics, glass and metal cans. In addition, recycling has been encouraged by the free provision of containers for, and free collection of, recyclable materials, and free or subsidised provision of compost containers.

Because the network of services comprises a set of collection routes, capacity is easily varied so that peaking of demand is not a serious problem. The costs of disposal vary to a modest extent with the distance to landfill sites, which in general is higher for garbage collected in the central areas of cities.

**Conclusions**

First, the demand for most physical infrastructure services includes a significant collective demand as well as a (usually predominant) private demand. Second, it is helpful for most services to consider separately the demand for volume of service and for access to the service. In some cases other quality dimensions such as reliability are also important. Third, except where individual services are close substitutes for one another, the elasticity of demand for individual services is low in the short term but much higher (though rarely greater than −1) in the long term. As a result it is easy for providers to increase their revenue by increasing prices, especially in the short run, but equally it is in the interests of users in general that prices should be regulated. Fourth, information about cross-elasticities of demand for services at different times and places is limited, but generally they too are low. They would be expected to be higher in the longer term. Fifth, it follows that, in the longer term, setting prices close to marginal cost is likely to result in significant saving of resources.

# 5 Objectives in charging for infrastructure

This chapter describes the main objectives to be met through the funding of physical infrastructure in urban areas. They provide criteria for choosing between alternative kinds of funding. The next chapter describes the characteristics of the alternative funding mechanisms and assesses them against these criteria. These two chapters provide the general principles which are used in Chapter 7 to derive optimal funding methods.

The four objectives of charging for infrastructure are:

1  Economic objectives: efficiency in the use of resources;
2  Environmental objectives: protection and enhancement of the quality of the environment;
3  Financial objectives: adequate, cheap-to-collect and predictable revenue; and
4  Equity objectives: a fair distribution of costs among users of the services.

## Economic objectives

From an economic perspective, charges send important messages to both producers and consumers. When consumers pay a price equal to the per-unit cost of a service, it is in their interest to use the service up to the level where the value to them of using another unit falls below the cost of supplying it. As a result, under some restrictive assumptions, the level of use of resources in production of the service will be optimal: up to this level, additional units of use would cost less than their value to users, but beyond this level they would cost more than their value to users.[1] To achieve this efficient level of use requires that the price at which the service is sold be set equal to the cost of expanding production by one unit: its marginal cost.

At that price also, producers have an incentive to increase their production up to the level where the cost of producing another unit, either by investing in additional capacity or producing more from the existing capacity, is just equal to the return they receive for it. Hence the golden rule of 'marginal cost pricing'. It can be shown that in a competitive market (and assuming that a number of other conditions hold) prices will equal the marginal cost of production. But we have seen that infrastructure services are provided under natural monopoly conditions and therefore cannot be competitive. Nevertheless, if prices are set equal to marginal costs, something like the optimal amount of resources will be used in providing the service, or at least a move towards marginal cost pricing is likely to improve the allocation of resources.

According to this rule, the price of water to a particular user should be equal to the cost of delivering another kilolitre to that user; the cost of telephone calls should be the cost of an additional call being made; the cost paid by users for connection to the telephone service should be the cost to the system of connecting an additional service; the cost to the user of making a trip along a particular road should be the total cost of an additional trip on that road; and so on. An alternative for comparison is a situation where water supply costs are all recovered from rates on property. Users have no financial incentive to restrict their use of water because their water bills are unaffected by how much they use, and suppliers, who can recover any level of costs by increasing the level of rates, have no incentive to adopt the best technology or to supply only as much water as users are prepared to pay for.

If charges are to lead to efficient resource allocation, they need also to be easily understood so that consumers know how much it is going to cost them to use another unit of a service. Otherwise they will not be able to make a rational decision about how much to use. Furthermore, if charges are complex it will be expensive just to calculate the bill to each user.

The complexity of the mix of joint products outlined in the previous chapters implies that setting the price of each product at its marginal cost would result in a very complex schedule of charges. It is necessary to make a trade-off between the complexity of the set of charges needed to reflect cost conditions and the simplicity of the charges needed for consumers to know how much it will cost to use an additional unit of the service.

The importance of getting prices right varies between services according to how large an effect the level of charges has on the amount demanded, and how the level of output affects the marginal cost of production. First, if demand for the service is very sensitive to its price, differences between price and marginal cost will cause the amount demanded to be much too high or too low and there will be a corresponding misallocation of resources. Second, if the marginal cost of production is very sensitive to output, differences between price and marginal cost will again cause the amount produced to be much too high or too low. Conversely, if demand is inelastic and costs vary little with output, as may be true for domestic sewerage services, getting prices right is less important. Both of these criteria are useful when alternative bases for charging are considered.

It requires only a little thought to recognise that the principle of marginal cost pricing does not always lead in a straightforward way to a choice of charging methods. The complications are mentioned briefly here and are taken up more fully in subsequent chapters.

First, as explained earlier, many physical infrastructure services provide a number of products which are not close substitutes in either consumption or production. For example, the marginal cost of roads needs to be considered as a marginal cost of providing road space to carry a volume of traffic, the marginal cost of the thickness of road pavements to carry heavy vehicles, and the marginal cost of additional length of road to provide access to additional properties.

Access to many services has a value to users that is quite distinct from the value of the use of the service, and the elasticity of demand for access may be lower than the elasticity of demand for use. This difference can be illustrated by water supply, where access to a small amount of clean water for drinking, to water at a high pressure and high rate of flow for firefighting, and the regular use of water for cleaning and transporting human wastes or irrigation meet quite different demands, and meeting each of these demands has its own distinct marginal cost.

Second, in many cases, including water supply and roads, costs of providing the service vary markedly with location. If the charging system is to encourage users of these services to choose a location that takes due account of differences in the cost of providing them, those cost differences between locations should be reflected in different charges. Some of these cost differences are stable over long periods, for example, the higher costs of providing roads in densely developed congested areas where the value of space is high, and the higher cost of installing sewers in a sandstone plateau or stormwater drainage in low-lying locations or locations remote from the coast. Others vary over time, changing with changes in the location of, for example, sewage treatment plants, water supply catchment dams, trunk mains and garbage disposal sites. Because of the complex effects of increasing demand at a particular location on the load on different parts of the network, the calculation of costs in each location is difficult.[2] Already we have three dimensions of output of services: quantity, access and location.

Third, in the short term, the capacity of infrastructure services can be regarded as fixed and the marginal cost of providing another unit of service depends on how fully the available capacity is being used. As the level of use approaches capacity, marginal cost increases because of, for example, congestion, risks of road collisions, falling water or gas pressure or electrical voltage, the increasing probability of a telephone call being unsuccessful or of cuts in electricity or water supply. In the long term, the cost of increasing output is the cost of expanding capacity. As was shown in Chapter 3, short-run and long-run marginal costs are equal when investment (capacity) is optimal. When capacity is larger or smaller than the optimum, as it may be for considerable periods, it is necessary to decide whether to set prices equal to long- or short-run marginal costs.

Fourth, one of the circumstances in which there is commonly excess capacity is outside the periods of peak demand. In off-peak periods the short-run marginal cost equals the variable cost of increasing production and is lower than the long-run marginal cost because there is spare capacity. Price in such periods should equal only short-run marginal cost so that users are not unduly discouraged from using the available spare capacity. At peak periods, however, the only way of increasing output is to increase capacity, and the whole of the marginal cost of capacity as well as marginal variable costs is attributable to peak use and should be covered by the charges for peak period use. Differences in the marginal cost between peak and off-peak periods are large for a number of infrastructure services because demand varies markedly between different periods, capacity costs are a high proportion of total costs, and the products are expensive (water, gas), if not impossible (travel, electricity, telecommunications), to store between peak and off-peak periods.

Fifth, another circumstance in which excess capacity commonly occurs is where the optimal path of investment over time requires few large 'lumpy' investments rather than a number of smaller investments each year. In the period after a lump has been added there is spare capacity until it is taken up by growth in demand. The conventional economic view is that in this circumstance, for the same reason as in off-peak periods, prices should equal short-run marginal cost rather than the higher long-run marginal cost. That argument, which would see charges following a saw-tooth course over time, has not found favour with suppliers. In Chapter 7 it will be argued that there are strong economic and political reasons for prices not to fluctuate over time.

Sixth, at least the approximate level of price needs to be known by consumers in advance of their use of the service so that they know the relative cost of alternative consumption decisions. But, because the level of use is unpredictable, marginal costs cannot be projected accurately. This is a problem in the short term in setting in advance the charge for using a congested road.

Seventh, in the longer term, one of the major determinants of the amount of capacity needed, and hence the cost of providing some services, is the reliability of supply. Reliability is a quality dimension of access. The cost of a water or electricity supply system which has a very high probability of being able to meet all demand at all times is much higher than the cost of a system which accepts a significant probability that on some occasions, due to drought, very cold weather or equipment failure, it will be unable to meet all demands. A decision about supply reliability is a collective decision, and that decision needs to be taken in conjunction with decisions about pricing and other rationing measures that will be taken in times of shortage.

Eighth, congestion represents a particular kind of cost of use in which marginal users affect the costs borne by other users of a facility. It occurs most commonly in transport services where a substantial part of the cost of the service is borne by users as costs other than direct charges, for example, vehicle operating costs and the value of the time of users. When the level of use of a service approaches capacity and an additional user attempts to use it, the quality of the service provided, in this case the speed at which vehicles can move along the road, declines for all users. Thus we see an external effect of an individual decision which is felt by other users but not by non-users. It occurs because short-run marginal costs to users rise as capacity is approached and therefore exceed the costs of the marginal user. Congestion should be taken into account in setting prices equal to marginal cost in the interest of narrowly defined economic efficiency (Walters 1987). Since it results from an externality *among road users* it is not reflected in a market price, but it is not an external diseconomy *of road use*. The revenue collected from a congestion charge is in effect a rent for the space occupied by the road user. Like any rent it increases as the scarcity of the space increases.

It follows that the marginal cost of production of individual infrastructure services is not a simple concept nor does it imply a single 'price'. There are marginal costs for each of the products the service provides, sometimes different short-run and long-run marginal costs, and marginal costs which vary with the time of day and year and with location. Because charges need to be simple, they need to be based on only a few of these cost determinants; the choice of which ones is an art rather than a science (Paterson 1991, p. 69). One of the tasks of this study is to determine which charging bases provide the greatest economic, environmental and social advantages.

If prices are set equal to marginal costs and if, because of economies of scale, those marginal costs are lower than average costs, the gap has to be covered from some other source. Ramsey (1927) demonstrated that the way to cover the deficit that would cause the least inefficient allocation of resources is to load it on to the cost of those services for which the elasticity of demand is lowest. Such charges will have the least impact on the level of demand and hence on the allocation of resources. This criterion has been used extensively in studies of cost allocation (e.g. Luck & Martin 1988).

It is possible to charge for infrastructure services in ways which have very little impact on demand. The extreme case is a property tax levied on the site value of all properties that have access to the service, whether or not they have a connection. Such charges have almost zero impact on demand for either access or use of the service. Almost as good, from this point of view, are fixed charges for connection to the service (especially when connection is compulsory, as it is with sewerage), whether paid as a capital charge during development (and usually passed on to buyers for reasons to be argued later) or as an annual fixed charge paid by owners of properties. Such a charge increases the cost of housing, and it will have some effect on the demand for the service since fewer people will be able to afford separate housing because of its higher cost.

Chapter 3 argues that the need for special measures to pay the overhead costs of infrastructure services not covered by marginal cost pricing has been exaggerated. For reasons canvassed briefly in Chapter 2 and expanded in Chapter 3, the economies of scale that justify a single network do not imply that costs will fall as the network expands, and there are diseconomies of scale in the headworks of a number of these services. If the overall returns to scale are roughly constant, marginal cost pricing will cover all costs.

Partly for historical reasons many infrastructure services are provided by single suppliers to large markets such as urban areas. The suppliers are either public authorities that are expected to meet performance standards such as a rate of return on assets, or private suppliers that are regulated to ensure that they do not make excessive profits by exploiting their monopoly positions. In neither case do they experience the competitive pressures, or even the threat of the potential entry of a credible competitor, to encourage them to adopt the most efficient technologies available. Charging systems should, if possible, provide an appropriate incentive.

**Environmental objectives**

The environmental (external) costs and benefits resulting from the provision of infrastructure should, like the internal costs and benefits, be taken into account in setting prices if resources are to be allocated in an economically efficient manner. Environmental objectives are, for the most part, a component of economic efficiency objectives. Environmental costs and benefits also have different impacts on different groups of people and therefore are related to equity objectives in two specific ways. First, some environmental effects have an impact over a very long term and therefore affect the distribution of welfare between generations. Second, since environmental benefits cannot be bought and sold directly, their distribution tends to be affected by where people live and work (the poor can only afford to 'buy'—live in—a lower quality environment), and by administrative decisions about the location of infrastructure investment. For example, inner-urban freeways are often built through, and reduce the amenity of, low income suburbs because that is where space is cheapest.

Nevertheless, for three reasons it is useful to discuss environmental objectives separately from economic objectives. First, environmental impacts are externalities, which means that they are not bought and sold in a market and therefore cannot be valued in the same way as other costs and benefits. Second, many decisions about the supply of infrastructure services which are justifiable on economic grounds may damage the environment. Third, environment policy decisions are taken by communities collectively through political process for cultural, ethical and aesthetic reasons rather than being taken individually in the market for economic reasons (Sagoff 1988).[3] Unless effects on the environment are considered separately they are likely to be ignored, especially because individual buyers and sellers regard them as being of minor consequence rather than central to resource allocation decisions.

Since people vary greatly in how much they care about the environment and how much they value its protection and enhancement, and because there is no market in which individual valuations can be arbitrated, assessment of the external costs of infrastructure services in monetary terms falls back on indirect ways of estimating damage functions or contingent valuation, in which a market is simulated. To the extent that environmental objectives are ethical objectives pursued by communities, those methods of simulating what a market would decide may not be relevant to the decision. Even indirect measures such as estimating the impacts on property values are based on market simulation. Environmental objectives may be more important in the choice of a charging base than in determining the level of charge. If there are alternative charging bases, it is better to choose the one that discourages to a greater degree behaviour which is environmentally damaging. (For an example of environmental effects being used in assessing the level of charge, see Interstate Commission 1990.)

Pollution is typical of external effects of the use of infrastructure services. Unlike congestion, it affects non-users as well as other users through noise or a decline in the quality of air, land or water. Other externalities include the impact of urban water supply systems in flooding natural river valleys and reducing natural stream flows, which reduces the fish population and reduces recreational opportunities, and the impact of stormwater drainage in increasing the volume and peaking of flooding in urban catchments. The aim of choosing funding mechanisms to meet environmental objectives is to provide incentives to reduce such negative externalities.

For example, the environmental aesthetic and recreational value of water flowing in streams and of underground water in sustaining springs is recognised in many countries by charges for extraction of such water. The charges vary with the use of the water according to how far it will be evaporated or altered (for example, by heating or pollution) before being returned to streams (OECD 1987, Chapter 5). It is extraordinary that Australia, the driest vegetated continent, levies no royalties for water extractions. Like many so-called environmental charges, royalties for extraction of water can be interpreted as marginal costs. They reflect both the opportunity cost of water for other purposes, including environmental enhancement, and the marginal cost of expanding the capacity to supply water by developing the next (more expensive) catchment.

## Financial objectives

Financial objectives are both more varied and less complex than economic and environmental objectives. They include first, the adequacy of the revenue yield to cover the total costs of providing the service. Partly for efficiency and partly for equity reasons it is desirable that the total costs of physical infrastructure services are covered from revenue raised from the users of the service. If the responsible authorities have to cover their costs from users, they are less likely to indulge in excessive expenditure. As spelled out below, one definition of equity is that users of services should pay the total cost of the services they use. The alternative to covering costs from charges on users is to subsidise the service from revenue from all taxpayers, irrespective of whether or not the taxpayers use the service. Depending on the tax base, taxes themselves distort the choices of taxpayers to a greater or lesser extent. For example, income taxes affect choices between work and leisure, and reduce the efficiency of the allocation of resources. This is known as the 'excess burden' of taxation.

One difficulty in judging the adequacy of yield lies in defining the total costs of providing a service. Traditional accounting methods are based on historic costs and take no account of the current opportunity cost of the capital invested (its value in alternative uses). In recent years authorities supplying services have been required to value their capital (or that part of it that would be replaced if it was destroyed) at replacement cost depreciated according to age. Authorities have been expected to earn a dividend for their owner governments on the equity in their capital defined as the capital base, less the portion of it accounted for by debt. The rate should be the real rate of return earned by capital elsewhere in the economy. (These issues are discussed in more detail in Chapter 8.)

There are problems with this requirement, especially where most or all of the capital investment has been funded either from the net revenue of the authority, or from loans amortised from net revenue, rather than from general taxes. While it may be correct to require such a dividend for calculation of the level of charges, where the capital has been funded from charges on users the dividend should be paid to the users rather than to the government. There is a problem also with depreciation. With appropriate maintenance, some physical infrastructure capital can last indefinitely. It reaches the end of its economic life when it becomes obsolete due to changes in land use or the development of better technologies rather than through wearing out. In these circumstances, its life, and hence the appropriate rate of depreciation, may depend on the adequacy of maintenance.

The difference between this financial objective and the economic objective is illustrated in situations where there are economies of scale. In these situations the long-run marginal cost is less than average cost, and a price set equal to the former would not cover total costs. Such a price satisfies economic objectives but not financial objectives.

Second, the feasibility and cost of collection limit the charging bases that can be used. A charge for the use of a service is possible only if its use by each user can be measured and if those who do not pay can be excluded. For example, because it is impossible to exclude people from receiving the public health benefits of water supply and sewerage services, these 'products' cannot be financed from charges, though their cost may be covered by user charges which vary with the private benefits from the use of these services. It is difficult, and very costly, to exclude people from using access roads or local parks, or to measure the extent of their use. Furthermore, as long as there is spare capacity, there is no efficiency reason for restricting their use. Neither product is therefore a suitable base for charges that vary with the extent of use, despite the attractions of such charges from some points of view.

There is a great deal of literature showing the economic benefits of charging for the use of congested roads according to the costs of congestion imposed by additional users, but such charges would be very expensive to collect, using traditional methods of collecting tolls. Electronic means of charging, however, would permit such charges to be collected at much lower cost. These are described in Chapter 7.

In the past it has frequently been argued that the cost of installing and reading water meters was too high to justify charging domestic users for water according to amount of use. In recent years, however, the benefits of user charging have been more fully recognised and many cities have installed meters and read them at least once a year. Charging at a higher rate during the season of peak use requires reading at least twice a year and therefore greater cost. Whereas meters that distinguish between peak and off-peak use are feasible for electricity and telephones because electricity is already available at the meters, they would be much more costly for water and gas because they would require the provision of electricity at each meter. Finally, with the technology currently available it would be too costly to measure the volume or the composition of sewage discharged from individual homes.

Third, stability and predictability of revenue is desirable for physical infrastructure services because of the high proportion of their costs that remain fixed from year to year irrespective of the level of use. Funding of water supply readily illustrates the issue. In cities where much of the water is used to irrigate gardens and lawns, its use varies significantly with the weather. In a cool wet year the demand is much lower. If volume charges were the only source of revenue, water suppliers would find their income, but not their costs, to be lower in wet years. This provides an argument for access charges which produce stable revenue. That argument needs to be weighed against arguments for user charging. It is not entirely persuasive because the authorities can cover their costs over several years by carrying forward modest surpluses or deficits rather than being required to cover costs every year.

Fourth, borrowing by governments is subject to controls in the interests of macroeconomic objectives. In periods when a higher level of saving is desired, perhaps because deficits in the national government budget result from the government spending more than its revenue, borrowing by public authorities is frequently restricted. In addition to such controls, borrowing may be restricted by the credit rating of the authorities or of state or local governments, and by high interest rates. Borrowing restrictions and the cost of borrowing may force infrastructure authorities to seek other sources of funding for their investments. The main alternatives are revenue surpluses or requiring new users to contribute to the capital costs of expanding capacity in order to serve them. This can include the cost of both the network expansion needed to connect them and the expansion of headworks and capacity in other parts of the network required to meet their demand for services. The latter are collected through developer requirements and contributions. They have the advantage that they limit the need to borrow, but they may be inequitable by requiring that too much of the cost of durable capital be paid for by current users and first-time home buyers.

## Equity objectives

It can be held that equity should not be an objective in deciding the method of charging for physical infrastructure services. Thus in Chapter 2 it was argued that these services are provided by government because they are natural monopolies, and not because, as is the case for social infrastructure services, they should be available to everyone, irrespective of ability to pay. That argument implies that equity objectives should be less important in deciding how to fund physical than how to fund social infrastructure.

On the other hand, the choice of methods of charging inevitably influences the distribution of costs among users and taxpayers. Since most of the services are provided by public authorities or publicly regulated firms, the political process ensures that the distributional effects of different methods of charging are likely to be taken into account, especially when some kind of tax unrelated to the use of the service is involved. Furthermore, if charges that are set at the marginal cost of use do not cover the total cost, as may be the case with public transport, equity is an important consideration in deciding how the deficit should be met. The charges levied to cover the deficit should have few effects on resource allocation, and should be equitable in their incidence.

One meaning of equity that is consistent with economic efficiency is the view that it is equitable that users should pay the additional cost of providing the services they use. This view supports the case for marginal cost pricing.

A second meaning of equity is that charges should be levied according to the benefit that different users (and in some cases, non-users) receive from the provision of infrastructure: the so-called benefit principle. For example, since the provision of physical infrastructure increases the value of property, it seems equitable that the owners of the property served should meet the cost.

This argument can be used to justify attempts to achieve 'land value capture', or to charge for infrastructure through a tax on land or property in the service area. It can be used also to support the requirement that development charges pay the cost of providing infrastructure to new developments. The next chapter examines the success of various attempts to capture the increase in the value of land which results from the provision of infrastructure and considers development charges in more detail.

A third meaning of equity is that charges should vary according to ability to pay. Pursuit of this objective results in lower charges for many services for children, pensioners, the unemployed and other identifiable low income groups. It is often argued that this means of achieving equity objectives results in inefficiency because the incentives of charging mechanisms are weaker for the groups that have to pay lower charges. A counter argument is that lower charges on low income earners affect behaviour as much as higher charges for high income earners. It may also be inequitable compared with other measures because it provides the greatest benefits to the largest consumers and because the subsidies for low income consumers are funded from the largest full-charge consumers rather than those with the highest incomes. Nevertheless its advantages may outweigh its disadvantages. Property taxes, being wealth taxes, albeit crude (because they seldom allow for debts incurred to buy property) and partial, are often justified as charging according to ability to pay.

Another dimension of equity is raised by the question of whether or not borrowed funds should be used for investment in infrastructure. Borrowing spreads the cost of such investments over the lifetime of the loan. With refinancing it is possible to spread it over the lifetime of the asset financed, and across all users that are served by the infrastructure provider. A major alternative, capital charges on new developments, levies charges directly on the development of newly serviced property. For the most part these charges appear to be passed forward as increases in the price of new housing, and those price increases in turn raise the price of established housing.

Established home owners are not affected by the price increase but tenants and first-time home buyers have to meet higher costs. A shift from financing through borrowing to development charges also results in lower future user charges or property rates since there is a lower level of loan funds to amortise. At the time such charges are first introduced they therefore cause a redistribution of wealth to current owners/buyers from non-owners/buyers.

A further equity issue arises when development charges are used to fund much of the cost of the infrastructure needs of newly developed property, but similar charges are not levied to cover the cost of major maintenance, upgrading or replacement of existing infrastructure. This occurs in part because, for reasons given earlier, replacement occurs more commonly as a result of obsolescence or inadequate capacity than because the facilities wear out: much of the cost of maintenance is designed to defer replacement, perhaps indefinitely. Furthermore it is much more difficult to attribute the cost of replacement or upgrading than the cost of new infrastructure to particular properties. It is also more difficult to levy capital charges on established property owners than on developers of new property where development approval can be made conditional on payment of the charges and their cost can be included as part of the cost of development and recovered from buyers.

Equity is not independent of efficiency. The 'efficient' allocation of resources will vary if the distribution of buying power among consumers changes. For example, if some parts of a city that are well served by public transport are taken over by higher income families, since they can afford to spend more, it will be 'efficient' to allocate more resources to public transport in those localities. An argument frequently mounted against user charging for infrastructure services is that only the rich will be able to afford services for which a user charge is levied, or in less extreme terms, the charges will have a more adverse effect on poor than on rich users. Such a criticism can have two alternative meanings, depending on the strength of the assertion.

Its stronger form means that the demand of the poor is more sensitive to price changes than that of the rich. A given level of charge will have a greater impact on the consumption of the poor than of the rich: in conventional economic terms, the elasticity of demand of the poor is higher. This is more likely to be the case for luxuries, such as long-distance telephone calls, road use for leisure travel, or water used for garden irrigation or swimming pools, than for necessities such as journeys to work or water used for drinking or cleaning. It is an argument that needs to be taken into account when charges for particular services and products are being considered: most physical infrastructure services provide more necessities than luxuries.

Its weaker form means that, because the marginal utility of wealth decreases as income increases, poor people's utility declines more than that of the rich as a result of being charged for a service that was previously 'free'. The same level of charge costs the poor more in terms of the utility of other goods and services forgone. If the alternative to user charges is funding services from a progressive tax, the poor will be made worse off each time a user charge is introduced for an additional service. Of course this argument applies to all goods and services, but that does not lessen its force when a decision about a change from one method of funding urban infrastructure to another is being considered.

When a society considers whether a given distribution of money income is acceptable, arguably it takes into account the range of goods and services which are distributed 'free' according to some criterion other than ability to pay. For example, some infrastructure products are distributed according to unconstrained demand (water when no volume charges are made), some criterion of need (drainage services are provided in poorly drained and flood-prone areas), or willingness to wait in a queue (public transport) or to spend time on a congested road. If the range of unpriced services is reduced, the poor are made worse off relative to the rich. One way to overcome that problem is to combine the introduction of user charges with compensating income redistribution measures through the tax or welfare system, for example a larger tax-free level before income tax is payable. That too has its problems, as 'poverty traps' become more serious the more benefits are reduced or taxes are increased as the income of the poor increases. Another is to have increasing block tariffs which recover more revenue from large relative to small users.

Progressive taxes (which I will assume are the source of general government revenue) are used to fund relatively few physical, as distinct from social, infrastructure services. The main service for which they are used extensively is public transport through the subsidies provided by state and territory governments. Charges that are related in some way to access to or use of the service are much more common, including property taxes, fuel taxes and development charges, and are described in some detail in the next chapter. These sources of revenue may be more or less regressive in their impact than charges that vary directly with the level of use.

In addition to the long-term equity effects discussed above, there are important transitional problems in shifting from one charging mechanism to another. The owner (often poor) who purchased an old gas-guzzler when fuel prices were low is disadvantaged when prices rise because the car becomes less valuable. The family, often large, that bought a house with large gardens and lawns will be even more seriously disadvantaged when the price of water is increased.

## Conclusion

The four objectives of infrastructure charging—economic efficiency, environmental protection, adequacy of revenue and equity in distribution of the cost burden—provide criteria for choosing among alternative charging methods. The four criteria are interrelated, but they are not entirely comparable. It is necessary to raise adequate revenue from some source, otherwise the services will not be provided. But the raising of that revenue provides an opportunity to pursue the other goals. The next chapter looks in some detail at the alternative methods of raising revenue.

# 6 Alternative charging mechanisms

The first part of this chapter describes the advantages and disadvantages of the main categories of charges used to finance the provision of infrastructure: user charges, access charges, developer contributions, and taxes. The second part deals with several general issues relating to methods of financing: the equity impacts of charges compared with taxes; the question of whether community service obligations are best met from tax revenue or by cross-subsidies among users; charges that vary with location; and charging when major items of capacity are lumpy.

## CATEGORIES OF CHARGES

### User charges

The simplest user charges are those which are set at a uniform price per unit volume of use of the service. For reasons given in Chapter 5, user charges set equal to the marginal cost of supplying the service encourage an efficient level of use of resources. In the case of services such as electricity and gas, the definition of volume of use is relatively straightforward. For most services, however, the volume of use has different dimensions and, because of the need to keep charges simple, user charges should aim to influence the demand for those dimensions which have the greatest effect on cost.

The main advantage of user charges is that they encourage the use of the service up to the level where the cost of supplying an additional unit would be greater than its value to consumers. Because most goods and services are paid for per unit volume, user charges are more likely to result in the best allocation of resources between infrastructure and other sectors of the economy. In addition, user charges are the only funding method that can be varied according to the time of use to reflect differences in cost of supply at different times. They can be varied between locations relatively easily according to the cost of providing the service at different locations.

User charges are equitable in the sense that consumers have to pay for the cost of what they use, though they suffer from qualifications about their equity discussed in the previous chapter and later in this chapter. Since the environmental damage produced by most services depends heavily on the volume of use, user charges are environmentally desirable because they discourage excessive use. Environmental impacts are external costs and they justify user charges that are higher than financial (internal) marginal costs.

Their disadvantages vary greatly between different services. For some services, for example, roads, sewerage and stormwater drainage, it is difficult, costly or even impossible to measure the volume of use by an individual or household. For others, it is relatively expensive to measure use and more expensive the more frequently it is measured. Measurement of use during particular hours of the day when cost per unit volume is high or low is very expensive (water, gas). Since demand often varies with temperature and rainfall, the revenue raised cannot be predicted accurately. This is a problem for suppliers of many goods and services and competition between private suppliers makes their revenue even less predictable.

The equity advantage of user charges—that each consumer pays for the cost of what they use—holds strictly only if the distribution of income is believed to be ideal. If it is too unequal, such charges allocate too many resources to the production of goods and services consumed by the rich. In such circumstances, user charges do nothing to redistribute towards particular deserving groups. Finally, when they are set equal to marginal cost, they do not yield enough revenue to cover the total costs of services that are produced under increasing returns to scale. In such circumstances, revenue needs to be supplemented from some other source. It was argued in Chapter 3 that this problem arises infrequently in the provision of physical infrastructure services in urban areas because marginal costs usually equal or exceed average costs, especially when marginal environmental costs that increase with the level of output are included as part of marginal cost.

User charges are sometimes set at higher levels for the first units of the service used by a consumer in a particular time period—declining block tariffs—or at higher levels for higher levels of use—increasing block tariffs. Declining block tariffs incorporate a kind of access charge. The initial high-priced block is usually small enough that all consumers use at least that number of units. In those circumstances, total accounts will be the same as if there was a fixed access charge plus a uniform price per unit of use. The advantages and disadvantages of access charges are discussed below.

Increasing block tariffs are usually an equity measure, resulting in less of the cost burden falling on small users and more on large users than under a flat rate charge. The assumption is that small users are likely to be poorer. That is not always the case, as can be seen by comparing the use of water or energy by occupants of high and low density housing or by large and small families. They are a crude equity measure, and any desirable equity effects need to be compared with the inefficiency that results from the incentive they give for excessive use by small users who do not use up their 'free' allowance. They can be adopted also for environmental reasons, reflecting, perhaps, a moral view that large users should reduce their consumption.

Finally, user charges can distinguish between different classes of user, for example, commercial, industrial, residential and government. Some kinds of users can be served at less cost than others, for example, industries which use electricity at a constant rate throughout the day and the year. A lower overall price is used in lieu of charges that vary between peak and off-peak periods. Similarly it is cheaper to supply electricity in bulk at high voltage. Different levels of charges are often adopted for equity reasons: it is assumed that commercial users can afford to pay more than residential users. Another interpretation of the reason for the differential is political: residential charges affect many more voters directly.

## Access charges

Access charges take three main forms (a fourth form, requiring developers to provide access, is discussed in the next section):

1 A fixed and uniform charge per user, which may be combined with a uniform price per unit of use in declining block tariffs;

2  A charge which varies with capacity to use the service; and
3  A charge which varies with the value (either site value or total value) of each property which has access to the service.

Most access charges have traditionally been levied on property value, and sometimes (stormwater drainage, garbage, residential sewerage) the total cost of the service has been covered by the revenue from access charges. There has been a move recently away from property based access charges towards either fixed charges or charges that vary with the capacity of the access provided. In North America in particular this has been associated with a move towards corporatisation and privatisation of responsibility for the provision of these services. Other non-property access charges include motor vehicle registration fees which give vehicles access to the road system, and driving licence fees which give drivers access to roads.

Since it is costly to provide access, access charges could be a kind of marginal cost price, and could have the desirable effect of providing appropriate signals to potential users when they decide whether to buy access to the service. Decisions about the provision of services to the properties in a locality are usually taken at the time the land is subdivided, by the developer as a matter of choice or under compulsion from the local government, or by the provider of the service. For services such as roads, sewerage and electricity, connection is compulsory, or is necessary to be able to sell building lots. That is not true of telephones or gas. In all cases, once the networks are installed, the additional cost of providing access to individual properties is small. Under these circumstances, with the exception of gas and possibly telephones, there is very little opportunity for an individual consumer to make a decision about access that has any impact on the level of use of resources. The one decision which does carry such an implication is the decision to buy a separate property, especially a house. Since the cost of providing access is incorporated into the price of housing, a higher cost of providing it will increase housing prices and reduce the demand for housing. As a result there could be expected to be some elasticity of demand, but it will be low because the cost of access to an individual service is only a small part of the cost of a house.

The inelasticity of the demand for access is an advantage when access charges are considered as a way of raising funds that do not distort resource allocation. This makes access charges attractive as a component of a two-part tariff: a user charge set equal to the marginal cost of use and an access charge to cover the overheads.[1] Where access is compulsory, however, an access charge is a tax; and where it is a flat charge per user, it is a lump sum tax on the occupation of a separate property or dwelling. A flat rate access charge does, of course, raise the cost of housing relative to other goods and services, so it is not neutral with respect to resource allocation.

Access charges that vary with capacity to use a service include vehicle registration charges that vary with the size of the vehicle, and periodic charges for water and sewerage that vary with the size of the supplying/collecting pipe, or the number of toilets. Varying registration charges are justified on cost grounds because larger vehicles cause more damage to roads and occupy more road space. They do not, however, vary with how much the vehicle is used. Access charges for water, sewerage and electricity are partly a benefit charge. The cost of access pipes varies little with the size of the pipe, but size does reflect the maximum peak use of the service, which affects system costs. Combined with a volume charge, such access charges may encourage reductions in the extent to which demand is peaked. It is a charge on 'capacity to receive/ discharge water', one of the dimensions of water supply and of sewerage services.

Property taxes used to finance individual services have some of the features of general taxes, and are discussed below. If they are hypothecated (earmarked for a particular use), however, they are best considered as an access charge. If the base is the total value of the property, they are a partial gross wealth tax ('gross' because they ignore mortgage debt), and can be justified on equity grounds, especially in the absence of other wealth taxes. Ownership of property, however, may be a poor indicator of wealth, especially if it is heavily mortgaged, and a poor indicator of ability to pay in the case of retired people with low incomes. If the base is site value, it is an even smaller proportion of wealth and a poorer indicator of ability to pay, but a site value tax is a non-distorting tax and more of it will be capitalised into the value of land (a matter that is taken up again later).

The advantages of access charges are that they raise a predictable amount of revenue and have some equity advantages. Their disadvantage is that they provide little incentive for efficient use of resources. In summary, access charges are more useful in achieving financial than economic objectives. Charges that achieve both are generally preferable. Access charges provide almost no desirable environmental incentives and their equity advantages are modest.

## Development contributions

Starting in the 1950s in Australia, water and sewerage authorities, and the local councils that were responsible for access roads and local drainage, were short of funds for servicing the large areas of new developments. This led to delays in subdivisions being approved. Local councils began to require developers to provide sealed roads, footpaths and gutters and to donate a percentage of their land for local open space. Local stormwater drains were added to the list a little later. Councils refused to approve development applications unless developers agreed either to provide the services or pay to the council its costs of doing so.

About the same time reticulation of water and sewerage became a requirement; subsequently, developers have been required to contribute also to the cost of off-site services needed to serve their new subdivision. Over time the contributions required towards off-site costs have increased substantially, including some social as well as physical infrastructure.

Development contributions can be divided into two classes:

1 Responsibilities for the provision of access to services for properties within a subdivision plus paying the cost of connection to the existing networks; and

2 Cash contributions to the additional, usually off-site, costs of providing the additional trunk and headworks capacity needed to meet the demands from properties in the subdivision.

The responsibilities under (1) are commonly met by developers themselves installing the services although in some cases they pay the costs to the local council or the service authorities. The charges under (2) are almost always paid in cash. Development contributions can be seen as a kind of access charge but they are distinguished from other access charges in that they are levied as a capital sum. They cover the cost of initial installation but of neither depreciation/renewal nor maintenance costs, which continue to be met from the general revenue of the supplying authority.

Water, sewerage, drainage and local roads are the main services for which much of the cost of reticulation and some trunk main and headwork costs are recovered through developers. In some circumstances, the smaller reticulation costs of electricity and tele-phones also are met from this source, and it is more common for the additional cost of underground electricity to be met by the developer. For water and sewerage, development contributions are the main alternative to loans, amortised from revenue from property taxes and user charges, for meeting the capital cost of providing water and sewerage to new areas of urban development. They partially replaced loan funds when they were introduced. Local roads and drains are mainly provided by local authorities and do not yield direct revenue that can be used to amortise loans. In these cases developer charges are an alternative to funding from property taxes and, to a lesser extent, fuel tax revenue collected by national or state governments and paid to local councils.

One of the arguments for this kind of charge is that access to all of these services increases the value of property, and part of that increase in value is captured by these charges. For this to occur, the charges levied on developers must be passed back as prices for unserviced land that are lower than if the costs were met from tax revenue. The general view, however, is that the charges are passed forward as higher prices for serviced land. Snyder and Stegman (1987, Chapter 8), and empirical studies in North America (e.g. Skaburskis & Qadeer 1992), suggest that the costs are fully passed forward. This happens for three reasons.

First, tax incidence theory suggests that such a charge will be passed forward or backward depending on the relative inelasticity of supply and demand: backward if the supply of raw land is less elastic and forward if the demand for serviced land is less elastic. The demand for serviced land is likely to be inelastic because servicing costs are only part of the cost of land, land is only a minor part of the cost of housing, and the demand of households for separate dwellings is itself relatively inelastic.[2] The supply of raw land, however, is likely to be elastic, especially in the face of price reductions. Owners of land which can be readily connected to urban service networks (who may be developers also) recognise that the supply of such land is limited, and if they defer sale for develop-ment, eventually the price will rise. If enough owners defer, of course, the price will indeed rise.

Second, development charges were introduced in a situation when public funds were scarce, so that servicing by developers relieved the financial constraint on service providers and was expected to bring forward the date at which land could be developed, tending to increase rather than decrease the value of the raw land to which they were applied. Third, the charges were commonly introduced throughout metropolitan areas at the same time so that developers had no opportunity to move to locations where the charges were lower or absent.

The only situation in which development charges seem likely to be passed back to owners of raw land in the short term is when developers themselves have stocks of land at the time they are introduced and when demand is slack relative to supply. The long-term incidence is more difficult to assess. The charges could be passed back in the long term if borrowing constraints limit the price people can pay for housing. For the most part this applies only to first-time buyers, the majority of whose borrowing is limited by their repayment capacity rather than the value of the security provided by the house they are buying.[3] Such buyers have to save longer before they can buy, a tendency which was becoming evident in Australia by 1991 (Bourassa et al. 1995). It does not apply to second- and third-time buyers.

If these charges are passed forward, the price of new housing will rise, and with it the price of its close substitute, existing housing. Existing home owners will be made somewhat more wealthy and their housing costs—mortgage payments, maintenance and insurance—will be unaffected. Renters and prospective home buyers, however, will be disadvantaged by the increase in price. Since established home owners generally have higher incomes than renters and first-time buyers, a change from funding infrastructure from taxes or user charges to developer charges will have regressive distributive effects.

There are different interpretations of this change in the method of funding infrastructure. Each interpretation helps to provide a critical understanding of the reasons for, and the consequences of, the change.

First, the change represented privatisation of the provision of infrastructure—a shift from costs being shared across the jurisdiction of the supply authority to being shared only within the subdivision. They are privatised in that new home buyers are forced to borrow more to become home owners. Under funding from a property tax or a user charge the cost of extending infrastructure to newly settled areas was shared among all of the owners of taxable property or users in the area covered by the service authority: local government, metropolitan area or state.

Before the change, a home buyer's purchase of a house stopped at the boundary of the property; after the change the buyer also purchased a share of the roads, pipes and drains that served the property within the subdivision and sometimes beyond. (They did not, however, have to pay a share of either maintaining or eventually replacing services.) As a result of privatisation there was also a shift from charging for services according to a crude measure of ability to pay (as represented by the value of taxable property) to charging according to the cost of providing access to the service.

Second, it involved a shift from paying for the capital cost of services, from an annual charge used to amortise the loans borrowed for the purpose to a capital charge. This and the previous aspect of the change did not need to go together. Under the special assessments and special district financing of infrastructure services in the United States, property owners in each subdivision pay its servicing costs through annual charges. United States' development fees, however, like Australian developer charges, require those within a subdivision to pay the capital cost of the services required for their properties. The advantage of a capital charge is that it reduces the need for public borrowing. The ability of local councils and service authorities in Australia to borrow was frequently constrained by limits to state borrowing, first to achieve macroeconomic objectives and later to avoid what was claimed to be 'crowding out' of private investment; a part of the neoclassical economics policy agenda.[4]

One of the impacts of these two changes can be seen by comparing the situation in different times and places. In periods of slow growth in the number of households and in towns where there is little growth, developer charges are less likely to be passed forward, and even to the extent that they are passed forward for new housing, they will have little impact on the price of existing housing. In times and places where growth is rapid, the changes cause marked increases in house prices.

Third, the change involved the current cohort reneging on an implicit inter-cohort contract. Under the traditional system of financing from loans, each cohort of home owners contributed through its rate payments and user charges to amortising the loans used to pay the capital cost of the infrastructure needs of earlier and subsequent cohorts as well as its own. Each cohort of first-home owners was assisted by previous cohorts who shared the cost of the provision of urban infrastructure, and in turn it assisted following cohorts. Development charges sheet home to the cohort of renters and first-time home buyers the capital cost of their decisions to form separate households which create the need to expand infrastructure. The cohorts that were already home owners by the late 1950s had been assisted because the infrastructure needed for their homes was funded from property tax revenue to which all contributed. Following cohorts, though, were expected to fund increasing proportions of the capital cost of the infrastructure needed to serve their homes through up-front charges built into the prices and rents they paid.

The cost of the new contributions required from developers affected the prices of all housing, because new and existing housing are close substitutes. As a result, existing home owners received capital gains; or more correctly they were unaffected by the change since their housing costs were unchanged and their increased equity allowed them to buy another home as easily as before the change. But as prices increased, the rents of non-owners increased, and it became more costly to become a home owner for the first time. That this occurred has been demonstrated by Snyder and Stegman (1987) using a simple quantitative model. The inequity was compounded because first-time home buyers after the change, who had to pay for their own infrastructure through a higher price for their home, still had to contribute to amortising the loans used to finance the capital cost of the infrastructure which served earlier cohorts by paying the same annual taxes, access charges and user charges.

In Australia the second interpretation was uppermost in the minds of those who decided to move in this direction: capital funds were scarce and a reduction in the need for public borrowing was attractive. Supporters of the change have appealed also to the first interpretation, that those who create the demand for the new facilities should pay for them. The third interpretation shows that the change in method of funding has been unambiguously inequitable.

It must be recognised that these charges had been in force for 25 to 40 years by the mid-1990s so that many of the equity effects of the transition have worked themselves out. The suggestions about funding in this book do not attempt to turn back the clock; it would be too difficult after more than 30 years to correct all the inequities that have arisen, and a large proportion of current home owners have become owners since development charges were introduced. Moreover, governments are still short of capital funds for investment. Nevertheless, since the extent of charges on developers for off-site social as well as physical infrastructure costs is continuing to increase (see, for example, Briggs 1992), the question about what if any expenditures should be funded through development charges is still salient.

It remains important to re-examine the view that the cost of physical infrastructure should be incorporated into the cost of new housing. If the total capital cost of off-site as well as on-site infrastructure were to be charged to developers, eventually only operating costs, maintenance and depreciation/replacement costs would need to be funded from other sources. One possible result would be that user charges would be relatively low, although as infrastructure assets age replacement and maintenance are likely to become more important relative to other costs. I have argued earlier for a different policy: that on efficiency and environmental grounds, user charges should cover most of the capital as well as operating costs. Another result of charging developers the full capital cost of infrastructure needed to serve new development is that different funding for new and replacement infrastructure would unduly discourage investment by developers in new suburbs relative to established areas. Authorities, however, would have an incentive to encourage new development, which would provide its own infrastructure funds, relative to redevelopment and infill for which they would be responsible.

What are the equity implications of funding most of the capital costs of new off-site capacity through developer charges compared with funding most through loans amortised from user charges? Developer charges increase the capital cost of housing, and hence the mortgage interest payments of purchasers. Recent research by Bourassa (1995) has shown that few renters in Australia can afford to borrow enough to become home owners, and increased prices would exacerbate that problem. Increased purchase prices would result also in a rise in the level of rents paid by tenants. User charges, on the other hand, increase annual outgoings in proportion to the use of the service. Without information about the income elasticity of demand for the individual services to compare with those for housing, it is difficult to be clear about the lifetime incidence of the alternatives among different income groups.

One difference is clear. Compared with user charges, developer charges increase costs during the part of the life cycle when households are tenants and recent purchasers, and lower costs when their equity is high or they are outright owners. Since other claims on household incomes are higher during the former periods, developer charges are in that sense more regressive.

The equity impacts described above may be acceptable if development charges increase the efficiency of resource allocation. In this respect it is important to distinguish between contributions to cover category (1) above, mostly on-site, and category (2), mostly off-site, servicing costs. On-site contributions have several favourable effects. First, the charges greatly increase the investment land developers must make to provide lots which can be sold for building. As a result, lots have become too costly for developers to hold for very long. One result is that the scattered building of houses on subdivisions with very few services, which was a feature of the suburban fringe in the early post-war period, has disappeared. Second, developers are required to install services in advance of building, which costs less than installing them at a later date.

Third, on-site charges encourage development in locations where the reticulation of services within the subdivision is inexpensive. Before they were introduced it was politically difficult to refuse applications to develop sites that were costly to service. Land-use controls were the only policy measure available; when they were unsuccessful, the high cost of servicing had to be borne by the servicing authorities. When developers became responsible, however, they had an appropriate incentive to develop areas that were cheaper to service. They were encouraged also to design their subdivisions in ways that economise on servicing cost.

An undesirable effect of on-site development charges on resource allocation results from the separation of responsibilities for capital investment in reticulation and local roads, from responsibility for their maintenance and future replacement. Developers have an incentive to provide facilities that are less than optimally durable and that have only sufficient capacity for immediate requirements. They are prevented from doing so by standards and design specifications set by the service authority. But the authorities have an incentive to require over-design to minimise their future maintenance and replacement costs, widely known as requiring 'gold plating' of infrastructure services. This, in turn, has required legislation which prohibits excessive standards and provides developers with an avenue of appeal, for example s. 94 of the New South Wales *Environmental Planning and Assessment Act* 1979 .

Off-site charges can usefully be separated into first, those needed to connect a new development to the established network, such as extending water and sewer mains or an arterial road, and second, contributions to amplification of headworks and trunk networks in general. The former discourages subdivision remote from, or difficult to connect to, existing services, and therefore provides desirable location incentives. Since the effect of an individual subdivision on general off-site costs is difficult to estimate, the second component of the charges is commonly levied at a rate per dwelling or per hectare and rarely discriminates between subdivisions.[5] As a result these charges have no impacts on the choice of location and are essentially a revenue raising device. Both kinds of off-site charges make housing more expensive, which produces the adverse equity impacts described above.

In summary, all developer contributions help to achieve financial objectives but have equity effects which are generally regressive. Requirements that developers provide reticulation services and local roads within their own subdivisions, and link their subdivisions with existing networks, provide also desirable location incentives and incentives for efficient subdivision design. Requirements that developers contribute to costs of headworks and general amplification of the networks have no such desirable effects.

Judgments about whether developer contributions should or should not have been introduced and whether they should be maintained or expanded need to take account of the historical context in which they were introduced and the reasons they are continued. They were introduced in the 1950s and 1960s at a time of very rapid urban growth when local councils and water and sewerage authorities were having difficulty keeping up with the demand for additional services and at the same time providing services in suburbs which had been settled without a full range of services.

Developer charges continued to be levied even after the growth had slowed and the unserviced areas had been serviced, partly because they are a convenient source of funds. Two other arguments have been used for their maintenance and expansion. The first is an efficiency argument: unless the cost of new suburban development includes the full cost of provision of public services, there will be too much new development relative to redevelopment and infill. That argument would be valid if it could be assumed that there is spare capacity for every service in areas where redevelopment or infill occur, or that the cost of any amplification in such areas is small. Manifestly this is not true, as was argued in Chapter 3 and can be seen from overflowing sewers, flooding and traffic congestion. The argument would still be valid if contributions of the full cost of its servicing were required when redevelopment and infill occur, but they are not, partly because of the difficulty of estimating them. Furthermore, from an equity point of view there seems to be no good reason why first-time home buyers should pay for the additional physical infrastructure required to service new households, any more than we expect parents to pay the full cost of schools.

The second argument derives from the ideological view that taxes should be lowered and government control over resources minimised in order to increase competition and hence efficiency. This argument is not persuasive in a context in which the alternatives are government provision of infrastructure or private provision of the same infrastructure under government control. This issue is taken up again in Chapter 9.

## Taxes

Taxes can be used, first, as a general source of revenue, part of which funds the provision of a service (e.g. drainage), second, as a user charge (e.g. the tax on motor vehicle fuel), third, as an access charge (e.g. taxes on property to fund water and sewerage), and fourth, to subsidise the provision of a service (e.g. public transport).

Property taxes have advantages as a source of funding for most services. First, they bear some relationship to the increased value of property resulting from provision of infrastructure. Second, they bear some relationship to ability to pay. Third, they spread the cost of services over different cohorts and over all property owners within the servicing jurisdiction. Fourth, site value taxes on all property with access to a service cause little if any distortion in the allocation of resources. The latter characteristic makes them almost ideal for achieving financial objectives, but of zero value in achieving efficient resource allocation.

Fuel taxes vary reasonably closely with the amount of road space occupied by a vehicle, but vary little with the wide differences in the scarcity, and hence the marginal cost and value, of road space between congested and uncongested locations and times. By themselves fuel taxes on vehicles with heavy axle loads are too low to reflect the damage they cause to roads. They do, however, vary in proportion to the amount of air pollution which vehicles cause and, partly for that reason, are seen also as a good tax base for raising general revenue. Costs of collection are very low.

Other taxes can be considered together since they are seldom used as either access or user charges but rather as a source of funds for subsidies. Their advantage is that they presumably reflect the way the society wishes to distribute the cost of raising revenue among its members, and therefore are equitable. Their disadvantage is that they do nothing to encourage efficient levels of use of the services. Furthermore they reduce the efficiency of allocation of resources throughout the economy because of the so-called excess burden of taxation. This burden arises because all taxes, except lump sum taxes on individuals and site value taxes, distort choices between different goods and services, between consumption and investment or between work and leisure. General tax revenue is used to provide subsidies which achieve financial objectives with a minimum of inequity. They are most appropriate for funding 'community service objectives', which are concerned mainly with equity, and for the funding of parts of infrastructure which produce public goods. For this reason they are appropriate for funding social infrastructure but should be used sparingly for physical infrastructure.

## A COMPARISON OF USER CHARGES, ACCESS CHARGES AND TAXES

A change from taxes to user charges has distributional impacts both at a general level and for particular services. First, at the general level: when goods and services are sold they are distributed in accord with the intensity of demand of different consumers and their ability to pay. The rich can afford the most. When they are distributed free, and funded from tax revenue (which I assume to be progressive), as is the case with open space, primary and secondary education and public health services, ability to pay is not a criterion, and distribution between different income groups is more even. Whenever additional goods and services are shifted from the free list to the priced list, the relative position of the poor deteriorates. Their limited income has to be used to buy a wider range of goods and services and, because their incomes are low, they gain little from the reduction in taxes that results from fewer services being funded from tax revenue.

The same point can be made another way. When, through political processes, we make a collective decision about the extent of income redistribution through taxes and benefits, we do so on the assumption that a well defined range of goods and services is available irrespective of ability to pay. If we believe that the amount of redistribution is about right, and then decide to shift goods and services from the free to the priced list, we should increase the amount of income redistribution. Unless we do that, our decision will have made the poor worse off relative to the rich, and the distribution of income will be no longer 'about right'. The efficiency advantages of the greater use of pricing need to be compared with the efficiency costs of the greater redistribution which needs to accompany it. Otherwise we are not comparing like with like.

Yet a third way of explaining the same point is that general tax revenue, a large part of which comes from income taxes, takes a higher proportion of the income of the rich, while charges for the use of urban infrastructure services take a higher proportion of the income of the poor. For example, in 1988–89 the proportion of the total expenditure of the lowest income quintile of Australian households accounted for by income tax, was only a fifth of that for the highest income quintile. But the proportion of the expenditure of the lowest income quintile that went on electricity, gas, postage, telephones and bus and tram fares was over twice that of the highest quintile.

These differences reflect the fact that low income people spend a higher proportion of their income than higher income people on most urban physical infrastructure services (income elasticities of demand for them are less than 1.0). Taxes, however, are presumed to be progressive: they take a higher proportion of the income of the rich than of the poor. In 1988–89, as Figure 1 shows, total taxes accounted for an increasing proportion of the total expenditure of households as incomes increased, except at the bottom end of the distribution.[6] It is clear from the figure, however, that the progressivity of tax revenues as a whole is very largely the result of the direct (income) tax being progressive. Indirect taxes are very slightly regressive with respect to total expenditure.

The argument that a change from taxes to prices is generally regressive is quite powerful in relation to services that are funded from general tax revenue, such as open space and the recreational opportunities that go with it, education and to some extent health services and public transport. It is less powerful in relation to services such as water, sewerage, stormwater drainage and roads, for which the alternatives to user charges are specific taxes or access

**Figure 1    Tax as a percentage of total expenditure by income deciles, 1988–89**

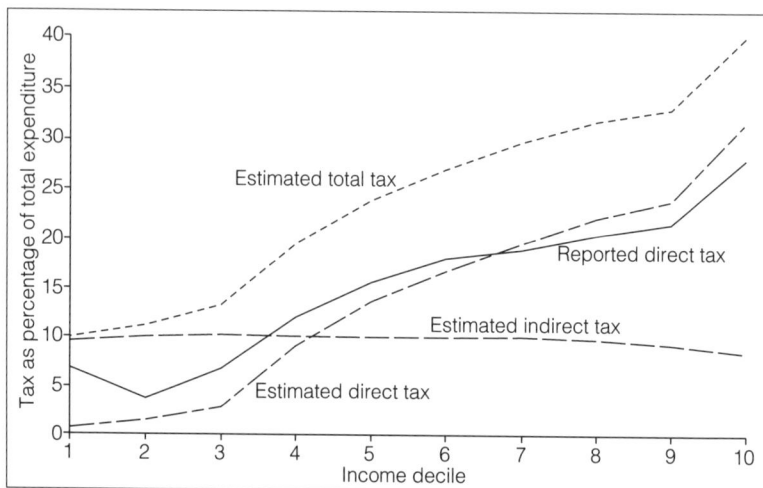

*Source*: Australian Bureau of Statistics, *Household Expenditure Survey, 1988–89*

charges. The impact of a change to user charges for these services needs to be considered on a case by case basis.

While funding services from income tax is clearly more progressive than user charges, that is not necessarily true for other taxes. For example, in 1988–89 water, sewerage and drainage rates were the main source of revenue for providing those services, the only other being development charges. Water, sewerage and drainage rates as a proportion of total expenditure for the bottom quintile was 2.4 times that for the top quintile. Clearly they were a regressive source of finance. At that time water, sewerage and drainage rates were predominantly access charges variously levied on the unimproved, improved or annual value of properties. For general property rates, used to fund local roads, drains, open space, etc., the ratio was the same. Even the purchase of petrol, the base for the fuel tax which is the main source of revenue for road expenditure by the states and a significant source for local government, accounted for a higher proportion of the expenditure of the lowest than of the highest income quintile, in the ratio of 1.2:1.

Some useful comparisons can be made with services which were funded mainly or entirely from user charges. The comparable ratios were: electricity, telephones and postage 2.6:1, gas 2.3:1, bus and tram fares 2.1:1 and for rail fares 1.05:1. It is not possible to judge whether a shift from petrol taxes to congestion charges would have progressive or regressive effects.

Public transport deficits, however, are funded from general state revenue, and a shift to a greater reliance on user charges would be more regressive, especially in the case of bus and tram fares which account for over twice the proportion of the expenditure of the lowest compared with the highest income quintile. It would be less regressive in the case of trains, which are used as much by higher income commuters as by households on lower incomes: train fares account for about the same proportion of the expenditure of the top and bottom quintiles.

It can be argued that property taxes are not as regressive as these data imply. They are a tax on an imperfect measure of housing wealth, first because they take no account of mortgage debt, and second, to the extent that landlords pass on their property taxes as part of rent, which seems likely, they are levied on tenants without any housing wealth. They should be judged on progressivity with respect to wealth. They appear regressive relative to income partly because they are levied on many retired people with low incomes but considerable housing wealth.

A number of infrastructure services are funded in part from a fixed access charge per property or per user, for example, telephones, vehicle registration, water and sewerage, garbage. Such fixed charges are more regressive than user charges except in those rare circumstances where poor people use more of the service than richer people.

From the point of view of their distributional impacts between income groups within a particular cohort, development charges have many of the features of access charges. Those development charges which recover off-site costs, especially those which are at a fixed rate, are, like other fixed access charges, likely to be more regressive than user charges.

It follows from the above discussion that for these physical infrastructure services (except for bus and tram travel) a shift from the current sources of funding—special taxes, access charges and development charges—to user charging might not be a regressive policy measure. Estimates of the distribution of the burden of user charges generally assume that levels of use will not change with their introduction. The efficiency argument for user charges, of course, is based on an assumption that they will fall. To the extent that they do, user charges are likely to become less regressive than is suggested by current levels of consumption, since the poor may be expected to reduce their consumption proportionately more than the rich. User charges at least give the poor the opportunity to save by using less, including by changing their location, time of travel, kind of housing and consumer durables. Access charges do not offer this opportunity.

## DIFFERENTIAL CHARGES ACCORDING TO LOCATION

One of the popular objectives of spatially oriented social justice strategies is that people should have equal access to services at the same cost no matter where they live. Australia has often tried to provide services such as postage and telephones to people living in remote areas at the same price as in large cities. In some states the price of electricity has been uniform throughout the state. Such policies raise important questions of equity, as well as efficiency, in relation to regional policy, which are beyond the scope of this study.

One reason that government took over from private water suppliers in nineteenth-century London was that in times of shortage the water companies found it profitable to cut off the supply to low-income suburbs. It is widely accepted that public utilities, whether public or private, have obligations as well as privileges, but how far do those obligations extend? A community service obligation of Telstra has been to provide telephones to people in remote areas at the same cost as in more settled areas, but that is being watered down, and whether the proposed broadband services will be made available in remote areas, and if so who will bear the costs, is unclear.

Some of those questions arise also within and around urban areas. Is it desirable on equity grounds to have uniform charges across an urban area? Around the urban periphery, how far should urban services such as garbage collection, sewerage and public transport be extended to ex-urban settlements and areas of very low population density? These two questions are related because the answer to the second might be that the services should be extended as long as the individuals or communities served are willing to pay their full cost.

The core issue is the appropriate definition of equity. My argument is that, since these services are provided by the public sector mainly because they are natural monopolies, a charge that varies between locations to reflect variations in costs is equitable as well as encouraging efficient use of resources. First some qualifications. This argument would not hold:

1  For services that were publicly provided because there was a collective judgment that they should be equally available to all, irrespective of ability to pay (for example, education and health services), in which case charges should be uniform or should vary with ability to pay; or
2  If most of the benefits from providing these services flowed to all people living in the city rather than to the individuals or households who use them, in which case they should be provided from tax revenue.

There are external benefits of type (2) (and external costs) from the provision and use of these services. But in most cases charges that are set to cover the marginal cost of providing the private benefits, adjusted up to allow for the environmental costs, will also cover the cost of providing public benefits. In these cases it is appropriate for user charges to be based on cost. Where, as in the case of sewerage, garbage and stormwater, the external benefits are large, but the costs can be attributed to individuals who generate the unwanted wastes, it seems reasonable that they should be required to pay for its disposal ('the polluter pays' principle).

The argument that user charges should vary between parts of a city with differences in cost can be illustrated by examples. The cost of road use within urban areas is determined mainly by the level of congestion in different areas, which in turn is determined mainly by the cost of land needed to expand road capacity in different parts of the city. The same land cost differences are major determinants of the cost of building space in different parts of a city. It is accepted that people pay more for building space in inner-city areas and along main transport arteries. Because space is more valuable in the inner parts of cities it needs to be used more intensively, roads should be more congested, buildings higher and dwellings and public open spaces smaller. In such areas, users should be charged a higher price for the parking space and road space they occupy, as they are for floor space or land. Congestion pricing is not simply a way of allocating road space in the short term until congestion is eliminated by expanding road space. Rather it is a way of allocating space that is scarce in the long term.

Similarly, the fact that roads are narrow and sewers are inadequate in some of the older parts of cities may not be a result of inadequate investment but rather a reflection of the very great cost of increasing their capacity. Short of demolition of all buildings and re-subdivision, which itself would be both economically and socially costly, such differences in service quality should probably continue.

Likewise, if people choose to live in the west of Sydney or Brisbane or the north of Melbourne they accept that it will cost them more each time they visit a beach. It will also cost more to transport or treat the sewage they produce and to dispose of treated effluent, and to prevent the run-off from their properties during heavy rain from causing flooding and pollution. There seems little reason why both kinds of cost differences should not be met by people who live in those areas.

This second example highlights the equity dilemma because the west of Sydney and the north of Melbourne are primarily low income areas. People do not 'choose' to live there; they live there because they cannot afford to live anywhere else. Will higher charges for sewerage further impoverish them, reduce the attractiveness of those areas to anyone who can afford to live elsewhere, and increase segregation? This might occur if cost-based user charges were to be higher in low income areas in general. But a few examples will show the contrary. It costs more to supply water to more elevated, steeper sites, which are usually occupied by the rich. Most long peak-hour journeys to city centres on congested roads or by heavily subsidised public transport are made by those with high incomes.

One of the factors which ameliorates the distributional impact of a policy of locationally differing charges within a city is that the differences are to some extent capitalised into the value of land. Because it costs more to buy services in one part of a city, buyers will be prepared to pay less for housing, and home builders will be prepared to pay less for land. This kind of capitalisation will happen to a greater extent with differences in capital costs (development charges), which are reflected directly in house prices, than with differences in annual costs (user and access charges).

The variations in cost of some services between parts of a service area are likely to be too small to justify different charges, especially in small towns and cities and, in the case of electricity, gas and telephones, in large cities. This seems unlikely to be the case for hydraulic services, roads or public transport in large cities.

## Non-contiguous development

An important equity question arises whenever it is proposed to extend urban network services beyond the edge of contiguous urban development. This may involve extension to settlements or ex-urban large-lot subdivisions which have been in existence for many years, or to a proposed new development which involves 'leap-frogging' over vacant land. The major services at issue are water supply, sewerage, roads, garbage collection and sometimes public transport.[7]

If it could be assumed that there would be no further development of the leap-frogged vacant land, the equitable and efficient rule would be for such services to be supplied on the condition that users, through capital, user, and access charges and taxes, pay the total additional cost compared with a contiguous development. This would require charges that differ within service areas. The possibility (or probability) that the leap-frogged vacant land in the vicinity will subsequently be developed changes the situation in two ways. First, the authority will want to provide sufficient capacity, especially in the connecting mains, to cope with the expected demand from the future development. Second, the users that are supplied in the first instance should have to pay the full cost of the connection only until such time as demand from further development in the area takes up its share of the capacity. At that time the costs should be divided among the different users in an equitable way.[8] There is a strong argument that the developer or the users who want the service extended should cover the holding costs until the intervening area is developed and thus take the risk that development of the intervening land will be delayed, or may never occur.

In Australia there is a strong tradition of universal access and uniform prices for public services within a service area. As a result small and non-contiguous settlements have often lobbied to be supplied and have strongly opposed being charged at a higher rate than users elsewhere in the service area. This might be overcome if there were more widespread variation between locations in levels of charging with variations in cost.

## Costs and benefits of locational variation

Requiring developers to pay for reticulation of services on their subdivision and for linking their subdivisions with existing networks is an efficient way to vary some charges with cost. Contributions from developers to the other off-site costs can vary with location, but for two reasons that seldom occurs (Snyder & Stegman 1986). The first is that it is difficult and costly to estimate costs in different locations. The second is that these relative costs can vary over time with, for example, the capacity of sewer mains and arterial roads serving an area. Varying and unpredictable charges would not provide useful signals for developers choosing where to develop.

The extent of locational variation in charges depends on institutional arrangements. In Australia such charges may vary between local councils or be uniform over urban areas. In the United States it is not uncommon for districts to be formed within a city for the provision of a service, and for charges or property taxes from that district to be used to fund its provision. Thus charges vary between districts with costs.

Where the marginal cost of providing a service varies spatially because of long-term cost differences, it is desirable that charges should reflect them. One example is the difference in cost of sewerage between locations close to the coast and inland locations. Pollutants generally, and nutrients in particular, do less damage when released into the ocean than into inland waterways. Sewage generated in inland locations must either be piped long distances for less costly treatment and discharge into the ocean, or treated more fully at greater cost prior to discharge into inland waterways. A second important example, discussed above, is the cost of roads.

## CROSS-SUBSIDIES AND COMMUNITY SERVICE OBLIGATIONS

If the government requires a service authority to provide services at less than full cost, they can be funded either by cross-subsidisation from other parts of the operation or by a government grant from tax revenue. Cross-subsidisation of the cost of infrastructure services occurs in a number of ways, including the following:

1  The tradition of uniform charges, even when the cost of services for different users is different, results in subsidies from users that can be serviced cheaply to those that are expensive to service. While some cross-subsidies benefit poorer users, many have regressive effects. For example, it is commonly cheaper to provide roads and hydraulic services on sand or clay plains

where most low income housing is built than on rocky hilly areas where more of the rich live. Flood protection, on the other hand, is more costly in low-lying flat areas, but much of the water that causes the floods drains from the hills and higher land upstream.

2 A different kind of cross-subsidisation occurs when services are provided mainly for low income customers at less than cost, for example, off-peak public transport for those without access to cars, though there is a cross-subsidy only if the off-peak fares are less than variable operating costs. Provision of water to low income households that use little water may produce a lower return on investment than providing it to higher income households that use a lot, though the use of water per hectare may not be so different if lower income people live at higher density. Uniform user charges in these circumstances could result in regressive redistribution.

3 An even clearer case of cross-subsidisation occurs when deliberate decisions are made, usually by the government, to charge some users at a higher or lower level for equity rather than cost reasons. One example is the concessional rates at which pensioners are charged for services such as water, sewerage and drainage and public transport. Children also are commonly carried at concessional fares on public transport. On the other hand, businesses frequently have been charged for hydraulic services and electricity at a higher rate than households, even when the cost of servicing them was the same.

Type (1) cross-subsidisation seems undesirable because it gives incorrect signals about the cost of alternative location decisions. The conventional economic view is that the cost of government-determined types (2) and (3) concessions should be paid by the government rather than from revenue raised from other consumers such as those that suffer under type (3) discrimination.

Some type (2) community service obligations have much in common with some of the obligations of providers of public services. For example, it may be seen as an obligation of any such monopoly authority not to charge higher prices to low income consumers, even though the return from serving them at the same price is lower. An analogy can be found in community rating for health insurance, under which insurers are required to charge the same premiums to the old with high risks of requiring medical services as to the young whose risks are much lower. Providing concessions to pensioners, school children or off-peak users are not usually seen as part of that obligation.

Notwithstanding the conventional wisdom, there seems to be no reason in principle why the contract between the government and the service authority should not specify which concessions are to be provided as one of the obligations of the authority. The cost of meeting those obligations would be taken into account in determining permitted levels of charges. Cross-subsidies from higher income users are less redistributive than subsidies from income taxes, but they may be much cheaper to administer.

If some kinds of users are subsidised because they pay property rates or other access charges which do not cover full costs, the main effect is on income distribution and there is little impact on the use of resources. Any other kind of redistribution of charges among users will also affect the use of resources. For example, cross-subsidies from developer charges that are uniform while costs vary can distort location choices, as noted above. If user charges for some consumers are too low to cover their costs, the result will be excessive use of the service. Even access charges that vary between users or (especially) between locations, will distort land use and location choices. These effects need to be compared with the costs of other means of achieving the same equity objective.

## CHARGING WHEN SHORT-RUN AND LONG-RUN MARGINAL COSTS DIFFER

One of the most useful rules for managers of urban infrastructure is that efficient allocation of resources will result in short-run marginal costs (SRMC) being equal to long-run marginal costs (LRMC) under most circumstances. The reason for this can be explained intuitively. The level of production of a service can be expanded either by using additional variable inputs to get more output from the existing capacity, or by increasing capacity. The cost of the former is the SRMC, and of the latter is the LRMC.

A good manager will increase output by whichever means is cheaper, so that an optimal production program will have the two equal. If there is spare capacity it will be cheaper to increase variable inputs until that capacity is used, at which stage it will be cheaper (necessary) to increase capacity. If SRMC were to remain constant as capacity was approached and suddenly became infinite when capacity was reached, the equality of SRMC and LRMC would be neither interesting nor helpful. For most forms of infra-structure, however, capacity is more elastic: it becomes more costly to increase output by adding variable inputs as capacity is approached, and at some stage the cost of adding such inputs (SRMC) will exceed LRMC. At that stage it will be cheaper to increase capacity, as long as capacity can be efficiently increased by small amounts. Where increments in capacity can be made efficiently only in large lumps, it is necessary to discount future benefits (savings in variable cost) and compare them with the cost of adding to capacity. SRMC is likely to be well above LRMC by the time benefits exceed costs.

This rule provides an answer to a debate in the economics literature about whether prices should be set equal to short- or long-run marginal costs. The answer is that if investment is at the right level the two will be the same, so it does not matter which is chosen. In this section I will argue that in situations where the two can usually be expected to be the same, prices should be set equal to long-run marginal costs because they are easier to measure. There are some situations, however, in which the investment rule (that they should be equal) cannot be followed, and in those circum-stances it is necessary to consider carefully whether charges should equal short- or long-run marginal costs.

The equality of short- and long-run marginal costs provides the general link between optimal charging policy and optimal invest-ment policy: charges should be equal to marginal costs and invest-ment should be carried out up to the level where the cost of increasing output by increasing capacity is equal to the cost of increasing output by using more variable inputs.

When capacity is approached, successive marginal units of use first cause a decline in the quality of service to all other users. Users therefore should be charged the marginal cost of the service to all users considered as a group, which is the cost borne directly by the marginal user plus the costs this user imposes on other users. When demand has reached the level where that cost, of increasing output by one unit using the existing capacity (SRMC), has risen to exceed the cost of adding a marginal unit to capacity (LRMC), capacity should be expanded.

The investment rule is more difficult to apply, however, first because estimating the unit cost of the capacity needed to meet demand requires an estimate of the future level of demand. Whereas capacity has a long life and often cannot be used for any other purpose, variable inputs, by definition, can be increased and withdrawn at relatively short notice. Because investment in infrastructure capacity is durable and specialised, the outputs of services it produces at different times are joint products. Not only is the capacity to produce during peak hours also available in off-peak hours, but the great majority of the capacity that is available this year will still be available next year and in five years' time. While long-run costs are easier to estimate, investment decisions based on them are inherently forward-looking and must make assumptions about future demand, and hence they are risky.

There is a further difficulty in using the equality between short- and long-run marginal costs as an investment criterion. It is very difficult to measure SRMC at levels of output close to full use of capacity because, as the full use of capacity is approached, not only does the money cost increase but so too do user costs as the quality of service falls. This also suggests that it is more practicable to set charges equal to LRMC rather than SRMC for infrastructure services in most circumstances. The fall in quality is well recognised in the case of roads, where it is reflected in the additional time costs incurred in using increasingly congested routes. This can be converted into an estimate of the dollar value of rising SRMC by imputing a value to the additional time. But even this dollar measure of SRMC is an artefact. As will be pointed out in Chapter 7, because the time costs involved are borne by road users themselves, their value is not reflected in a cost increase that is observable in the market.

Though a decline in the quality of other services clearly occurs, estimating its cost as a rising SRMC is even more difficult than for roads. For example, as the use of electricity approaches capacity, the probability of a power cut or a decline in voltage increases. The cost of the increasing probability of failure is difficult to estimate. Similarly, the costs of an increased probability of a decline in water pressure or of the imposition of water restrictions, of sewers or sewage treatment plants overflowing during rainstorms, of being unable to make a telephone connection because all lines are busy, of a decline in pressure or a cut in gas services, of being unable to get on a bus or train because it is full, or having to stand in crowded conditions, are all difficult to measure. The difficulty of measuring the cost of the decline in service quality is partly because it cannot be accurately predicted.

In order to avoid these problems, SRMC has often been identified as marginal 'avoidable' costs (more commonly called 'variable' costs in the economics literature) (BTCE 1988): those costs which could be avoided if the use of the service ceased. Since that measure of short-run cost assumes that the decline in quality when capacity is approached has zero cost, it is not surprising that, even when capacity is considered to be at an appropriate level, avoidable cost is below the LRMC, which includes the cost of capacity. The revenue which would result from estimates of prices based on this definition of SRMC always falls well short of covering total costs even when capacity is fully used. Such a revenue shortfall results not from economies of scale but from an incorrect measure of marginal cost.

As demand fluctuates over time, there are periods in which it is optimal to have spare capacity and when, as a result, SRMC is below LRMC. Less commonly, the opposite occurs: there is a chronic shortage of capacity and LRMC is below SRMC. In both of these circumstances there is a question of whether prices should equal short- or long-run marginal costs. The standard view (Vickrey 1980, 1985) is that prices should always be set equal to SRMC because they encourage users to make the best use of existing capacity. I will argue, on the contrary, that in some circumstances, when SRMC and LRMC differ, prices should be set at LRMC.

The following are some circumstances in which SRMC and LRMC can be different even when correct investment decisions are made.

**Lumpiness**

The special case of lumpy capacity occurs most clearly in water supply dams, though lumpiness is a feature of all the pipe and wire services and parts of transport systems, as described in Chapter 3. Because lumpiness is most easily recognised and most important in the case of dams, and because much of the discussion in the literature deals with this case, it will be used here. The problem that it raises is that, in a growing market, short-run marginal cost (SRMC) differs from long-run marginal cost (LRMC) most of the time. SRMC is lower, from the time immediately after a dam has been completed when excess capacity comes on stream, until demand grows to the extent that capacity begins to restrict supply. For reasons described in Chapter 3, SRMC rises as capacity increasingly limits supply and eventually exceeds LRMC. From that time until a new dam is completed, which should occur when the present value of the benefits from increased future capacity exceed the present value of the cost of building the new dam, SRMC exceeds LRMC. The discussion of pricing policy in these circumstances has mainly been concerned with efficiency, and has ignored equity and environmental considerations. Equity considerations are unlikely to be very large because the questions concern intertemporal price questions rather than differences between prices charged to different users.

The prescription that has been most common in the economics literature is that prices should be set equal to SRMC (Ng 1987). The argument in favour of following this course is that, during the long periods when there is spare capacity, users should not be discouraged from using the service as long as they are willing to pay the marginal operating cost (SRMC) of the dam plus, of course, the marginal cost of the remainder of the system. Any higher price would deprive some users of water which, given the existing capacity, costs less than they would be prepared to pay. Similarly, when the demand for water is approaching the full capacity of existing dams, the price should rise to ration the use of water and in due course it will be high enough to cover the cost of additional capacity. At that stage it will pay to invest in new capacity. But once the new dam is completed, according to this argument, the price should fall again to equal the new lower SRMC. The result is that prices follow a pattern over time that resembles the teeth on a saw, with the teeth more or less close together depending on the frequency of building of dams, and the saw on an upward slope if there is a shortage of good dam sites. The argument for this pattern of pricing is strongest where the lumps of capacity are large relative to the rate of growth of demand in a city and when future growth in demand is uncertain.[9] In those circumstances, the marginal cost of supplying water may remain below its long-run marginal cost for many years.[10]

The arguments against such a charging regime are of several different kinds. First, there is a simple but powerful administrative/political argument. A policy that results in prices which fluctuate over time in this way is difficult to administer and to justify to consumers. It is also difficult to argue politically for price changes that have nothing to do with the underlying cost of provision of the service. It seems perverse to require users to be willing to pay the full cost of a new dam before constructing it and then, immediately the dam is completed, reduce the price to much less than the full cost.

Second, it results in the price of water being below LRMC for most of the investment cycle. In strict economic efficiency terms, it will result in too much use of water. One result of this will be that supply authorities will be unable to cover their costs from the prices they charge. If the supplier borrows to fund the dam it will receive insufficient revenue to amortise the loan after construction is completed. Such funds have to be raised from property taxes, access charges or from surpluses elsewhere in the system. The price of water supply will be too low relative to other prices because investors in other sectors of the economy, where lumpiness is common, cannot raise either property taxes or access charges and would be forced to charge higher prices for their products. When businesses make an investment decision they have to recover the capital costs by levying charges that exceed short-run marginal costs after the capacity is expanded. The result is that when water supply authorities meet all the demand at these low prices, too many resources are used in the provision of water. Because the financial costs of a water supply authority do not include environmental costs, water prices should exceed long-run financial costs rather than being lower. Prices that are below LRMC most of the time encourage excessive use of water and damage to the environment.

Third, it results in inefficient consumer decisions about the use of water. The view that prices should equal SRMC assumes that decisions to consume water are predominantly short-term decisions, such as how frequently to take a shower or how long to water the garden. Such decisions can be varied daily according to the changing price of water. But in reality the most important decisions which affect the level of use of water are long-term investment decisions about the purchase of consumer durables and landscaping. The evidence for this is found in Chapter 4, where it was shown that the elasticity of demand for water is perhaps three times as high in the long run as in the short run. These investment decisions are based on expectations about the future price of water. Long periods when prices are below the long-run marginal cost of supply will encourage excessive water use, which is unlikely to change during brief periods of high prices. If consumption decisions are mainly long-term decisions, they are more likely to be optimal if they are guided by a relatively stable price which reflects the LRMC.

These arguments would be more significant if they applied also to the mains of the network, on the grounds that it is most efficient to increase their capacity in large lumps. Those who argue for prices to be set equal to SRMC, defined as avoidable or variable costs, are implying that they do. In fact, apart from the pipes or channels that transport water from the dams to the city, it is better to think of the capacity of the network as being continuously variable by the successive relief of constraining bottlenecks. Whatever the merits of charging only marginal variable costs of a dam with surplus capacity, they are much less persuasive when applied to other parts of the supply system.

Lumpiness also has impacts on investment decisions. SRMC and LRMC in a growing market will be the same only once in each investment cycle: at the time when SRMC rises due to increased operating costs and falling quality of service as output approaches the maximum possible with the existing capacity. The investment question is, when should the next lump of capacity be provided? In principle the answer is the same as it is for any other large and durable investment: when the present value of the benefits, in the form of lower costs to producers and users of providing the service in the future, exceeds the cost of the investment.

The returns from an increase in capacity, however, are difficult to measure. Some accrue to the producer as reduced operating costs but others to the users as a higher quality of service. The higher user costs of infrastructure operating close to capacity are well recognised on congested roads. Because non-price user costs are a smaller proportion of the costs of other services, they are less affected by the reduction in service quality. Nevertheless, the effects are significant.

Because infrastructure services are not sold in competitive markets, there is no direct commercial incentive for suppliers to provide a high quality of service. The difficulty of measuring the benefits to customers of improved quality of service is one reason why engineering standards have been very important in deciding on the appropriate level of service. Another reason is the importance of public health and amenity as objectives in the original decisions of government to provide many of these services, and their continued importance in relation to reliability. A third reason is that equity is a significant criterion in decisions about urban infrastructure. The argument that the services should be provided to all users at some given standard implies a more equal distribution of the benefits from their provision than if each investment decision was assessed on the basis of the willingness of users to pay its cost over an amortisation period. Service quality is determined frequently by regulation rather than by commercial judgment.

## Peaking in demand

Where demand fluctuates over time, the full capacity of a service is generally used only at periods of peak demand. Under such conditions the only cost of producing an additional unit of output in off-peak periods is the variable cost of labour and materials used. It follows that SRMC is less than LRMC in off-peak periods. This is a permanent situation and therefore it is appropriate that charges should equal SRMC outside the peak so as not to discourage use of the service by those who would be prepared to pay its marginal cost. Charges during the peak should equal LRMC, including the total marginal costs of capacity, since the chosen level of capacity is needed solely to meet the demands of peak period users. Likewise, off-peak demand is irrelevant to investment decisions. Capacity should be expanded when the benefits to peak period users exceed its cost.

The reason for a different pricing rule when there is surplus capacity in off-peak periods and when it results from the addition of a lump of capacity needs to be explained. Surplus capacity in off-peak periods is a permanent feature of the operation of many infrastructure services. It is desirable that consumers adjust their consumption patterns to this stable pattern of fluctuations in the cost of providing the service. Furthermore, over the cycle which includes peak and off-peak periods, total revenue will cover total costs. Surplus capacity which results from lumpiness in capacity is a temporary phenomenon and, to the extent that consumers make long-term consumption commitments, it is undesirable that they adjust their consumption to the lower marginal costs, especially as returns over the investment cycle will not cover the total costs of providing the service.

## Long-term capacity shortage

Where capacity is less than optimal and is expected to remain so over a long period, perhaps because of shortages of investment capital or other constraints on investment, SRMC will be greater than LRMC. Unless other methods of rationing are to be used for equity reasons, the price should equal SRMC to ration the available capacity. For example, it has been argued that the benefit: cost ratio from increasing the capacity of many congested urban roads in Australia is well above 1 (BTE 1984), which implies that SRMC LRMC. If this is true, rationing the capacity of the existing roads by levying congestion charges at the difference between private costs and total SRMC is more desirable than relying on rationing through congestion. It will discourage users who value their use of the road less than the cost of their use to themselves and other users.[11]

## Long-term surplus capacity

Where excess capacity is expected to continue for a long time because future demand was overestimated, or where demand has fallen, there is a case for charging only the SRMC, in this case the variable (including environmental) cost of providing the service, even though it is below LRMC. In this situation, the capacity costs cannot be recovered and should be written off. Any higher price would unduly discourage the use of capacity. It should be noted that the argument for charging a price which excludes the marginal cost of capacity depends not on the existence of spare capacity but on the expectation that spare capacity will continue for a long time into the future.

Like the owner of a water supply dam, the owner of unused capacity to provide other infrastructure services, where demand is expected to grow in the relatively near future, should compare the strategy of reducing the price so that all available capacity is used with the strategy of maintaining prices that cover marginal capacity as well as operating costs and waiting for growth in demand to take up the slack in capacity. Only when demand is sufficiently elastic that the lower price will yield enough additional revenue to cover the variable costs of the increased output needed to fully use capacity would it pay the producer to lower the price. Especially since suppliers are monopolists, such elasticity seems unlikely. From a social point of view, however, it is desirable that charges be lowered even if it results in a larger loss.

In summary, in those specific situations where SRMC and LRMC are not equal, price should be equal to short-run marginal cost where the difference is expected to continue for a long time:[12]

1  Where there is surplus capacity during off-peak periods and the difference in demand between periods is likely to continue;
2  Where shortage of capacity is expected to continue for a long period due to capital shortages; and
3  Where surplus capacity is expected to continue for a long period because of earlier over-investment or a decline in demand.

Price should equal long-run marginal costs in those situations where the shortage or surplus capacity is a temporary phenomenon, as when the lumpiness of investment in facilities such as water supply dams for a growing city causes successive periods of shortage and surplus capacity.

# 7  Optimal funding arrangements

Previous chapters have described the technical and economic features of urban physical infrastructure services. These features result in unusual aspects in both the cost of and the demand for these services. The alternative ways in which the provision of urban infrastructure can be funded, and the advantages and disadvantages of each, have been analysed. The equity implications of alternative funding sources have been discussed. The fact that these services are provided at particular locations has an important influence on the way they are considered in this book.

In this chapter the implications of the arguments in the previous chapters are summarised in the form of concrete proposals about the optimal methods of funding. The first part sets out some general propositions and the second part describes their application to the funding of particular services. Following chapters deal with additional issues, including the relationship between urban planning and infrastructure funding, technical innovations and their implications for funding, and financial and institutional issues.

The charging objectives spelled out in Chapter 5—efficiency in the use of resources, protection of the environment, adequate and cheaply raised revenue, and equity between different users—are not simple alternatives that can be assigned weights according to some policy judgment. Adequate revenue is essential: if the services are to be provided, the cost of providing them has to be paid from some source, even if it is from tax revenue. A substantial part of the cost of public transport is met from tax revenue, by default. It is unusual for a government to take a deliberate decision that taxes are an appropriate source of funds for public transport; rather the fare revenue is insufficient to cover costs and no access charges can be collected. There has been some suggestion that developers should contribute to the capital cost of public transport as they sometimes did in the nineteenth century, but little revenue has been raised from this source.

The other objectives are in one sense optional: they may or may not be actively pursued. In another sense, however, they are not optional: the choice of the system of financing will inevitably influence efficiency, the environment and equity. The questions that must be considered are *how* the costs will be covered and what is the *relative importance* of each of the other objectives in making decisions about how to fund these services. Chapter 2 contains a list of the reasons why infrastructure services are provided, or their private provision is regulated, by government: either they are natural monopolies, or they provide public goods or produce large externalities, or they provide goods or services that are regarded as essential and should be available to all regardless of their ability to pay, or they are regarded as merit goods. In some cases more than one of these reasons applies. The first part of this chapter builds on that discussion.

## THE RELATIVE IMPORTANCE OF CHARGING OBJECTIVES

The users of services that are provided by governments solely because they are natural monopolies might be expected to cover their full costs: the natural monopoly argument for government, or regulated private, supply does not, in itself, justify government subsidy. The requirement that such natural monopolies cover their costs from prices (user charges) is itself a valuable discipline on their decisions, even if that discipline is relaxed where specific obligations are imposed by the government on the supply authority. Prices are of most value as a guide to resource allocation when there is competition between suppliers. But even though it is recognised that there will not be competition under conditions of natural monopoly, user charges are still valuable because they provide information to suppliers about the value users place on their services.

Since it is not possible to charge for public goods, the alternatives are to finance them from general tax revenue or from taxes or charges on those who benefit from their provision, if possible access charges that do not vary with the level of use. The main criterion for making this choice is equity. For example, since police and fire services protect property as well as people, part of their cost might come from a property tax. Since the provision of access roads and parks increases the value of properties that have access to them, it may be appropriate that the owners of nearby property cover their cost through a property tax, or that subdividers provide the roads and parks and pass on the cost to home buyers.

Part of the costs of some infrastructure services for which equity is an important objective are covered from user charges and part from general tax revenue in order to achieve redistribution. User charges that covered the total cost would exclude those who could not afford to pay and therefore prevent public provision from achieving its equity objectives. Consistent with the redistributive objective, access to some of these public services, or to the subsidy in their provision is means-tested, for example, public housing and some welfare services.

Although equity considerations are rarely dominant in determining the means of funding physical infrastructure services, they are generally one of the considerations, especially where the services are required to meet community service obligations. These are obligations, imposed on service providers by governments for equity reasons, to provide services at less than full cost to particular users. Often the cost of these obligations is met by cross-subsidisation from profits made on other services supplied by the authority or on the same services supplied to different consumers. The conventional economist's view is that they should be financed from tax revenue so that the costs of meeting the obligations are distributed according to ability to pay rather than being met by other users of particular services, but there are arguments for cross-subsidisation (see Chapter 6).

If the provision of a service has major impacts on the environment, charges that increase with the user's contribution to adverse external impacts will discourage behaviour that is environmentally damaging. This is not to imply that charging mechanisms should be the only or even the main means of controlling negative externalities.[1] It does, however, imply that they can be a useful part of the policy response. Governments generally want their citizens to consume more merit goods than they would if they had to pay their full cost and as a result the provision of such goods is commonly funded partly by user charges and partly from tax revenue.

## GENERAL FUNDING PROPOSALS

Since physical infrastructure services are either in the public sector or regulated by government mainly because they are natural monopolies, the main (non-financial) objective is efficient use of resources rather than equity. Because there are important externalities from the use of physical infrastructure services, preserving and enhancing the environment is an important secondary objective. Fortunately, because the main determinant of both the use of resources in providing them and the environmental harm that results is the volume of use of these services, user charges that encourage efficient use of resources also discourage environmental damage. Volume of use is not, however, the only determinant of either use of resources to provide the services or of the environmental damage that results from their use. For example, the location at which the services are used will influence both how much resources are used and the environmental impact of their use. The time of use will also affect the use of resources but not, as a rule environmental impact. Both the provision of access and the quality of the service provision (for example, the security of supply) have significant resource costs.

Raising of funds to pay the cost of urban infrastructure should be regarded as an opportunity rather than a problem. The need to raise funds provides a policy instrument that can be used to achieve economic and social objectives. All methods of funding will contribute to achieving the financial objective, albeit at different costs of collection. Funding methods should, wherever possible, contribute to at least one, and preferably more than one of the other objectives. Funding methods that do nothing more than help to cover the cost should be used only as a last resort. In addition, any adverse effects on achievement of the other objectives need to be taken into account in the choice among funding methods.

The following general recommendations are made for funding physical infrastructure in urban areas. They are followed by more detailed recommendations about the funding of individual services, showing how the general recommendations can be implemented in each case.

### User charges should be the major source of revenue

User charges should, as a general rule, be set equal to the long-run marginal cost of providing the service. They should, in a sense, take precedence over other sources of revenue. One of the disadvantages of other methods of funding, as Snyder and Stegman (1987) point out in relation to development charges is that, because they cover part of the cost of capacity, users need not pay the full marginal cost of the service and will therefore tend to use the service excessively.

Efficiency, equity and financial arguments have been used to argue that user charges are inappropriate as the major source of funding. These arguments have been examined in previous chapters and found wanting. The first efficiency argument against user charges is that, when they are set equal to short-run marginal cost, they will not cover total costs because of increasing returns to scale. But, for reasons given in the previous chapter and summarised below, prices should be set equal to long-run rather than short-run marginal costs. And it was shown in Chapter 3 that in cities larger than a moderate size, there are not large economies of scale when the enterprises that provide most of these services are considered as a whole. In the parts of the production process where there are scale economies, as in the sections of networks that provide reticulation within subdivisions, developer charges are an appropriate alternative funding mechanism, for reasons set out below, and they are commonly used for this purpose. It follows that in larger cities, apart from capital costs within subdivisions, charges set equal to the long-run marginal cost would cover the total cost of providing most services. They may even yield a surplus.

Where such user charges do not cover total costs, the difference may be covered in different ways. One is simply to increase the level of user charges, a policy that is defensible since these services (with the exception, for the most part, of telephones) produce adverse environmental impacts, and some, including water, sewerage and solid waste disposal, use up exhaustible resources. For these reasons there is a strong case for user charges to be set above internal marginal costs. The use of most of these services results in environmental costs which are broadly proportional to the volume of use. If an allowance for environmental costs was added to the marginal financial cost estimates used to determine levels of user charges, the probability of a surplus would be higher.

If a surplus results when charges are set equal to marginal social cost, one alternative is to use it as a source of tax revenue for general government purposes. It is an environmental tax of the Pigouvian type, which appropriately discourages the use of services which damage the environment.[2] The alternative is to refund it to users in a lump sum by providing a free allowance of the service to all users; a form of negative access charge. This would be administratively easy for services such as water and electricity for which there is periodic billing but not for services such as roads where the costs are paid continuously.[3] It also would have favourable equity effects, as pointed out above.

The conventional view has been that charges should equal short-run marginal costs (SRMC), which have then, erroneously, been equated with variable or avoidable costs. Because variable costs ignore the marginal cost of capacity entirely, user charges based on them would produce revenue that was less than total costs for many services. It has been argued in earlier chapters that, except where (a) SRMC is less than long-run marginal costs (LRMC) because there is surplus capacity that is expected to persist for a very long time, or (b) SRMC is greater than the LRMC because of a chronic shortage of capacity, or (c) SRMC is less than LRMC outside periods of peak demand, user charges should be set equal to LRMC. In most situations where the capacity level is close to optimal, properly defined SRMC will be very similar to LRMC. Setting user charges (average charges where demand is peaked) equal to LRMC ensures that the marginal cost of capacity is included.

The second efficiency argument against user charges is that the cost of measuring the volume of use by individual users of some services is high relative to the benefits of user charges. But as the next part of this chapter shows, the costs of measuring the volume of use of most services by individual users are no longer so high as to preclude efficient charging. The equity argument against them is that user charges for most services are less equitable (more regressive) than the alternative methods of charging such as property taxes, access charges and fuel taxes. The previous chapter shows that user charges are not necessarily more regressive. Furthermore, because user charges give low income people the opportunity to reduce their expenditure by using less of the services, they could well be more equitable. The financial argument against user charges is that revenue from them fluctuates, especially in the case of water, and makes financial planning very difficult. But the fluctuations in revenue can be handled by permitting service authorities to carry over deficits as well as surpluses from year to year.

LRMC will vary, in some cases significantly, with location within an urban area and between periods of peak and off-peak demand. Whether or not user charges should vary with location depends on whether the gains from discouraging development and the use of services in parts of the city in which services are costly to provide are greater than the cost of estimating the different costs in different locations, and charging accordingly. The benefits will be greater the greater the intra-urban cost differences and the greater the responsiveness of location choices to price differences. If, for example, land-use controls are very tight so that development is permitted only in places where services can be supplied at low cost, the gains may be small. This issue is taken up in Chapter 10. The costs are mainly the cost of calculating and administering different levels of charges in different areas.

The larger and more topographically diverse the urban area the more likely it is that the cost differences will be substantial. A city which draws its water from a small number of surface catchments will also experience more cost differences than one that relies on underground supplies. Additionally, the overhead costs of setting up a system for estimating and charging the different costs in different parts of a city will be spread more widely in a large city. For one service, roads, we know that costs vary greatly between congested parts of large cities where land values are high and uncongested parts where they are low, and it seems almost certain that differing charges are warranted.

The marginal cost of services where the cost of capacity accounts for a high proportion of total cost, and where demand fluctuates widely between peak and off-peak periods, are much higher in peak than in off-peak periods. In these circumstances, the level of capacity provided is determined solely by the need to meet peak period demand and all of the marginal cost of capacity should be charged to peak period use. The additional costs of measuring peak and off-peak use separately need to be compared with the gains in efficiency that would result from different peak period prices.

**Developers should provide on-site reticulation of services**

Requiring developers to provide reticulation of roads, water, sewerage and drainage services within each new subdivision provides desirable incentives for development in places and in forms which make efficient use of resources. The same should occur within areas being redeveloped. Such a policy has the added advantage that it recovers at least the initial capital cost of the parts of the service network in which economies of scale are largest: the marginal costs of capacity in these parts of the networks are very low and, as a result, excess capacity is common. In addition to these arguments, local access roads and local drains provide public goods and there is no economic way of charging users. Loading the cost on to development costs effectively charges beneficiaries. Development charges have the equity disadvantage of increasing the cost of achieving home ownership by increasing capital costs that have to be met at a period in the family life cycle when little capital has been accumulated and other demands are high. These on-site costs were the first costs of public infrastructure to be imposed on developers and they have been the responsibility of developers in many countries for many years.

The only reason for excluding electricity, gas and telephones from this list is that their reticulation costs are lower proportions of their total costs and vary less with location within an urban area and with the form of development. In addition, connection to the last two is optional, and recovering their reticulation costs from access charges provides an appropriate disincentive to connecting.

Decisions about the location and the form of development of new subdivisions are taken at the time of development and are taken by developers who try to anticipate the preferences of their clients. Buyers seem likely to be more sensitive to capital charges, which they will be required to pay as part of their purchase price in some locations and with some forms of development, than to the expectation that they will be liable to continuing higher user charges or access charges. It is certainly true that once decisions about, for example, the density of development and the extent of impermeable hard surface for parking and the like are taken by the initial developer, subsequent changes are difficult and expensive. For these reasons also, requiring developers to cover the cost of reticulation of services within subdivisions seems to be desirable.

Initial development largely sets the hydrological characteristics of the subdivision, which in turn determine the extent and speed of run-off following rain. Developers need to have an incentive to minimise the volume and speed of run-off and to maximise the retention of rainfall on the subdivision either through absorption into groundwater, retention basins or temporary storage for future re-use. Specific proposals which provide such incentives are outlined later in the chapter.

## Development charges should cover out-of-the-ordinary off-site and on-site costs

Where the location or other characteristics of a development make the capital cost of infrastructure unusually high, it is desirable that developers pay the additional costs, whether or not they are incurred on site. One example is developments at high elevations which require additional service reservoirs and additional pumping capacity. A second is when developers want to develop out of sequence and therefore require trunk services to be provided earlier than they would be required for incremental growth of the city at its fringe. This requires unusually long mains and connecting roads between the new development and the established urban area. There are now well-established procedures under which developers are required to finance the additional cost of out-of-sequence development until the intervening area is developed and takes up the spare capacity, as laid out in the 1992 Victorian Ministry for Planning and Housing draft, 'Guidelines for assessing out-of-sequence development'. A third example is where developers decide to install electricity mains within their subdivision underground to provide a higher quality of environment. A fourth is the provision of a new trunk sewer to cope with the load resulting from a proposed redevelopment at higher density.

The proposal under discussion here, that only the *additional* cost of unusually expensive developments be charged to developers, would result in a major reduction in the level of charges for off-site infrastructure capital currently levied in many cities. It has the advantage that it gives appropriate disincentives for out-of-sequence development and for development in locations that are costly to service, while minimising the adverse equity effects. In this case the criteria for equitable charges also provide efficient charges.

It may not always be simple to distinguish situations in which costs are 'out of the ordinary'. Nevertheless it should be possible to develop workable guidelines for implementing this proposal for the most important cases.

### Access charges

Whether in the form of a property tax, a flat charge, a declining block tariff or a charge which varies with capacity, most compulsory access charges do nothing to discourage excessive use of the service.

Although property taxes in a crude way reflect ability to pay and the increase in capital value that results from the provision of services, generally they do little if anything to achieve equity. Their main merit is that they provide predictable revenue. For most services it is appropriate to use them in only two circumstances: first, as an alternative to developer charges and requirements, where they have the merit that they spread service reticulation costs over the household life cycle, although they provide none of the desirable location incentives of developer charges; second, to pay the maintenance and replacement costs of reticulation mains and roads within subdivisions, though such costs will commonly be covered by user charges; and third, in the circumstances (for example, some low-volume non-access roads) where correctly calculated user charges and developer charges do not cover total costs.

Where the owner or occupant of a property has a choice about whether or not to connect to a service, an access charge that reflects the cost of providing access encourages potential users to make an optimal decision. Of the services covered in this book, only telephones and gas supply can now be regarded as optional for most developed urban properties, and it can also be argued that telephones have become a social necessity. In the future, however, access to some other services may become optional. For example, approved composting toilets and storage tanks for sullage for subsequent use in irrigation could mean that access to sewerage becomes optional. People who compost or recycle nearly all solid wastes might opt out of access to garbage collection services. Small scale wind or solar energy generation might make access to mains electricity optional. More widespread use of rainwater tanks might make access to water supply optional. If these changes occur, there will be a stronger argument for funding the costs of providing access from access charges.

Access costs vary depending on whether or not they include the share for each property of providing access to the suburb or the subdivision, as well as access to the individual property. If they do not, access costs are almost trivial. The broader definition of access costs makes decisions about getting access comparable with the kind of decision that a commercial investor would make in similar circumstances, but it requires that decisions be made for a whole subdivision. It is legitimate to include other costs unrelated to the level of use of the service, such as meter reading, billing and maintenance, as part of the cost of access.

At present, however, connection to all of these services except gas and telephones is compulsory, and access charges for them are therefore almost solely a method of raising revenue. As a means of raising revenue they have the advantage that they are likely to have less influence on demand than user charges in excess of marginal cost; they satisfy the Ramsey (1927) criterion of being sources of funds that distort resource allocation relatively little. That is, however, also their weakness: they do nothing to discourage excessive use of resources or damage to the environment. They should be used as a means of funding these services only when optimal levels of user charges and developer charges do not bring in sufficient revenue to cover total costs.

## Benefit taxes or charges

The term 'benefit tax' describes a particular *rationale* for taxes and charges rather than a particular *kind* of charge. Benefit taxes are levied on individuals or owners of property who benefit from the provision of infrastructure. In this sense they are seen to be equitable. They can take the form of annual payments, such as property taxes or access charges, or of capital payments, such as developer charges that are passed on as higher prices of developed property. Annual charges can be used to amortise loans raised to pay for the infrastructure and also to cover the cost of depreciation and replacement of the assets.

If they are levied on the unimproved value of all land within a defined area benefit taxes have little effect on resource allocation, but if they are levied only on developed sites or sites connected to a service they are simply an access charge. If they are levied at the time of development, property owners or developers can pass on the cost to buyers of developed property by deferring development until the market price of the developed property rises enough to cover the cost. Like access charges, they should be used to cover off-site infrastructure costs only when user charges based on marginal cost plus development charges (as defined above) do not bring in enough revenue to cover all the costs.

One situation in which such a charge may be both needed and justified is in paying the deficit on public transport which mainly serves the city centre. This case is argued in the section dealing with public transport.

## General taxes

In most situations general tax revenue also should be used to cover the cost of regular services only when the revenue from optimal charges on users and developers yields insufficient funds to cover all costs. General taxes can be justified also where the government wishes to use infrastructure services to achieve specific redistributive objectives. Notwithstanding the argument advanced earlier, that redistribution is not a major reason for the public provision of physical infrastructure services, there are situations where free or below-cost provision is appropriate. In much of the literature these requirements of government are called community service obligations (CSOs) imposed on the provider of a service. Examples are public transport services for the disabled, school students and pensioners, or telephone services for people living in remote areas.

Subsidies from general tax revenue may be justified also where there are external benefits from infrastructure services for which it is not possible or desirable to charge. Reduction of public health risks and of public nuisance were important reasons for the introduction of a number of physical infrastructure services, including the provision of potable water, water-borne sewerage systems, stormwater drainage and garbage removal. All of these services also, to a greater or lesser extent, provide benefits to individual property owners. Subsidies may not, however, be necessary even where there are external benefits. If charges for those services are set equal to their full marginal cost when provided at a standard that avoids health risks, nuisance and flooding, and if the reticulation costs are paid by developers, their total cost will commonly be covered. If they are not, either general taxes, access charges or benefit charges should be used to cover the deficit.

The external economies argument has frequently been used to justify subsidising public transport. Because the use of roads causes so many external diseconomies, it has been argued, public transport should be subsidised to encourage fewer people to use the roads. It is not a very powerful argument, partly because the choice between private and public transport is not very sensitive to relative price and partly because public transport has its own externalities. In any event it is much better to charge motorists at a level that reflects their full long-run marginal costs, including the rental value of the land occupied by the roads.

Benefits of other kinds are provided to non-users also. One is the value of an option to use a service even when it is seldom if ever actually used. Thus many urban residents who very seldom use public transport may value it because it provides a means of travel when their cars break down or need to be serviced. That benefit is much greater than the fares they pay for their occasional journeys. Similarly, owners of property value having water mains in their street which provide sufficient volume and pressure to fight a fire, even if the need never arises.

Uncongested roads, and in particular access roads in urban areas, are public goods in that their use by one driver does not restrict their use by another. Since their main purpose is to provide access to individual properties, it seems appropriate that they should be paid for by the property owners concerned through developer charges and/or annual benefit taxes. Arterial roads provide access and also carry through traffic. In some cases the revenue from an optimal congestion charge plus an appropriate developer charge on some lightly used arterial roads will not cover their full cost. In that situation their costs, like the cost of similar rural roads, may need to be subsidised from revenue from a tax on road use, such as a fuel tax.

## FUNDING OF INDIVIDUAL SERVICES

The implications of these above proposals for individual services are spelled out below. Special attention is given to defining the user charges and to problems of measuring user cost responsibility.

### Stormwater drainage

The principle that should be adopted in the case of stormwater drainage is to charge for the costs which property owners and developers impose on the drainage system when it rains heavily. Developers of new subdivisions should be required to provide drainage facilities adequate to cope with maximum load. A major problem in implementing this policy is deciding to what extent developers are to be required to provide pondage and infiltration areas to reduce the peaking and total volume of flow and to improve the quality of stormwater discharge from the subdivision. The standard adopted in some parts of North America is zero impact: a subdivision is required to have no greater volume and peakedness and no worse quality of discharge following development, than it had before development. If that is not achieved the developer is required to pay the capital cost of the off-site facilities needed to achieve those standards before the stormwater is discharged to main drains or natural watercourses. Such a policy would give developers an incentive to provide for on-site absorption, short-term storage and re-use on the site. Since the costs will vary greatly depending on location, developers will have incentives to subdivide land where stormwater can be dealt with relatively cheaply. There may be difficulties in calculating the cost of off-site facilities, but these would be no greater than making the cost estimates needed for implementing some other aspects of developer charges. The above principles provide the basis for an appropriate set of charges.

The main disadvantage with such a charging policy is that it could significantly increase the cost of development and hence of housing. The alternative, an annual charge on property owners rather than a capital charge on development, lessens the equity problem but also lessens the impact of the charges on the marketability of the site and hence the incentive for developers to make on-site provision for stormwater.

This kind of charging policy leaves the maintenance, depreciation (replacement) and the remaining off-site costs of stormwater facilities to be covered by an annual charge. There remains also a need for revenue also to cover the cost of maintaining the stormwater system in established urban areas, and to augment that system as the proportion of the surface of a catchment covered by hard surfaces—roads, parking, driveways, paths and roofs—increases, causing greater volumes and peaking of run-off. It is unlikely to be practicable for developer charges to be levied for all of the increases in hard surface in established areas.

One efficient and equitable way to fund both maintenance and replacement costs in new areas, and the total cost in established areas, is an annual user charge, calculated on the basis of the total hard area on a property (mainly roofs, driveways, parking and a share of access roads) with a discount for on-site absorption or storage. In addition there should be a surcharge on the outdoor use of water for irrigation, car washing, etc. to cover the environmental cost of run-off. The method of distinguishing indoor and outdoor use of water is dealt with in the next section.

The level of the annual charge per square metre of hard surface would vary between catchments, and in some cases between parts of catchments, depending on two factors. First, where developers have been charged the full cost of dealing with stormwater, as described above, the annual charge would be lower. Second, the cost of dealing with stormwater in order to reduce flooding and pollution varies greatly with location. For example, the cost will be much lower in a suburb which drains directly into a part of the ocean which is flushed by strong currents than in an inland suburb which drains via flood-prone and polluted creeks into rivers or lakes also subject to serious pollution and flooding. The above proposals do not include any incentives to discourage litter and other waste materials being left in places where they will be washed into drains when it rains. This problem will have to be handled in another way.

## Sewerage

Most of the cost of sewerage should be covered from (1) a charge on discharge to the sewers, and (2) requiring developers to meet the capital cost of reticulation within subdivisions and connection to the existing network. Ideally charges should vary, first with the volume of discharge and second with its composition (usually called trade waste charges): the quantities of a range of substances that are difficult or expensive to separate in treatment facilities, likely to cause damage to sewers or likely to cause environmental harm because they are not extracted during treatment. Such a set of charges provides appropriate incentives for decisions about measures such as on-site separation and recycling of industrial wastes, which will reduce the costs of discharged sewage.

With currently available technology it is cost-effective to measure both the volume and the composition of the discharge from industrial and large commercial properties, and from smaller businesses which discharge wastes that are likely to be costly to handle, but not to measure either the volume or composition (which varies little) of domestic sewage, or of small commercial establishments that discharge essentially domestic-type sewage.

The volume of domestic discharge to the sewers is essentially equal to indoor water use; water used outdoors for irrigation or washing cars and paths is either absorbed into the groundwater, transpired from plants or run off into stormwater drains. Indoor water use, which tends to vary little between different times of the year, can be estimated from the level of use of water during the time of year when outdoor (and hence total) water use is lowest: for example, during winter in southern Australia. Charges for domestic sewerage should be based on the volume of use during the period of minimum use of water. Levying such a charge requires at least quarterly reading of meters and may require some other approximations, but even with such approximations it is much better than a charge that is invariant with discharge as occurs at present. It is also better than the second-best policy, simply adding a surcharge to the price of water consumed, unless conservation of water is such a high priority that its price should be raised above its resource cost. Such a surcharge is inequitable towards people with gardens relative to occupants of flats. The arguments for increasing and decreasing block tariffs are the same as they are for water supply and will be discussed in the next section.

A sewerage charge based on water use during the period of lowest use would provide an incentive for developers to install composting toilets and methods of dealing with grey water which together would enable properties to avoid connection to the sewerage system. An alternative is for developers to install a local sewage treatment facility, the effluent from which could be used for irrigation.

Where the operating cost of providing sewerage varies significantly between parts of an urban area, the charges per unit of volume and the level of trade waste charges should vary also. Cost may be higher because of the need for maintenance of sewers over a long distance in areas remote from treatment facilities, the need for pumping from low-lying areas and the need for high levels of treatment where the treated effluent is discharged into environments that are very sensitive to pollution.

**Water supply**

Aside from the contributions from developers to cover the cost of on-site reticulation and connection to the existing network, the great majority of the cost of supplying water should be recovered from a flat charge per unit of water used. The charge should equal the marginal cost of supply, including the marginal cost of the capacity provided by assets used for collection, storage, trunk transmission and treatment. The marginal cost of headworks capacity is the annualised capital cost, per kilolitre per year, of the most efficient available increment in capacity. Frequently this will be more costly than the highest-cost capacity currently in operation. If it is considered to be inequitable to charge for the next source of water supply before it is being used—charging the current cohort of consumers for the costs of supplying the next cohort—one alternative would be to have a smooth rate of increase in price over the period from the completion of one dam to the completion of the next, so that by the time each new source is developed consumers will be paying for the marginal cost of the water the dam supplies.

The marginal cost should include also a component for the opportunity cost of water being used for urban purposes. This would include the forgone value of the water for recreation, irrigation and environmental improvement, which results from the flooding of storages and the decreased streamflow below the dam. In large cities the total revenue from user charges and developer charges is likely to cover the total cost supplying water and may yield a surplus, but in smaller towns where economies of scale are not exhausted it may also be necessary to use access charges or tax revenue to cover total costs.

A relatively high price for new water will encourage economy in use, saving of rainwater and the use of collected stormwater and the effluent from sewage treatment, especially for irrigation and especially in public open space areas.

Although, as the previous chapter showed, flat user charges have a more progressive distributional impact than flat access charges, they can still be regarded as inequitable. One way to increase the progressivity of volume charges is to replace a flat volume charge with increasing block tariffs under which the first block of use carries a lower, possibly zero, price. This is, however, a fairly blunt equity measure since many factors other than income and wealth affect the level of use of water. It also increases the variability of revenue to supply authorities between wet and dry years.

It is possible that the revenue from optimal charges for water and sewerage could exceed the cost of provision, even including environmental costs. In that event, the use of water would become, like the use of motor fuel, a tax base. That might seem to be inequitable if it applied only in large urban areas where environmental costs are high and sources of water are scarce, though it would reflect some of the environmental costs of living in large cities and would have a modest effect in discouraging excessive concentration of population. It would be only one of the many differences in government charges and expenditures between parts of states.

The case for different levels of user charge in different locations is generally weaker for water than for sewerage because costs do not vary as much geographically. Water is supplied under pressure and uses smaller mains than sewerage, which flows mainly by gravity. Nevertheless, there may be situations in which water supplied to higher altitude areas and to areas remote from large storages requires sufficient pumping that it should be priced at a higher rate.

There are three reasons why it may be desirable to charge at different rates at different times. The first, which was discussed and rejected in the previous chapter, is that charges should vary depending on whether or not there is spare capacity in the catchment at a particular time. This will vary between periods soon after a new dam has been completed, when there is spare capacity and periods when capacity is nearly fully used, just before a new dam is built. As argued previously, private investors do not charge for the use of capacity in this way; were water-providers to do so, water would be under-priced relative to other goods and services.

The second reason is that the cost of supplying water is higher in periods of peak demand than in off-peak periods. The cost of meeting the daily peaks is the cost of providing the necessary additional capacity in service reservoirs which refill each night and are gradually emptied during the day, and in the mains between those reservoirs and users. Where those costs are high, peak-hour pricing may be justified. In most Australian cities which rely on large storages to meet demand, variations between different seasons of the year in both supply and demand make the cost of supply much higher in some periods during the year. Often water is collected during a wet season and used much more heavily during a dry season. Demand during the whole year determines the need for storage capacity, but demand during the season of peak demand determines the capacity of the pipes that transport water from the storages in the catchments to the city, the treatment facilities and the large mains which feed the service reservoirs. Whether the marginal cost of the capacity of those facilities is high enough to make differential seasonal pricing worthwhile would need to be assessed for each city.

The third situation when time differences in prices should be considered is during periods of drought, when demand for water is high and the supply is low. Consumption has to be rationed by some means during such periods, the usual approach being to use water restrictions which become more severe as the water level in the storages falls. Such restrictions are equitable in the sense that they treat all users in the same way, whereas a price increase is less of a burden for the rich. The disadvantage of restrictions is that they force reductions in consumption that take particular forms, for example, restrictions on the use of sprinklers during particular days or times of the day, rather than giving users a choice about how to make the savings, or indeed whether they want to make savings or pay a higher price. The ideal would be some combination of price increase and restrictions to be implemented progressively as storages fell to specified percentages of capacity. The rationing strategy would be decided in advance of a drought. The means of rationing during shortages should be a collective decision by the community supplied.

## Roads

Urban freeways and most of the costs of arterial roads should be funded from congestion charges which vary with the level of congestion between parts of the city and between times of the day and week.[4] They should vary also with the type of vehicle, depending on the road space it occupies and its acceleration capacity. The simplest method of levying such charges would be to install in each vehicle a meter, rather like a taxi meter, activated by signals from electronic loops in the road (of the kind which are currently used to activate traffic lights). Each time the vehicle passed over a loop the meter would register a charge per kilometre travelled; that charge would continue for each kilometre travelled until the vehicle passed over the next loop. The rate per kilometre would vary during the day depending on the severity of congestion. The driver would 'feed' the meter either with tokens available from petrol retailers or by inserting a debit or credit card. Smart-card technology would permit the meter to show the driver the rate at which the charge was accumulating. Whether or not the meter was in debit could be read from outside the vehicle. When the debit exceeded some specified level the charge might accumulate at an increased rate and a debit above some higher level would provide cause for legal action to collect the debt. Hau (1992) provides more detail on the options that are available and their relative merits.

An alternative already in use on some bridges and tunnels (Hau 1992) is electronic numberplates (bar codes) attached to vehicles and read by sensors beside or in the road. Such sensors are connected to a central computer and accounts issued periodically to the owner of the vehicle, who could opt to pay by direct debit. The disadvantage of this second method is that it provides a means by which the movement of individual vehicles can be tracked, and is therefore seen as an invasion of privacy.

The cost of levying charges electronically by either of these methods is much lower than of manual collection of tolls (Hau 1992). As tolls are charged for increasing lengths of urban roads, tunnels and bridges, the introduction of an electronic system is looking increasingly attractive for their collection. Hau records examples of electronic charging in a number of states in the United States, in France, Spain, Italy and Norway. Congestion charges have the great advantage over fuel taxes that they permit higher charges where and when the marginal cost of road space, and hence the cost of road use, is high. Since the economies of scale in provision of roads, as measured in relation to the volume of traffic they carry, are low (Small et al. 1988), optimal user charges which include an assessment of environmental cost (pollution, noise, damage and injury from accidents) would almost certainly cover the total cost of the provision of major urban roads, including a rental return on the land occupied by roads that reflects its marginal opportunity cost. Such charges would provide an appropriate disincentive not only to travel on congested roads but, in the long run, also to living or locating a business in places which required travel on such roads.

Two pieces of information are required to estimate the appropriate level of charges. The first is the relationship between the speed of traffic and the volume of flow. This shows the effect that an additional vehicle on the road will have, through increased congestion, on the speed of all other road users. The result of that calculation can be multiplied by the number of other users to find out the total delay in minutes per kilometre caused by an additional vehicle using the road. There has been much research on this relationship, and for a range of types of roads the total delay caused is quite closely related to the speed of vehicles using the road. Converting this to a cash amount requires that some value be placed on the time of road users. There is a large literature on this subject (surveyed briefly by Small 1992, pp. 36–45) and it is a matter about which there are some disagreements in principle. The optimal congestion charge is sensitive to the value of time used in the calculation. Difficulty in deciding on a precise value of time is not a good reason for not adopting congestion charges: the value of time is not zero, as is implied by the current zero congestion charges.

Congestion charges are a much more appropriate method of rationing road space than any used at present. During periods of peak demand, rationing of freeway space is by queuing, either to get on to the freeway or to get through the bottlenecks on it. The result, as described by Walters (1987), is that too many people try to use the road because the price is too low. Like any funding change that introduces greater rationing via pricing, road pricing disadvantages low-income road users, though this disadvantage would be offset at least in part by the removal of registration charges which are themselves more regressive than the fuel tax, the best indicator we have at present of how regressive congestion charges might be.

Are there situations in which short-run and long-run marginal costs (SRMC and LRMC) of road space are different, so that a choice has to be made about which to use as the basis for setting prices? Each of the four situations mentioned in Chapter 5 applies to some degree to road pricing.

1 There is a degree of *lumpiness* in the provision of road capacity in that there are circumstances in which it is necessary to add a complete lane in each direction to a road as the minimum efficient addition to capacity. This is most likely to be the case when urban freeways are being expanded, but it is seldom a serious problem, for two reasons. First, there are many ways of increasing the capacity of roads by small increments: by widening lanes, by adding lanes or increasing intersection capacity only at bottlenecks, or by adding a lane only on the side of the road on which vehicles are travelling up hill. Second, urban roads provide a network. Expanding the capacity of a single road has some effect on level of congestion on other roads as vehicles are attracted from alternative routes. Seen from another perspective, a road will seldom have spare capacity even immediately after it has been widened because it will attract traffic from competing routes. The capacity of the network as a whole is commonly best expanded by successively relieving the most severe bottlenecks. Widening congested main urban arterials is seldom the best way to increase the capacity of the network. Since the LRMC of providing roads includes the cost of acquisition of property needed to widen it, and the land abutting urban arterial roads is frequently occupied by very valuable buildings,

it is cheaper to build a new road following an alternative route where land costs are lower.

2   Use of roads in *peak periods* is much higher than during off-peak periods. Since congestion charges are set at estimated SRMC, they automatically vary significantly between different times of the day, depending on the extent to which capacity is used. But if the capacity of the road is optimal, the weighted sum of the SRMC for different periods during a week should equal the LRMC for the week as a whole.

3   It is widely believed that there is *insufficient capacity* in many parts of urban road networks.[5] If that is true in the sense that SRMC exceeds LRMC and is expected to do so for a long time, the congestion charge should be set equal to SRMC. A popular view is that the existence of any congestion is evidence that there is under-investment. But since there are few if any low-cost routes available in the inner urban areas, it is only when congestion (and SRMC) rises to a very high level that it will equal the very high cost of increases in capacity (LRMC) (which might involve tunnels or overhead roads), that extra investment is justified. Even when capacity is at its optimal level, roads in these areas will and should be congested.

4   Where there is *excessive capacity*, which is expected to persist for a long time, congestion charges should be low or even zero. This appears to be the situation in low density suburban areas, and especially in rural areas, where vehicle speeds are relatively high and congestion, by inner urban standards, is low or non-existent.

It seems paradoxical that large sums of money are still invested in increasing the capacity of roads that operate well below capacity. On the face of it, that seems to be inefficient. Why not just let more vehicles use the existing roads, since it seems that would be cheaper than adding to capacity? One result of the policy of operating such roads at much below capacity is to cause authorities such as BTCE (1988), who equate SRMC with avoidable costs, to confidently assert that charging according to SRMC will yield much less revenue than the total costs of rural arterial roads.

It is not, however, necessarily inefficient to invest in roads in which it is asserted that optimal charges will leave a deficit. Roads could be subject to such strongly increasing returns to scale that even charges equal to LRMC would not cover costs, though United

States studies by Small et al. (1989) and others do not support that view. They do suggest, however, that there are major increasing returns in providing thicker pavements: the marginal cost of providing thicker roads is relatively small. The major costs of building roads are, however, in providing wider roads, and there are only modest increasing returns in providing more road space: the marginal cost of increasing road width is not much below the average cost. Taking both cost functions into account, together with economies or diseconomies of scope (see Chapter 3), charges set equal to LRMC of both dimensions of road services would come close to covering total costs.

There seem to be three main explanations for the apparently excessive investment in rural and outer suburban roads:

1  Land and construction costs are relatively low in rural and outer suburban areas so that optimal levels of congestion will be much lower than in inner urban areas.
2  Free-flow vehicle speeds on these arterials are high; they can be significantly reduced by the limited passing opportunities ('congestion') that occur even with low volumes of traffic on two-lane roads, especially where many fully laden heavy vehicles have limited acceleration capacity.
3  Investment in these roads may be made more to increase safety in using them than to increase their capacity. In comparison with a two-lane road, passing is almost risk-free when there are two lanes in the direction of travel. Especially where roads accommodate trucks, buses and cars, the reduction in the need for risky passing seems to be a major benefit from increases in capacity of arterials in rural and outer suburban areas.

If the above arguments are valid, and if decisions about investment in improving rural arterials are optimal, a considerable risk premium should be included in estimates of the SRMC of the use of two- or three-lane roads, especially in rural areas. Such risks are of the same nature as congestion (US FHA 1982, E37): just as increasing the density of traffic on a road causes vehicles to slow down to avoid running into one another, it also causes more collisions between vehicles when they do not slow down enough. If we assume that the probable cost of collisions between vehicles suffered by a user increases proportionately as the density of traffic on a road increases, collision costs are very much like congestion costs:

part of the increase in the cost of collisions between vehicles as a result of an additional user is experienced by the marginal user, but most is imposed on other road users. Like congestion costs, they are externalities to the individual road user but not to road users as a group. They should be added to time costs and other user costs in calculating road user charges.

The fact that some sections of rural arterial roads that have high accident rates, such as the section of the (Sydney to Melbourne) Hume Highway crossing the Cullerin Range between Goulburn and Yass, were improved before more congested sections, such as that through Yass itself, supports the above arguments. The publicity resulting from head-on collisions frequently results in decisions to convert a rural arterial with one lane in each direction into a dual carriageway. Notwithstanding the difficulties of measurement, the increased probability of collisions that result from an increase in the volume of traffic on rural and suburban arterials is one of the important components of short-run marginal cost. If they are sufficient to bring SRMC up to LRMC, apparently extravagant investment in widening uncongested rural and outer suburban roads would be justified.

Given that the capital cost of access roads will be covered from developer charges, the costs that remain to be covered are the maintenance costs of access roads and that part of the capital and maintenance costs of those relatively uncongested arterial and collector roads that are not within individual subdivisions. The latter roads will yield some revenue from congestion charges, but not enough to cover total costs, because they operate on the downward sloping part of their average cost curve. The alternative sources of revenue are access charges (vehicle registration and driver's licence fees), property taxes and fuel taxes.

Fuel taxes are a suitable source of funds to cover costs which vary with the volume of traffic on uncongested roads. Almost certainly they will be required to provide most of the revenue needed for rural roads and, since they cannot readily be levied at different rates for travel at different locations, they would be a suitable source of revenue for the above purposes. Indeed, it is likely that congestion charges will be levied at the appropriate rate less the cost per kilometre of that part of the fuel tax which is levied to pay for road use. Access charges and property taxes have no particular merit as sources of funds for these purposes.

Road damage costs relate to the thickness of pavement. There has been much research in many countries on a method of charging heavy vehicles which reflects the damage they cause to road surfaces (e.g. Interstate Commission 1990). The short-run marginal cost of heavy vehicles using roads is the cost of the damage to the road, either the cost of repair or the cost of a poor road surface to other users. The long-run marginal cost is the cost of making the pavement thicker. The ideal means of covering these costs is through a charge based on the axle weight (raised to an appropriate power) and multiplied by the distance travelled. These charges would be levied only on medium and heavy trucks and buses.

**Public transport**

For a number of reasons fares for public transport in Australian cities are currently too low.

1 Public transport operators serving the city centres nearly all lose money. This is not conclusive evidence that fares are too low but it is suggestive, especially for bus transport where economies of scale appear to be relatively small.
2 Fares for bus public transport do not take account of the congestion caused by buses and would need to be increased, with the introduction of congestion charges to pass on to passengers the road user charges paid by bus operators.
3 Travel by public transport is heavily concentrated in serving the city centres during peak periods and very unbalanced in direction during those periods. This is one of the reasons why so many public transport operators serving the city centres make losses. Peak period fares should be high enough to cover most if not all of the capacity costs of the systems.
4 Fares for long journeys are too low relative to short journeys: they seldom rise with the length of journey as rapidly as costs.
5 Fares take no account of the environmental costs of public transport. Indeed public transport subsidies are sometimes justified because it is regarded as environmentally benign relative to travel by private car. That difference applies to electric-powered modes only in relation to air pollution within the city. It is now generally accepted that, taking account of the environmental effects of the generation of electricity, public transport generally, and rail transport in particular, results in almost as much production of greenhouse gases per persons kilometre travelled as

the use of private cars (Troy 1996). The emission of greenhouse gases during the generation of electricity is, of course, a global rather than a local problem. One reason for this situation is that there have been large increases in fuel efficiency in private cars in recent years by reducing the weight of materials, efficiencies that are more difficult to achieve in public transport.

Even if fares were raised to take account of factors 2, 3, 4 and 5, it is doubtful whether long-distance urban bus, and especially train, services would cover their costs. It depends on the elasticity of demand for their services and the economies of scale, especially in fixed rail transport. It may be that the demand curve is below the average cost curve for fixed rail transport at all levels of price and output, in which case funds from other sources will always be needed if the service is to operate, no matter what pricing policy is adopted. There are a number of possible origins of the deficit.

First, it can arise from the community service obligation to provide out-of-hours services or services at less than cost to disadvantaged groups and school children to achieve redistributive objectives. Where revenue from optimal fares does not cover total costs, the cost of these obligations should be covered from general tax revenue. Second, the losses may arise because public transport fares are politically sensitive, and operators are not permitted to raise them to levels that would cover costs. This appears to be the case in some Australian cities.

Third, the losses may arise from the high fixed costs of rail systems, the highly peaked directional flows on buses and trains serving the city centres, and the relatively low volumes of traffic they carry over large parts of their networks. These in turn result from the location of the great majority of jobs and services outside city centres in numerous and dispersed suburban locations (for example, some 35 per cent of people in Sydney and Melbourne work in the local government area where they live). It also results from the relatively low residential density at which most Australians choose to live. Public transport can cover the costs of providing limited services to suburban shopping and employment centres in such cities. But at present the majority of its resources are used to provide services that feed the city centres and it does not appear to be able to cover their costs. Public transport provides for only a very small share of the trips from residential suburbs to dispersed workplaces, shopping and service centres.

If the revenue is sufficient to cover all variable costs but not to cover the sunk costs that would have to be met whether or not the trains or trams ran (there are few sunk costs in providing bus services), the sunk costs should be written off and the system should continue to be operated until the 'sunk' assets wear out. How to cover the amortisation of those sunk costs is a purely financial question to which we will return.

If the losses are such that not even the variable costs of the services can be covered, and in the previous case when fixed assets funded by the sunk costs need to be replaced, a decision has to be made about whether to continue the service. This question is not purely financial, since it involves continuing commitment of resources. If the users of the services are unwilling to pay their cost, the services should be continued only if the benefits to the community more generally are sufficiently large to justify a subsidy to cover the deficit.

One class of indirect beneficiaries, it has been argued, is the private users of roads, which would be even more congested if public transport were not provided. This would be true on the main roads to the city centre if the same number of people were to travel to and from the city centre each day whether or not public transport is provided. But this is very unlikely, since the level of congestion appears to limit the volume of traffic on those roads at peak periods. A more likely result of the withdrawal of public transport services would be that people would travel at different times and to different places. In the longer term they would also live and work in different places.

A second class of beneficiaries from public transport is the residents of the metropolitan area as a whole, since electric trains and trams, in particular, create much less *local* air pollution than the equivalent number of person-kilometres of travel by private car. They also will benefit only if it is assumed that the same journeys would occur whether or not there were buses, trams and trains serving the central cities.

The third class of beneficiaries is the owners of property in the city centre. Without public transport (and especially fixed rail) services, the demand from business to locate in the city centre would be significantly lower and the property there much less valuable. This group appears to be by far the largest beneficiary and it follows that it would be equitable, and would promote more efficient location decisions, if the owners of property in the city centre were taxed to cover the losses on public transport serving the city centre. A tax on property in the city centre, as is levied for example in Paris, would be an appropriate source of funds to cover both the short-term deficit which may result from the inability to cover sunk costs and the long-term deficit resulting from the need to replace fixed assets.

## Electricity

The cost of the urban network of electricity mains, especially where the lines are overhead, is a much smaller proportion of total costs of supplying the service to consumers than in the case of hydraulic services or roads, so it is easier for electricity authorities to include most of their network costs in user charges. There are also modest fixed costs per customer of meter reading and billing. Given the substantial environmental costs of producing electricity, even the small access charges, which usually take the form of declining block tariffs, should probably be replaced by higher flat user charges per kilowatt-hour to discourage excessive use. Greater use of lower off-peak pricing also would be appropriate, given the much lower production cost of off-peak power. Additional costs of underground mains in both commercial and residential areas are, and should be, generally covered by developers. In residential areas this permits home buyers to choose whether they want to pay the additional price for the additional amenity which results.

## Gas

The current situation and the proposed changes are much the same for gas as for electricity, though the case for off-peak *hour* pricing is not as strong because gas can be more cheaply stored. Where the demand for gas is more seasonal, as in colder areas where a major use is for space heating, there may be a case for off-peak *season* prices.

## Telephones

As pointed out in Chapter 2, the telephone service is the one service where network capacity costs are probably the highest proportion of total costs. There are also substantial economies of scale in providing higher capacity in sections of the network. It is difficult to judge whether the current fixed charge of, for example, $195 per year for a Canberra residential service, returns too high or too low a proportion of total revenue. Telephony is also the service for which environmental costs are lowest, so that there is not a strong case for increasing user charges to cover them.

## Garbage collection and disposal

Rather than recovering the cost of these services through a fixed charge or from revenue from a tax on property values, as is common at present, it would be preferable to charge for the volume of garbage collected. This can be done by offering, at different charges, a weekly or twice weekly pick up and/or by varying the charge according to the size or number of bins to be collected. This is the practice, for example, in Seattle, and occurs to varying degrees in Australian cities. It encourages recycling and reflects differences in the costs of collection and disposal. Most Australian garbage is disposed of in landfill sites near or beyond the urban fringe; the cost of transport to the disposal site varies slightly with the distance of a local council from the landfill site, which may result in some geographic differences in levels of charges.

The cost of disposal at landfill sites is not insignificant. It includes the value of the sites used for landfill, the environmental impact of landfill operations and the scarcity rent which should be paid in recognition of the fact that suitable sites are scarce and exhaustible (Bureau of Industry Economics 1993). Optimal charging for garbage disposal must take account of the effect charges have on people's propensity to litter and dump garbage illegally and the cost of surveillance to limit illegal dumping. This can be especially dangerous in the case of toxic wastes.

---

### CASE STUDY: ROAD PRICING IN HONG KONG

Singapore, the first place in the world to introduce road pricing in June 1975, opted for an area licence scheme. Drivers entering the Restricted Zone during the morning peak (7.30–9.30) were required to have a daily or monthly licence which cost about $US1.25 per day. Complementary measures,

---

including increased parking charges and the provision of park-and-ride facilities, were introduced to reduce the level of congestion in the city centre. Initially the scheme was entirely manual, with the distinctive yellow licences displayed so that they could be observed when vehicles crossed cordons. Any such area licencing scheme is a crude measure in that the charge is unrelated to the amount of travel within the congested area, does not allow for different levels of congestion in different parts of the Restricted Zone and outside it, and is only crudely related to the time of travel.

Hong Kong announced in 1983 that it intended to test the technical, economic and administrative feasibility of electronic road pricing. The trial was completed in 1985. It opted for a form of automatic vehicle identification in which each vehicle in the test was fitted with an electronic numberplate. The test was a technological success in that well over 99 per cent of vehicles were correctly identified. Details of the test are described by Harrison (1986) and Hau (1990, 1992).

Three different schemes were designed, with differing numbers of zones, and correspondingly different numbers of toll sites. A different level of toll was set for the peak periods (morning and evening), the interpeak period during the day, and the morning and evening shoulder periods before and after the peaks respectively. The three schemes were assessed as producing between 59 and 74 per cent of the total benefits achievable from a theoretically optimal scheme. In May 1982, the Hong Kong government had taken radical measures to reduce the volume of traffic by trebling the annual licence fees, doubling the first registration charge for new cars and motor cycles to 70–90 per cent of the import price, and doubling the duty on petrol (but to only $US0.18 per litre). The benefits of road pricing were compared with this suite of measures, whose main effect was the reduction of car ownership.

Hong Kong is an ideal place for such a test. Despite a very low car ownership (70 per 1000 population in 1982), its number of vehicles per kilometre of paved road (280 in 1982) was higher than in Singapore and more than three times the United Kingdom level (Harrison 1986). At the time the system was nearly closed, with very few vehicles from China using the roads. Between 1973 and 1982 the number of registered vehicles increased by 67 per cent while the length of roads increased by only 22 per cent. Hong Kong is built on a very confined site and the density of development in the built-up area is very high. Land values and the cost of expanding road capacity are correspondingly high, so that the optimal level of congestion and the optimal price for road use are high also. Under these circumstances the benefits from road pricing would be expected to be high also.

Compared with the then current policy of car ownership restraint, the theoretically optimal scheme of road pricing was expected to produce benefits of $US160 million per year and the three alternatives between $US94m and $US118m. The annualised capital cost was $US3.85m and the annual operating cost $US2.54m. This resulted in projected benefit–cost ratios of between 14.7 and 24.1. By comparison, the benefits from either car ownership restraint measures or an area licensing scheme were much lower.

But Hong Kong did not adopt any of the schemes, which its own trial had showed to be very advantageous. Hau (1990) advances a number of reasons why the proposal was not adopted. The more general reasons are summarised below. Some of the reasons are specific to the time or the place and others to the particular technology used. The fact that electronic road pricing for a complete urban area, as distinct from the cordon type schemes used in Singapore and Norway, has not been adopted anywhere, suggests that there may be other underlying reasons.

1   In 1984 and 1985 both the Island line of the Mass Transit Railway and the Eastern Island corridor freeway were opened, significantly reducing the level of congestion on at least some roads in the business area.
2   The 1982 stock market crash resulted in a decline in the rate of growth of incomes, and together with the additional taxes on car ownership, resulted in a significant decline in the demand for private cars. The average speed in the urban area increased from 20 to 28 km per hour between 1979 to 1984.

3   Because it was decided to exempt taxis from paying the road price, even though they account for more of the volume of traffic in the central area (Harrison 1986, p. 13), car drivers felt discriminated against.

4   Opponents argued that the likely growth of population and of traffic had been exaggerated, leading to excessive estimates of both the level of charge and the benefits from the charge.

5   Privacy considerations were important, especially in the period immediately after the joint Sino–British declaration on the future of Hong Kong had been initialled.

6   Residents were not convinced that the Government would carry out its undertaking to reduce annual licence fees and first-registration fees to offset its increased revenue from congestion charges. They were seen to be a source of additional revenue for the Government rather than a different way of collecting revenue which would result in less congestion.

Of these reasons, the last two have general importance. The only schemes which involve central recording of the travel of individuals that have been implemented anywhere have been voluntary schemes of replacing manual tolls by those collected through automatic vehicle recognition, including several at road tunnels in Hong Kong. Those who are concerned about privacy can continue to use the manual toll booths. The newer in-vehicle technology, commonly known as smart-card technology, avoids the privacy problem, though it may not be easy to convince privacy conscious motorists that that is the case.

Among the successful schemes are a number where the revenue from the charges is committed to either paying for an existing facility, and therefore seen as replacing a manually collected toll, or hypothecated to designated improvements in urban transport. It is legitimate for users to oppose congestion charging unless it is clearly going to be a different way of charging for the use of urban roads rather than an additional source of revenue. Motorists in some countries, including Australia, believe that they already pay more than the full cost of the provision of urban roads. For the reasons described above, that may not be the case in congested areas. Nevertheless congestion charging has to be seen by users as a different way of charging, and the only way to do this is through a package of measures which reduces other charges on motorists at the time congestion charges are introduced.

In 1989 the Hong Kong Government issued a Green Paper on Transport Policy which again raised the matter of electronic pricing; primarily because of the controversy about privacy, the ensuing White Paper committed the Government only to monitor technological developments. Apart from introducing automatic vehicle recognition at some tunnels as an alternative to paying a cash toll at manual booths, nothing has been done. In order to contain congestion, first-registration taxes, annual licence fees and tolls in the tunnels under the harbour were further increased in 1994. The Government is still committed to introducing electronic road pricing and in June 1996 a feasibility study was announced for electronic road pricing with a commitment to spend some of the revenues for transport purposes.

# 8 Financial issues

Because of the durability of urban physical infrastructure assets and the fact that their capital cost accounts for a large proportion of the total cost of providing the services, financing issues are very significant. In paying for durable capital, there is a distinction between the two questions: How are services to be funded? How are they to be financed? Funding is needed to pay for the annual cost of resources used to provide the service, including the cost of capital. Finance is needed to pay the capital cost of the assets used in providing the service. It is usual for such assets to be financed in part at least by borrowing.

There are two components of the annual capital cost of providing durable assets: (1) the cost of the capital invested in the assets, which is (a) partly interest paid to lenders on the loans used to pay the capital cost of the asset, and (b) partly interest forgone if the supplier's own funds are invested, which, as its equity in the assets increases, is paid to the owners of that equity; and (2) the cost of the 'using up' of the capital asset each year reflected in the reduction in the assets' productive capacity as they age and wear out and become obsolete. In the supplier's accounts, the cost of reduction in productive capacity will show up as depreciation.

Three loosely related financial questions need to be answered in relation to the provision and funding of infrastructure. One is: How should the investment in durable capital assets be financed? This question mainly concerns the role of borrowing and the consequent distribution of capital costs over time. The second question is: How should depreciation (2 above) be calculated, especially when many of the assets have an indefinite life if proper maintenance is carried out on a regular basis? The third question is: What return on what assets should be earned by a public provider of infrastructure services and to whom should it be paid? The first part of this question is concerned with how the capital costs of providing infrastructure services should be calculated, especially 1(b) above. The second part concerns to whom the returns on investment should be distributed, which depends on whether the appropriate level of government or the users of the services are the owners of the equity in the assets. Although these questions are loosely related, they can be considered independently.

The first part of this chapter deals with borrowing and equity as alternative sources of financing of capital assets. It deals also with the implications of developer charges and transferred assets, major alternatives to borrowing which have become more important in recent years. The second part deals with depreciation and how it should be calculated, a matter of some difficulty in the case of some infrastructure assets. The third section deals with the question of who owns infrastructure authorities, and the slightly different question of who is or should be the beneficial owner of the equity in the assets under their control.

## Borrowing and equity

Borrowing is a way in which the time distribution of the payments by users for durable infrastructure assets can be changed, from a capital payment at the time the infrastructure is installed to a flow of annual payments over a number of years. It is most commonly, and most legitimately, used to pay the capital costs of infrastructure services which are self-financing in that they are funded through user charges or hypothecated taxes, for example, water, sewerage, drainage, electricity, telephone and gas. Borrowing is much less common for those services that are funded from general tax revenue, such as roads and garbage collection, which do not receive revenue directly from users, and public transport, where revenue often covers much less than full operating costs and therefore is not sufficient to amortise loans. There is no reason in principle why roads should not be funded from loans amortised from revenue raised from fuel taxes, especially if a proportion of the revenue was to be hypothecated for the funding of roads. If road pricing were to be introduced, it is likely that roads would increasingly be financed from borrowing. This already occurs when they are privately provided and funded from toll revenue. It is quite common in other countries for loans raised by local governments for the provision of roads and drains to be amortised from tax revenue. It is not, of course, sound financial practice for loans to be used to pay operating costs.

If the financial responsibility of an infrastructure supplier is to cover its financial costs, including making appropriate provision for renewal of the assets, and it is not required to pay a dividend on the net value of its assets, the distribution of the cost of payment for assets markedly affects its total costs in any one year. Three different policies may be adopted.

1  If assets are paid for from net revenue raised before the investments are made, the capital costs fall on consumers in the year(s) when the net revenue is earned; consumers in those years will be subsidising consumers in later years who will not have to pay interest on the capital cost of the facilities used to provide their services. Of course the latter, in turn, will have to pay charges that are high enough to earn sufficient net revenue for the next round of investment and thereby contribute to the capital costs of later cohorts of users. The overall effect is that the supplier builds up a much larger equity than if investment is financed by borrowing.

2  If assets are paid for from loans which are then amortised from revenue, the costs are borne by consumers who use the infrastructure during the period over which the loans are amortised. Once the loans have been paid off, no interest payments will be needed.[1]

3  If the assets are paid for by developers either constructing and transferring the assets free of charge or paying for the cost of their construction, the whole cost is likely to be borne by buyers of the newly serviced property. As described elsewhere, as these charges work their way through the housing market they will be borne by renters (as higher rents) and by first-time home buyers as a higher purchase price. If those buyers are able to take out a larger loan to cover the additional cost, they can spread the cost over time. If not they will have to save longer or buy a cheaper home.

But if the supplier is expected to pay a dividend on its equity in the assets to the government (the value net of any outstanding debt on them), it is necessary to make a return on all assets, whether or not they have been financed by borrowing. Even with a dividend requirement, developer charges will increase the price of housing and disadvantage renters and first-time buyers relative to established owners. Later in the chapter the question of whether authorities should be required to earn a dividend on capital that has been funded by developers is discussed.

If a dividend is required, and if interest rates on borrowed capital are the same as the opportunity cost of capital—the rate which the supplier is expected to return on its equity in the enterprise—the extent of borrowing has no impact on the annual cost of capital. The greater interest cost of higher borrowing is offset by a lower expected dividend because of lower equity. The dividend might be expected to be at a higher rate than the interest cost of borrowed capital because the owner might expect a premium for risk. It could be argued that, especially where the supplier has a degree of monopoly in the market, the higher the supplier's debt relative to equity the greater the owner's risk and therefore the higher the rate of the dividend. When governments guarantee the loans of infra-structure authorities interest rates are likely to be lower, another reason for them being lower than the appropriate rate of dividend. Taxpayers are then bearing most of the risk of borrowing. Some governments are now charging their infrastructure authorities a fee for the guarantee. An alternative would be to remove the guarantee.

One truly neutral financing regime for a supplier that is owned by a government is for its only equity capital to be that contributed by the owner government. All expenditure on new capital would be funded by borrowing and the loans would not be paid off but would be continually refinanced. Replacement of capital assets would be funded from depreciation reserves, resulting from depreciation pro-visions based on the replacement cost of the assets. The supplier as such would own no equity.

It is common in many countries for the government to control the borrowing of infrastructure authorities. Partly because they are guar-anteed by governments, their loans are regarded as part of public sector borrowing. They have been limited as an inflationary control measure and to maintain a high credit rating for the government. When the loans are used to finance revenue-producing assets, those reasons for limiting the borrowing by governments in general are irrelevant. Such loans have the same macroeconomic impacts as private sector borrowing. Nevertheless, these borrowing limits have had a major effect in forcing infrastructure suppliers into financing more of their investment from net revenue from their operations.

A very conservative rule which is frequently used is that the loans used to finance an asset should be repaid over the life of the asset. If this rule is combined with an appropriate charge for depreciation, at the end of the life of the asset it can be replaced from the revenue from depreciation without raising any further debt. Under such a conservative rule the authority builds up equity because of the surpluses needed to amortise the loan and provide for depreciation. Because on average loans are paid off before the end of the life of the asset they funded, equity increases even more rapidly. Another reason for the large equity of many authorities is that much life-prolonging maintenance is financed from current revenue. For example, Melbourne Water's equity in its water and sewerage assets was 67 per cent of their value at June 1992, and the equity of the Water Board (Sydney, Illawarra, Blue Mountains) in 1994 was 87 per cent of the value of its assets.

These figures exaggerate the extent of equity as they do not take account of a large amount of unfunded depreciation. Some idea of the magnitude of unfunded depreciation can be obtained from the fact that current depreciation, calculated on a straight-line basis, is 2 per cent of the written-down replacement value of assets of the Water Board. If, on average, the age of assets was half their expected life, the written-down replacement value would be half the full replacement value and unfunded depreciation would be about equal to their written-down replacement value. In that case the debts plus unfunded depreciation would be about 56 per cent of the replacement value of its assets, and its equity 44 per cent. In reality the average age of the assets with long lives (200 years for dams, 150 years for reservoirs, canals, tunnels, etc.) will be much less than half their expected lives, because over half of the growth of Sydney has occurred in the past 40 years. If their average age was one-third of their expected lives, the Board's debts including unfunded depreciation would be 41 per cent of the replacement value of its assets, and its equity 59 per cent. On either assumption the Board has a very large equity. In effect the amortisation of loans is seen as an alternative to keeping depreciation reserves or, to put it another way, the depreciation reserves are being invested in the assets of the authorities.[2]

## Depreciation

The standard view is that depreciation should be based on the current replacement cost of the assets and their expected life. Thus if a straight-line method is used, an asset with an expected life of

100 years and with a replacement value this year of $1 million, should be depreciated by $10 000 this year. If the replacement cost increases to $1.02m next year because of cost inflation, depreciation should increase to $10 200. This system is being used by many infrastructure authorities, and presents an appropriate estimate of the total resource cost of providing the services.[3]

The concept of depreciation applies most readily to industrial machines or motor vehicles which wear out after a certain amount of use. It also applies readily to those parts of infrastructure services such as electricity generation, water treatment or sewage treatment or pumping equipment which are like specialised factories. It is less easily applied to many infrastructure assets, because with appropriate maintenance any wear can be made good, for example, resurfacing a road or relining a pipe. Similarly a dam does not wear out, though if there is erosion in its catchment it will eventually fill up and its storage capacity will disappear.

A second element of depreciation occurs as a result of the effects of time. Some kinds of pipes corrode, possibly as a result of electrolysis. Pipes move because of movements of the ground in which they are laid, and because of the growth of tree roots. This is particularly serious for sewer pipes which rely on gravity for flow, because pools of sewage collecting at low points can produce acids which corrode the pipes. Movement of water pipes can cause joints to open and leakage to occur. Some of the materials of which pipes are made corrode because of the effects of components of sewage, or because of soil acids.

A third, and important, reason for depreciation is obsolescence: for some reason the assets become unsuitable or uneconomic to use. One important cause of obsolescence is technological change. This can be seen most clearly in the case of electricity generation, where advances continually improve the efficiency available from new capacity. As a result the older capacity is first relegated to producing only in peak periods, and eventually phased out. Technological advances affect many aspects of infrastructure, for example, the replacement of metal water pipes and terracotta sewer pipes with plastic, and replacement of copper telephone wires with fibre optics. When the capital and operating costs of the new equipment are less than the operating (including maintenance) costs of the old equipment replacement is economically worthwhile. Technical advances can also permit existing dams to be made higher, increasing their storage capacity.

A second reason is changes in demand. For example, changes in vehicle design and traffic volumes have made many urban and rural roads obsolete as trunk routes, leading to rebuilding at higher standards or to through traffic functions being diverted to new freeways. Increased demand may make it uneconomic to draw water from small-capacity dams, and may result in the replacement of small pipes by larger ones. Demands for higher environmental standards have required either replacement or radical upgrades of both sewers (to reduce leakage) and sewage treatment facilities (to improve the quality of the effluent discharged into the environment). Improved estimates of dam safety may show that existing dams pose unacceptable risks to property and lives and require that they be strengthened. Some dams become unstable over the course of time. When localities or whole urban areas experience reductions in population or economic activity, parts of the networks that served them become obsolete.

For all of these reasons infrastructure investment does have a limited life, though the using up of that life is rarely captured by estimates of the average life of particular assets. One reason is that it is very difficult to predict the economic lives of many assets. Moreover, it is seldom efficient to replace an asset with a comparable asset, and much more common to carry out maintenance which prolongs its life, to upgrade it to operate more efficiently or to replace it with more efficient assets. In these circumstances, the prudent accounting standards that require asset depreciation according to a schedule of average lifetimes have important financial implications.

Infrastructure providers in growing urban areas with a lot of their capital invested in long-lived assets are likely to be cash-rich for a long time if they follow conventional accounting and financial practices. This is true of those which collect revenue from users (which does not include road authorities), whether they fund their capital investment from loans or from retained income, and is especially true in periods of inflation. The following are the reasons:

1  A high proportion of their costs are incurred in providing assets with a very long life, which can be further prolonged by appropriate maintenance. Appropriate maintenance makes the life of some forms of infrastructure capital almost infinite. The distinction between maintenance expenditure and capital expenditure, while clear in principle (any expenditure which prolongs the life

of an asset is capital expenditure), is difficult in practice. Neglect of routine maintenance will reduce an asset's life, and the most efficient expenditures to keep assets operating often also prolong their lives.

2   In order to assess the authorities' equity in their assets, and from that the dividend they are liable to pay, they are required to revalue frequently the replacement cost of those of their assets which would be replaced if they were to be destroyed. These values then provide the basis for calculation of depreciation. In periods of even moderate inflation the value of assets whose average life is about 100 years[4] often appreciates rather than depreciating. Although appreciation does not show up as a return, as it would if the authorities were investing companies, they are required to depreciate their assets by assuming a limited life. Setting aside depreciation calculated on this basis provides the authority with cash which should be invested in relatively liquid assets that can be sold to provide funds for replacement. They can, of course, be used to finance capital expansion, but the long-term risk of doing so is that when costly replacements are required the depreciation reserves will all be tied up.

3   For the first fifty or so years of a new authority almost no assets require replacement, so that depreciation provisions can be safely used for internal financing. In any city growing at a steady rate, the cost of replacing worn out or obsolete assets is likely to be small relative to provisions for depreciation on the current stock of assets.

The depreciation reserves that have traditionally been accumulated have been large, but not very large, mainly because they were based on historic cost rather than current replacement costs. Nevertheless they have been large enough to have two unfortunate effects. First, the authorities have found it relatively easy to finance capital- intensive extensions of their operations. They have had little incentive to look for technologies which are less capital intensive. Second, the depreciation reserves have been large enough to attract the attention of capital-starved governments, who began to milk them. This made it even more attractive for the authorities to invest their depreciation provisions, as the only way of ensuring that they did not lose them. The next step was that governments saw that authorities that could earn enough to accumulate such depreciation allowances could certainly pay a dividend to the 'owning' government, and would also be attractive to private investors. These two matters are discussed later.

As long as the most efficient technologies for providing infrastructure services continue to be highly capital intensive, the lack of liquid depreciation reserves may not create a serious problem. But there are a number of services for which new technologies and new approaches to meeting demands are being developed which require less capital. This is true for water (rainwater tanks, retention of stormwater, greater efficiency in use of water), sewerage (composting toilets, re-use of grey water), drainage (aquifer recharge), energy (small-scale solar and wind generation) and communications (mobile telephony, satellite). Such alternative approaches may be being adopted too slowly because of the incentives for authorities to continue to invest the funds they are accumulating as a result of depreciation charges.

More efficient charging mechanisms, which are being introduced for water, and which may be extended to sewerage, drainage and roads, are likely to reduce demand and accelerate the introduction of new technologies. Paradoxically, this may mean that investment in extending and increasing the capacity of the traditional networks, which have generally been thought of as very safe investments having a very long life, may become more risky because of the possibility of obsolescence. This can be met by using a higher discount rate in comparing investment proposals with longer and those with shorter lives. Authorities should not have incentives to make large lumpy investments which are based on old technologies and old levels of demand, and should be especially wary of the investment of depreciation provisions in the old technologies 'just because they are there'.

## Ownership

Two questions arise in relation to the ownership of the public authorities which provide most of the infrastructure in cities. The first is simply who owns them, a question which is as much one of equity and justice as it is one of law. The second is much more specific and relates to the ownership of assets that have been paid for by developers who then recover their costs from the buyers of developed property. These issues arise specifically in relation to the requirement that government business enterprises should pay a dividend to their (government) owner on the equity in their assets. The arguments for doing so have been spelled out above.

All of these authorities are established by local, state or national governments so that there is no doubt that legally they are owned by the relevant government. In one model set out previously (page 182), where the only equity was what the owner government had provided, and all other assets were financed by loans that were renewed rather than being amortised, the owner government would be the only supplier of equity and the only risk taker and there could be no doubt that any dividend should be paid to it. Road funding has some of these features, in that all expenditure by public road authorities is derived from taxes of some kind that are levied either throughout the state or throughout the local government. The ownership of roads becomes a little less clear when it is pointed out that taxes on motorists or on owners of property to which roads provide access are almost the sole source of funds spent on roads. It could be argued that state and national roads belong to the motorists who have funded them and the governments are simply acting as their agents. Since a high proportion of each state's population uses the roads, and property owners constitute the main tax base for local taxes, there are no major equity problems in assuming that state and local governments in Australia own the roads and should receive dividends on the (depreciated) current replacement value of road assets.

The case for government ownership is even stronger for urban public transport. It was pointed out in earlier chapters that the users of buses and trains pay for their use more directly than the users of roads. But most public transport enterprises also receive substantial subsidies from state revenue to cover operating losses and interest on capital. In such circumstances the government that provides the subsidies is the owner and risk taker. As long as public transport systems continue to make losses, the question about dividends is largely hypothetical.

Some authorities sell services to the public and for the most part cover their full costs. In Australia these include water, sewerage and drainage, electricity, gas, postal services and telephones. The great majority of their authorities' assets were either funded from operating surpluses, including depreciation reserves, or financed from loans which were then amortised from revenue. It is arguable that the users of such services should be regarded as the owners of the equity of the authority, and should be entitled to receive any dividends that are payable. They are, in terms of any equitable decision, if not legally, mutual organisations owned by users.

Apart from any grants or non-interest bearing loans that governments may have provided, the main claim the so-called owner governments could make for the ownership of these services is that they take the risks involved in providing them. First, since they have guaranteed the loans they bear most of the financial risk, but a loan guarantee is worth only a small percentage on the loan, which can be estimated by the difference between interest rates on guaranteed loans and those that are not guaranteed. Second, if the services provided broke down they would have to assume responsibility for ensuring that they were restored. Neither of these risks seems very high for a natural monopoly. Governments have also provided the power of eminent domain to acquire the land needed to provide the services. Eminent domain is provided by governments to any provider of such services, whether public or private. Governments have also provided access to water supplies, sometimes free of charge, and the right to discharge treated sewage into the environment. The appropriate way of dealing with this is to charge a suitable royalty for water extraction, and to regulate or charge for effluent discharge. None of these seems to provide a compelling case for government ownership when users have provided a large proportion of the equity capital.

Telephones, postal services and electricity generation are provided in an integrated manner across a state or across Australia, and the question of whether they are owned by users or governments does not make much difference. It can, however, be a matter for dispute if institutional arrangements change or if it is proposed to privatise the service.[5] The dividend paid to the government, i.e. to the taxpayers, can be seen as an indirect tax on the users of the service if such users paid for the equity capital. Where services such as water, sewerage and drainage, gas supply and distribution of electricity are provided for specific parts of a state by different authorities or under different accounts within an authority, a user owner model results in a very different distribution of dividends. For example, the dividends of Sydney Water should be distributed to its customers rather than to the taxpayers of New South Wales. While it is inequitable to pay the dividends from Sydney Water to state taxpayers, it is even more inequitable to do the same with the dividends of the Hunter Water Board, which serves the much smaller Newcastle urban area.

Given that it is desirable to charge prices for services which include a dividend calculated on the basis of the equity ownership of assets, how should that dividend be paid to users? A dividend paid to users that is proportional to use, like a lower price, will encourage excessive use, but a dividend that is unrelated to past payments will not be equitable. If there is a fixed charge, the dividend could simply be deducted from the fixed charge, but the argument in earlier chapters of this book suggests that there should be no fixed charges for most of these services. A dividend that is related to the average payment over the past $x$ years at least reduces the incentive to over-consume and may be the best solution.

The second question relates to assets provided at no cost by, or funded from charges levied on, developers. These assets become the property of the authority, which then has the responsibility for meeting operating costs and for maintaining and eventually replacing them. Should the authority earn, and pay to its owner, a dividend on its equity in such assets, its equity being calculated as the depreciated current cost of replacing them?

Although the assets are legally owned by the authority, an alternative arrangement which would better reflect responsibility for paying for them would be for the assets to be rented by the authority from the owners of property who effectively paid their capital cost. The rent would reflect the depreciated replacement cost. If this was the formal situation, the authority would be expected to earn a dividend on those assets, which it would then pass on in the form of rent to the owners of the property concerned. The rent could be paid in the form of a rebate on a water, sewerage or drainage account. If urban roads begin to be funded from road user charges, the same arrangements could apply.

In both cases it is legitimate to ask what is the rental value of reticulation of water, sewerage and electricity mains, telephone lines and access roads within a subdivision. Given that they commonly have excess capacity, the optimal charge for using them is low and therefore their earning capacity is low. On this view, the majority of the cost of providing services within a subdivision should be borne by the purchasers of the developed properties because it serves to increase the value of those properties. In that case the rental value may be negligible, and the dividend that is expected on the equity involved should be negligible also. This argument does not apply to charges levied on developers for the provision of off-site capacity, either in headworks or in trunk mains.

There is another side to this argument. From the point of view of the suppliers of services the reticulation of pipes, wires and roads within subdivisions are essential for delivery of services where they are needed. The value of those sections is at least as great as their replacement cost in most places and their rental value should be related to that depreciated replacement cost.

---

## CASE STUDY: A WATER AND SEWERAGE SUPPLIER

Some of the matters raised above are illustrated by Sydney Water, which supplies water, sewerage and drainage services to the Sydney region and adjacent urban areas in Australia. Sydney Water was established as the Metropolitan Water, Sewerage and Drainage Board in 1888, and until 1924 was funded by an annual appropriation from the New South Wales Parliament and had to pay all of its revenue into consolidated revenue. Nevertheless it was required to cover its costs. In 1924 it was established as a statutory authority with a significant degree of independence from the state government, most of its members being indirectly elected from local councils in the area it supplied. This independence was lessened to some degree from 1972 when all members of the Board were appointed by the Minister, though some came from a panel put forward by local councils (Butlin et al. 1982, p. 245).

At the time of its establishment the Board took over the rudimentary water supply and sewerage systems constructed by the state and by local councils and later took over some drains constructed by the state. In its Annual Report for 1984–85 the Board listed the value of funds received from grants and the value of assets transferred to it as at 30 June 1984. The total value was about $500 million, of which almost exactly three-quarters had been contributed, predominantly by developers, with smaller amounts from local councils to pay for specific projects. Of the other $100 million, about $56 million came from the New South Wales Government in grants or assets. This amount, which represented the state government's equity in the Board, accounted for only

---

1.66 per cent of the value of assets at the same date, $3376 million. The state could claim also that it contributes by permitting the Board at no cost to take water from the local rivers for water supply and to discharge treated effluent into some of them, although mostly offshore. There is a strong case for the government that owns those rights to charge a royalty for extraction, but no such royalty is charged for the right to extract water for other purposes, including the much larger amounts taken for irrigation.

Table 1 includes a number of figures extracted from the balance sheet of the Board in 1966–67 when it was acting in its traditional mode, in 1984–85 when it was beginning to be affected by the policies of the state government claiming 'ownership' of the Board, and in 1993–94 when the Board had been corporatised and was required to function in a (constrained) commercial manner.

**Table 1    Selected assets and liabilities of the (Sydney) Water Board, 1966–67 to 1993–94**

|  | ($ million at current prices) | | |
| --- | --- | --- | --- |
|  | *1966–67* | *1984–85* | *1993–94* |
| Value of fixed assets | 631 | 3 169 | 14 626 |
| Loans and advances | 514 | 2 266 | 1 750 |
| Loans & advances / fixed assets | 81.5% | 71.5% | 12.0% |
| Reserves | 218 | 764 | 499 |
| Investments | 99 | 889 | 461 |
| Equity | 0 | 1 480 | 12 528 |

*Source*:   Annual Reports of the Metropolitan Water Sewerage and Drainage Board (1967 and 1985) and the Water Board (1994).

Up to 1967 the Board's assets had been largely funded from loans. It did have substantial reserves, however, mainly for asset replacement (depreciation) and loan repayment. About half of the reserves were held in investments in government securities, though not in its own, and the other half, about $100 million, were in effect the Board's equity in its own assets, though there was no such item in its balance sheet. By 1985 the value of assets had increased about fivefold even though at this time they were still valued at their historic cost. Loans and advances as a proportion of fixed assets had fallen from 81 to 71 per cent. Since equity was shown separately, investments and reserves were by now more in balance, though about 70 per cent of the investments were now in the Board's own inscribed stock. Only the reserves held to meet short- to medium-term commitments for employee entitlements were held as external assets, to ensure that the funds needed to pay these entitlements were available when required. Although the largest part of the reserves were still for loan repayments, a much larger proportion than in 1966–67 was for employee entitlements, including a growing provision for superannuation.

Reserves had fallen from 35 per cent of the value of fixed assets to 24 per cent as a result of paying off loans, especially those from the state government, out of revenue. In addition the state government had restricted the Board's loan raising. Each of the Board's Annual Reports during the late 1970s and early 1980s reported the use of the provisions for repayment of its loans, which were required under its Act, to finance new capital expenditure, and promising their progressive restoration. Nevertheless the amounts involved increased throughout the period and eventually the practice of noting the progressive amount in each Annual Report ceased. By the mid-1980s the Board's accounts reflected a significant equity amounting to nearly half the value of the fixed assets.

By 1993–94 the basis for valuation of fixed assets had changed from historic cost to depreciated replacement cost. As a result their value had increased by a factor of 4.6 since 1984–85, even though revenue had not quite doubled. Over this period also, loan indebtedness had fallen so that loans as a proportion of fixed assets had fallen from 71 to 12 per cent. Equity had increased dramatically, mostly because of revaluation of assets ($9.1 billion), but also as a result of repayment of loans and financing new capital expenditure from revenue and from contributions of developers in money or kind to the cost of infrastructure needed to service their developments. Reserves had fallen in money terms, and all of them provide for employee entitlements for leave and superannuation. There are no reserves either for loan repayment or for depreciation, though it can scarcely be said that the Board's balance sheet is anything but very healthy.

If the state government ever decides to sell the Board, its market value should be substantial. If it did so, however, the Board's customers could legitimately claim that they were being asked to pay for the infrastructure twice. The first time was when they paid from the net revenue of the Board and through charges on developers for the great majority of the Board's assets, which it now owns debt-free. The second time would be through the user charges which a private buyer would have to use to pay interest or dividends on the capital sum it would pay for the Board's (or the Board's customers') assets.

Table 2 includes data from the Income and Expenditure statements for the same years. Like the balance sheets they are compiled on somewhat different bases in different years; in particular, in the first year they were on a cash basis and in the other two years on an accrual basis. The changes are large enough, however, that they are still clear. For the most part Table 2 confirms the changes described above.

Table 2    Selected Income and Expenditure Data for the Water Board: 1966–67 to 1993–94 (percentages of total)

|  | 1966–67 | 1984–85 | 1993–94 |
|---|---|---|---|
| *Operating income* | | | |
| Rates and fixed charges | 87.6 | 89.3 | 67.8 |
| Usage charges | 10.7 | 9.0 | 25.9 |
| Miscellaneous | 1.7 | 1.6 | 6.3 |
| | 100 | 100 | 100 |
| *Expenditure* | | | |
| Operations & services | 33.6 | 38.4 | 50.1 |
| Depreciation & debt | | | |
| repayment | 26.3 | 7.8 | 26.9 |
| Financing charges | 39.4 | 40.1 | 16.8 |
| | | | |
| *Provisions* | | | |
| Employee entitlements | 0.6 | 11.6 | 4.4 |
| Insurance | 0.0 | 2.1 | 1.8 |
| | 100 | 100 | 100 |

*Source*:  Annual Reports of the Metropolitan Water Sewerage and Drainage Board (1967 and 1985) and the Water Board (1994).

From the point of view of this chapter the more interesting changes are on the expenditure side. In 1966–67 substantial provisions were made for both 'Renewals' (depreciation) and for loan repayment. By 1984–85 depreciation was being charged systematically, but only on the historic cost of the assets, and nothing was being set aside for loan repayment: by this time loans were being repaid out of revenue. By 1993–94 depreciation was based on the replacement cost of the assets and was very substantial. Depreciation provisions ($292m), plus the operating surplus ($189m), plus capital contributions from developers ($75m), were used for financing capital expenditure ($287m), repayment of loans ($32m), making provision for a dividend payment ($57m)[6] and a notional tax payment ($47m) to the state government, and adding to accumulated funds. Financing charges fell dramatically between 1984–85 and 1993–94 in line with the fall in indebtedness. The most interesting change on the revenue side has been the dramatic increase since 1984–85 in the importance of charges related to use. Most of those charges are on the metered use of water but there is also significant revenue from charges the Board makes for acceptance of 'trade wastes' from non-residential properties. The state government has limited the increase in charges from one year to the next.

During the past thirty years the Board has changed from financing most of its new capital expenditure from loans to financing most of it from revenue, primarily from re-investment of amounts charged for depreciation based on the replacement cost of assets. Since its loans are small relative to the value of its assets, the Board has a large equity, most of which results from the revaluation of its assets to current replacement cost and the remainder from paying off loans and financing capital expenditure from revenue or by charging private developers. Re-investment of the large sums set aside for depreciation appears to be a good use of those funds, but if the Board ever has to carry out a large-lump costly renewal or replacement of assets, it may need to revert to increased use of loan funds for the purpose, at considerable additional cost. The Board's experience illustrates the increasing demands made by owner governments for infrastructure suppliers to pay dividends even when those governments have provided very little risk capital.[7] The result has been that the Board has in effect been collecting a tax for the state government from its customers.

# 9    Private sector involvement

This chapter discusses the question whether urban network services should be provided in the public or the private sector and critically evaluates the recent policy moves towards greater private involvement. In the context of this book it is important to recognise that shifting responsibility for provision of a service from the public to the private sector is not, in itself, a means of funding. Private suppliers, like public suppliers, have to fund the provision of the services they supply, and most of the sources of funding, with the exception of taxes[1], are available to both sectors. Also, either sector can finance the provision of the assets, either from loans or from net revenue. Private provision is a different institutional arrangement for provision of infrastructure services, and it has both advantages and disadvantages.

The right to provide infrastructure, and the responsibility to ensure that it is provided, are fundamental aspects of the functions of government. They are government responsibilities, first because they are 'essential services', an old-fashioned term used, for example, by Mathews (1967), and second because, given present technologies, the provision of these services requires collective decisions since unregulated competitive provision is inefficient. 'Essential' services include those that are needed by anyone living in an urban area and needed by the community to prevent the actions of individuals creating a nuisance to others. In accord with another meaning of 'essential', they are demanded by those with low incomes, as well as by those with high incomes: they have low income elasticities of demand. That governments have these rights and responsibilities is not questioned by any of the proponents in the debate about who should provide the actual services.

All involvement of the private sector in the provision of infrastructure involves a contract of some kind between a government that has the right and responsibility to provide the service(s) and a private firm which takes a specific role in their provision. The private firm takes over some or all of the responsibility for providing the service in return for a valuable consideration. That consideration might be one or more of the following: a single or regular contracted payment, the granting of development rights in property, the right to collect revenue from users of the service, and access to the government's power of eminent domain.

## Levels and modes of private sector involvement

The private sector can be involved to a greater of lesser extent in the provision of infrastructure services. Four different levels are readily identified, and there are other combinations of functions that can be franchised to private firms.

### *Level 1 Contracting out particular functions*

Government suppliers of infrastructure services have for a very long time contracted out particular functions to the private sector, where the functions to be performed could be specified quite precisely and their performance monitored at no great cost. The most obvious examples are the construction of capital works and functions such as cleaning, catering and the supply of particular inputs by competitive tender. Contracting out generally involves competition between contractors, which introduces some of the disciplines of the private sector.

The valuable consideration in most such contracts is a sum of money. Under a different form of contracting out, the government grants the right to develop a particular piece of property for a more profitable use in return for the provision of, or a contribution to the cost of, the infrastructure needed to provide services to the property. Since it will not be profitable for the owner of the property to develop it until the returns from development are sufficient to cover those costs, they are shifted to the buyer of the serviced property. This kind of contracting out, known in different countries as 'developer charges or requirements', 'land-use exactions' or 'development impact fees', has the government using its land-use control powers to shift part of the capital cost of providing infrastructure to private developers, and through them to home owners.

*Level 2 Contracting out construction and operation*

At this level the government decides what services and facilities are to be provided and contracts with a private firm for construction of the infrastructure and provision of the services, but pays all of the costs from its own revenue, which may be obtained by taxes on beneficiaries. Examples are the private construction and operation of water treatment and sewage treatment plants, and of specific links in a road network such as a tunnel or bridge. In all of these cases the government is the economic owner of the facilities. Effectively it uses the private sector both to raise capital and carry out construction, and as the operator. An interesting case is the Sydney Harbour Tunnel. Although the contract required that the contractors collect the tolls and legally own the assets, all of the revenue risks are taken by the New South Wales Government since the contractor's income is fixed in the contract and does not vary with its toll collections. Many such operations have been undertaken in the past as a means of reducing government borrowing and therefore avoiding restrictions on borrowing by public authorities.

*Level 3 Private provision of facilities and collection of revenue under government control*

The government decides where a new facility, for example, a link in a network of services, will be provided, and regulates the level of charges that will be levied on users of the facility, while a private firm finances the investments and operates the facility in return for the revenue from the charges. The best example in the classic infrastructure area is the provision of tollways. Australian cases are the M2 and the M5 in Sydney and the city-link freeway in Melbourne. A variation occurred on part of the M4 freeway closest to the city centre in Sydney which was built by government but then sold to a private operator which derives income from toll revenue. At this level of involvement the private supplier's income depends on the revenue it collects rather than being provided or guaranteed by the government. This form of operation is possible only where users are charged directly for the use of the service.

The distinction between this and contracting out construction and operation (level 2) essentially turns on who takes the revenue risk during the operation of the facility. That this may be a fine distinction can be seen by comparing the guarantee given by the New South Wales Roads and Traffic Authority of the revenue to the operator of the Harbour Tunnel, with the undertaking by the New South Wales Government to compensate the private operator of the M2 if the government permits the construction of any competitive road or railway during several decades following the construction of the freeway. Sydney Water contracted out the building and operation of a water treatment plant at its main balancing storage, Prospect Reservoir. The Board has asserted that it is not required under the contract to pay for the treatment of any given volume of water, but it is clearly understood that it will neither build a competitive treatment plant nor contract with another treatment plant at Prospect for those services. Often such understandings are formalised in 'take or pay' agreements in which the buyer of the services has to either take a certain volume of services or pay for them even if they are not needed.

*Level 4 Decisions about what services are to be provided and the level of charges are made by a private provider*

This is what could be called full privatisation, though the level of charging is generally regulated by the government. Water, telecommunication, gas and electricity supplies in many cities in the Western world are provided by private firms whose levels of charges are regulated but not determined in detail by governments, and in many countries there have been transfers of responsibility for services from the public to the private sector. In other countries some or all of these services are provided by private firms under franchise. Fully private provision of infrastructure services occurs mainly where it is possible to cover all or most of the costs from charges levied on users.

## Advantages of private sector involvement

Three important advantages are claimed for private sector provision of infrastructure services. The first two are expected to improve efficiency in the provision of the services (Economic Planning and Advisory Council 1995, Chapter 5). The advantages of private sector involvement can be read also as the disadvantages of public sector provision, and vice versa.

## Commercial discipline

A private firm that is not operating efficiently is likely to go out of business whereas public sector authorities cannot become bankrupt because their debts are guaranteed by the parent government. Also, it has traditionally been easier to dismiss a private sector employee who is not performing satisfactorily, though it should be recognised that such flexibility comes at a price since the secure jobs of the public sector generally attract a lower rate of pay. Insecure employees tend to be less committed to the long-term objectives of their employer. To avoid this problem, senior jobs in some private firms are at least as secure as their equivalent in the public sector.

## Competition

Both public and private firms must compete in the markets for factors of production, especially capital and labour. Private firms compete between each other for government contracts or the dollars of customers, and competition, in turn, stimulates greater efficiency.

## Reduction in public borrowing

Private provision of infrastructure means that any borrowing to fund investments is done by the private sector rather than governments. Governments try to restrict their borrowing for the following reasons: high levels of government debt reduce their credit rating and increase the interest rates they have to pay; government borrowing increases general interest rates and reduces private borrowing and investment, the 'crowding-out' hypothesis; borrowing is believed to be inflationary because it represents the government spending more than it is raising in revenue; borrowing increases future need for public funds to pay interest.

It will be argued later that the first two of these advantages are difficult to achieve from private involvement in provision of infrastructure because of the need for government regulation. The argument for reduction in public borrowing has little force if the borrowing is used to finance assets which produce income. Indeed, the economic effects are the same as if the private sector borrows to provide the same services, usually at a higher cost. Moreover, many of the risks remain with the government even when the services are provided publicly.

## Advantages of public sector provision

*Natural monopolies*

Because it is commonly inefficient, in the case of natural monopolies, to have competition between suppliers for the custom of individual consumers, the supposed advantages of private provision do not apply to many urban services. Under these circumstances any private provider has a captive market rather than competing with other providers, thus they need to be regulated to prevent profiteering. Such regulation unfortunately tends to reduce the opportunity and the incentive for innovation.

To some degree this problem can be overcome by an institutional arrangement which permits competition *for* the market rather than competition *in* the market. Such markets are said to be contestable even though they are not competitive. The markets for some infrastructure services, but not others, can efficiently be made contestable, a matter to which we return later.

*Essential services*

Given that governments have responsibility for the provision of essential services, there is a limit to how far they can transfer the risks involved in their provision to the private sector. Final responsibility remains with the government.

*Environmental objectives*

Services such as sewerage, drainage and garbage are provided primarily to achieve environmental objectives. Water supply is provided partly for public health reasons. The way in which all of these services, as well as energy supply and roads and public transport, are provided has major impacts on urban environments. Since normal market incentives do not ensure that private providers will achieve optimal protection or enhancement of the environment, it may be easier for governments to achieve these objectives if their own instrumentalities are providing the services than by regulating the performance of private providers.

*Equity objectives*

Although equity objectives are less important in relation to the provision of physical than social infrastructure, they are not unimportant, as shown by concessions for low income and other special groups of users of water, sewerage and public transport. In this case also it may be easier to pursue redistributive objectives through public providers than by regulating private providers.

*Lower cost of capital*

Public authorities can borrow more cheaply than private providers because the government guarantees their loans. The general view among economists is that this is not a genuine advantage of public provision, but rather is an artificial advantage since it reflects the availability of the taxing power of governments rather than the lower risk of governments providing a particular service.

The following sections of this chapter further analyse the advantages and disadvantages of private sector involvement by exploring the assumptions that underlie them.

## Rights, responsibilities and risks in the provision of infrastructure

One description of the role of government in relation to private firms that provide infrastructure refers to the government as the 'host' that deals with the private 'owner' of the infrastructure on the one side and with the public on the other (Gilligan 1995). The relationship of suppliers to their clients is not solely through the market. The host has responsibility to the public to ensure that the services are provided at an acceptable quality and price, and enters into a contract with the owner of the infrastructure to provide them. That contract is explicit and legal in the case of a private owner but is handled administratively in the case of a public owner.

While governments can contract with a private firm to provide a service by selling (franchising) the right to provide the service for a time, final responsibility for provision of the service, and the right to provide it, remain with the government. There are two reasons for these being rights and responsibilities of government:

- The legal reason is that only governments have the power of eminent domain to acquire and maintain the rights of way needed for networks, and to use them for the purposes of providing such services.

- The political reason is that, because these services are essential and because they are required to reduce the environmental externalities that would occur in cities if they were not provided, even though they are unable to eliminate them, voters hold governments responsible for ensuring that services are provided in an environmentally responsible way.

For the purpose of the following discussion we ignore the relative importance of legal and political reasons.

The responsibilities of government can be seen most clearly by considering the situation that would arise if a private firm holding a contract for the provision of a service failed to provide it in a way that was regarded as acceptable. Take the case of a privately operated freeway. If the private company which has the franchise to operate the freeway were to fail to maintain it so that the quality of service fell, it would be the responsibility of the government to enforce the terms of the contract to ensure that it was repaired. If the company could not do so without becoming insolvent, the government would have to renegotiate the contract or find another operator or take over the operation of the unprofitable business. Any capital loss which resulted would be a loss to the government. It would be politically unacceptable for the users of the road to have to make do with a parallel, lower capacity route, until another company was willing to take over the business and operate the motorway under the terms of the original contract. Similarly, if a private company franchised to distribute electricity were to fail, the government would be responsible for ensuring that supply was maintained.

Because of this nontransferable risk, governments have an interest in ensuring that private providers of infrastructure services do not fail. This is one reason for contracts with private providers being written in terms that leave either most or all of the risks directly with the government, as in the case of the Sydney Harbour Tunnel, or in terms that are sufficiently favourable to the private provider that there is little chance of failure. In some cases this requires adjustment to the terms of the contract after the facility has begun to operate. This occurred with the M5 motorway in Sydney, where certain proposed access points were deleted in order to increase its attractiveness relative to alternative unpriced routes. (For evidence on both of these facilities, see New South Wales Auditor General 1994.) The Auditor General found that, notwithstanding the formal legal situation, the New South Wales Government is effectively the owner of the Sydney Harbour Tunnel since the operating company's financial returns are essentially independent of the volume of traffic using the tunnel.

The risks involved in supplying these services are of several kinds.

*Construction cost risks*

These risks derive from unexpected changes in cost during the construction period. This is a risk which the private sector is accustomed to assuming and is more under the control of the constructing firm than of the 'host' government. Public suppliers usually shift the risk to private construction contractors through a fixed price contract.

*Operating cost risks*

The risk for a private provider of operating costs increasing over a longer period are usually covered by including some kind of escalation clause in the contract relating to the level of payments by the government or to the level of charges which can be levied on users. Alternatively such payments may be subject to periodic reassessment, which increases the risk to either a public or a private supplier. The government or the consumers are taking most of the risks, though the risks of changes in cost relative to the index used in the escalation clause are borne by the private supplier.

*Interest rate risks*

Such risks derive from unexpected changes in rates during the period of operation. This is another risk the private sector is accustomed to assuming. For infrastructure services, however, the long lives of the assets means that the interest rate risk is greater than for most other forms of private investment. This is especially true if the loans to build the assets are amortised over their full lifetimes. Governments have commonly handled this problem either by using tax revenue rather than loans for capital investment, especially in the case of roads, or by borrowing at fixed interest rates over long periods to fund the provision of income-earning infrastructure services such as electricity, telephones, water, sewerage and drainage. The Commonwealth Government has some control over short-term interest rates, but little control over long-term rates since financial deregulation, and state governments have none. It is not clear whether the public or the private sector is best able to take interest rate risks.

*Demand risks*

Demand risks results from the possibility of a lower demand than that predicted at the time the decision was taken to make an investment. The public sector has traditionally dealt with demand risks in several ways. The problem can be avoided by the government using its taxing powers rather than user charges to provide revenue: if the tax base is unrelated to the level of use, as in the case of property taxes used to finance water and sewerage, local roads and drainage, revenue is stable even if demand changes. As shown in earlier chapters, there are both efficiency and environmental disadvantages in financing many physical infrastructure services from taxes, and recognition of these disadvantages has led to taxes being progressively replaced by user charges as a source of revenue. The greater reliance on user charges has made private sector provision feasible over a wider range of services, though it has not necessarily made it any more efficient relative to public provision.

A second way to deal with demand risk has been to spread the risk across a wide range of investments and consumers, as in the case of funding of roads from nation-wide petrol taxes, and having single authorities which supply electricity over large areas. A combination of these two approaches has been frequently used in telecommunication, where there is a substantial fixed charge—a kind of tax—on users, and a nation-wide supply authority which spreads the risks.

Private involvement at level 3 or level 4 (see pages 198–200) generally means that taxes are no longer available as a source of revenue since only governments can levy taxes. In addition, any splitting of area-wide monopolies means that the capacity to spread the demand risk over a large, and to a considerable degree captive, market is reduced. This latter effect is more important than appears at first sight. For example, the future demand for water within a particular sector of a large urban area is less predictable than the demand in the urban area as a whole, and the demand within a particular suburb, especially one on the fringe of the city, is even less certain. And while those risks can be controlled by governments to some degree through land-use planning and controls, private suppliers of water have almost no control over them. Similarly the demand for the use of an individual road depends on land-use changes in the areas served by the road and on the capacity of competitive routes (those that can be used to make trips that would otherwise be made on the road) and complementary routes (those that feed traffic on to the road in question). It is much more difficult to predict the demand for use of a particular road than for the use of all roads within a state or a city. This is well illustrated by the M5 in Sydney, where one measure taken to improve its financial viability was to defer the building of access ramps between the northern end of the largely government-funded western link and the Hume Highway, in order to reduce the attractiveness of alternative routes. The political options available to the New South Wales Government were to make the M5 profitable or to take over its operation.

Those demand risks that result from uncertainty about future government decisions are more readily controlled by a government than a private provider. An attempt to control those risks can be seen in the provision in the contract to build and operate the M2 freeway in Sydney for renegotiation of the terms, with possible large compensation to the private contractor, if the government should build a road or railway competitive with it during the several decades after its construction.

*Government policy risk*

Risks result also from other unexpected policy changes during the life of the investment. In the light of new information or in response to political pressure from affected groups, the government may need to introduce more stringent standards for the quality of effluent from sewage treatment, higher standards of water purification or lower noise emission levels from motorways, for example, than were anticipated at the time a facility was commissioned, and incorporated in the contract. The government (as government) may have to require the government (as commissioner of the facility) to change the terms of its contract. It may be simpler and more equitable for the costs of higher standards decided in a political process to be imposed on public providers than on private providers of services.

Such a policy change creates a problem for the private supplier if the contract is written in such a way that the company has to meet standards as determined from time to time by the government. If, however, for legal or political reasons (for example, private providers may be a powerful political lobby) the standards required of the private provider cannot be varied, it creates a problem for the government in meeting its own environmental objectives.

Gilligan (1995) describes this problem as resulting from the fact that not all of the eventualities can be foreseen at the time a contract is written, nor provided for in the contract. As a result it is necessary for there to be a relationship between the owner and the host of 'mutual trust and respect'. The need for this kind of relationship rings alarm bells among those who believe that one of the advantages of greater private involvement is that it permits relations between the two sectors to be placed on a contractual basis which avoids exploitation of the public by the private sector—usually in the form of capture of the regulators by the regulated.[2] The need for relationships which cannot be specified in contracts is one of the main reasons for carrying out within individual firms, or indeed within governments, different functions that are related to one another in complex ways.

## Natural monopolies and the lack of competition

Infrastructure services are natural monopolies for three main reasons.

First, the less general, but better known, reason is that there are economies of scale in the provision of services as a whole, as in the building and operation of dams, sewage treatment works and electricity generating stations. These economies provide more compelling reasons for provision of the service by a single supplier if it is very costly to transport the service between cities, as it is for water and sewerage. That these economies are largely exhausted in the large Australian cities can be seen from the fact that each is served by more than one storage dam, water treatment plant, power station and sewage treatment facility. In smaller cities, scale economies in the provision of storage dams, and in smaller states scale economies in electricity generation, are not likely to be exhausted.

Only New South Wales and Victoria, and possibly Queensland,[3] have markets that are large enough to support several private and competitive producers of electricity. Transmission costs are too high for Australia to function as a single market for electricity and even for cities in a single state to serve as one market for water. There are economies also in being able to schedule the use of water from different dams depending on how much water they hold, especially in times of drought. Similar economies exist in being able to use the most efficient electricity generating plant to provide base load and to use older plant and hydro-generating capacity to meet peak demand. Markets would need to be very sophisticated in pricing electricity at different times, and with different risks of failure of supply, to be competitive.

Second, a more general and important, but less well-known, reason for natural monopolies is that there are economies of scale in the individual links within the networks through which the services are provided, and in the networks as a whole. In eighteenth century London, water supplies were first provided by individual water companies, each of which installed mains along many streets. It was partly the manifest inefficiency of this situation and partly the inconvenience of streets being continually dug up as consumers decided to change from one supplier to another which resulted in the creation of the London Board of Works to take over the system.

It is not efficient to have genuine competition in the provision of most of these network services in the sense of individual consumers being able to make a choice between competing suppliers. The fact that Melbourne Water is to be broken up into three retailing corporations, each serving a sector of the city, and one wholesaling corporation, cannot achieve competition as long as there is only one water main serving each street. Customers will not have a choice between suppliers. Nor will supply companies that buy a franchise to retail electricity within different parts of Victoria compete with one another. Similarly, the fact that freeways serving different parts of a city are owned and operated by different companies does not introduce competition between them: the fact that the service offered on one is better value for money than on another will seldom cause people to choose to live or work in the areas served by the former. Even in the case of telephone services, it is only on the long-distance routes between large centres and the heavily used commercial routes within cities that it is efficient to provide cables for more than one supplier.

The third reason is the economies from having a single decision maker, rather than competing suppliers, responsible for building and operating a network. These economies appear in different forms in different services. For example, the most efficient way to relieve a shortage of capacity in one section of a network of roads, public transport services, water or sewer mains might be to install more capacity in a different part of the network. That may be difficult to arrange if different parts of the network are under different ownership. A different aspect of network economies of scale has recently been pointed out in a simple example by Paul Mees (1996). He shows that, under reasonable assumptions, adding east-west bus routes to north-south routes in a rectangular street pattern can much more than double patronage. Such network economies are most likely to be achieved if all of the services are provided by a single authority rather than by competing suppliers, if only because of transfer privileges and the coordination of timetables.

One area in which competition does occur is between the suppliers of similar services: gas and electricity, road and rail transport, and different modes of public transport. But there is also an argument which says that the services of different public transport modes should be coordinated so that they complement one another rather than compete. Mees carries out an empirical test of his hypothesis that competition does not work well in public transport by comparing the experiences of Toronto and Melbourne. In Toronto all public transport is provided by the Toronto Transportation Commission and services have been provided in such a way that they complement one another: timetables are coordinated and transfer from one mode to another is facilitated by physical arrangements as well as by transferable fares. In Melbourne the bus services have been provided by competing private operators, tramways by one public authority and commuter railways by another. Consequently many services by different modes are provided over parallel routes and the operators compete with one another for customers. The end result is that Toronto has retained a higher level of public transport use and a lower level of subsidy than Melbourne even though it has a much smaller fixed rail network.

The Industry Commission (1994b, p. 25) concluded that 'the major factor promoting efficiency is likely to be competition rather than ownership *per se*'. Its study of the relative efficiency of public and private provision (1989, p. 20) found that 'where natural monopoly elements are present and extensive government regulations are in place the results are inconclusive'. It follows that the case for privatisation of such services is weak.

There are two ways in which competition can be introduced into the provision of infrastructure services that are natural monopolies. The first is through contestability *for* the market. This is achieved by allowing potential suppliers to compete for the right to supply the market as a whole for a given period. This form of competition is most effective when an existing supplier which is unsuccessful in bidding for the right to supply the market for the next period is readily able to recover the value of its investment in capital assets. If that is not possible, the established supplier generally will be able to outbid even a more efficient potential competitor. One situation in which that condition is met is where a bus company is providing services over a particular route; it can readily sell its buses and servicing facilities. But water and sewer mains, freeways, railway track and rights of way, electricity and telephone networks cannot be sold to anyone except the new supplier. The viability of the bid of any alternative supplier depends heavily on the price at which assets change hands, and the established supplier has an incentive to quote a very high price. The markets for the right to supply services that rely on large amounts of immovable and illiquid capital require a good deal of regulation of the terms of the 'contest' to make them contestable.

The second way is to allow third-party access to the networks provided by these immovable assets. In these circumstances the provision of the network itself remains a natural monopoly but different firms can compete in the provision of services through the network. The extent of competition for the service as a whole that results from third-party access depends on the value of the services provided by the network itself relative to the value of what is provided through the network. This can be illustrated by examples. The whole value of the service provided by roads is in the provision of the network: third parties in the form of road users have always had access to the road network, though it has been pointed out in earlier chapters that the terms on which users currently get access do not encourage efficient use of the network. The network of railway tracks and rights of way form a substantial part of the cost of rail services but the costs of provision and operation of the vehicles on the track is substantial also. The network of stormwater drains, pollutant traps and retarding ponds provide almost the complete drainage service. Most of the value of water and sewerage services is in the pipes that distribute water and collect sewerage. The collection, storage and treatment of water and the treatment of sewerage account for relatively small proportions of the total service costs. The costs of the network of pipes and wires that distribute gas and electricity, however, are much smaller relative to the cost of the gas and electricity that are distributed through them. Gas supply has been provided by different companies through the same networks in Britain for many years, and there are moves in many countries for competition between suppliers of electricity through a single network. Telephones are changing from a mainly network service to one where the value-added components are becoming increasingly important; with satellite and mobile phone communication, the network is being bypassed. Competition between suppliers is becoming relatively more efficient.

## Regulation and the restriction of competition

The related 'commercial discipline' and 'competition' advantages of private sector involvement at the higher levels imply that competition between suppliers will be relatively free. Regulations of various kinds, including setting of maximum prices, requirement of minimum quality standards and the provision of community services inevitably restrict competition. Regulations of a formal kind are, however, one of the costs of the separation of responsibility for provision of services from the responsibility for achieving other public policy goals through their provision, or dividing responsibility for providing different parts of a service. These regulations are needed for four main reasons.

### Avoidance of monopoly profits

Whether a natural monopoly is operated by a public authority or a private concessionaire, it is necessary for the government to regulate charges to prevent the supplier from exploiting its monopoly position by over-charging. Well established processes of ensuring accountability provide the information that enables governments to ascertain whether monopoly profits are being earned by public authorities, but commercial confidentiality and the supplier's control over cost information makes the same monitoring more difficult where there are private providers. For example, the New South Wales Auditor General has reported that he cannot assess whether the public interest has been adequately protected in the contract between the Government and the private builders of a proposed freeway because the terms of the contract are 'commercial in confidence'. Regulation of private providers inevitably reduces their flexibility, one of their main advantages in the production and marketing of these services.

Third-party access often requires one party that owns and operates a network, and provides services through it, to allow one or more competitors to use the network to distribute their services. For this access to be provided on terms that allow genuine competition, the initial owner must not charge too much for use of the network, and must not charge too little (predatory pricing) to consumers in order to freeze out any competitive use of the network. Baumol and Sidak (1994) have derived specifications of the level of charges that should be permitted to provide efficient access to a competitor using the local telephone network. In a review of their book, King (1994) argues, however, that the volume of information required to enable a regulator to ensure that the initial owner complies with such conditions is very large, and that the source of information is under the control of the owners of the network who have an incentive to distort it. Access to information is a problem for all regulation of natural monopoly, and is not overcome by providing third-party access. (See Skinner 1995 on cost information for water supply.)

*Ensuring adequate quality of facilities*

Any contract for the construction of facilities includes provisions to ensure adequate quality. When the market for the services is inelastic, which is often the case, the contractor has an incentive to reduce costs. The client government, however, desires the highest possible quality, especially to minimise subsequent maintenance and defer replacement. Where developers install reticulation mains and access roads which then become the property of local governments or service authorities, the problems of quality specification and control become acute because of the many small facilities provided. The government authorities have an incentive to require excessive durability and developers an incentive to cut costs. This has resulted in excessive standards being demanded, governments preventing developers from using lower cost techniques, and an appeal system. These regulations result from the separation of the responsibility for installing the facilities from the responsibility for operating and eventually replacing them. They are costly to administer and restrict innovation.

## Achieving environmental objectives

Private companies supplying urban infrastructure are likely to max-imise their profits by selling as much of their respective products as possible as long as the price at least covers the cost of provision. Yet there are large environmental costs in the use of roads, railways, water, electricity and gas, and most of those costs are borne by neither the users nor the supplying companies. Supplying companies have incentives to sell too much and to supply the services in ways that are not sensitive to their environmental impacts. The same incentives will have an impact on public suppliers, but public suppliers are finally responsible to the same political masters as determine environment policy.[4] Indeed, there is now plenty of evidence that public suppliers can and will respond to political pressures: public water authorities are urging consumers to save water and looking at innovative ways of re-using it, and electricity authorities are urging their customers to insulate their houses and take other measures to conserve energy (e.g. ACT Electricity and Water, *Environment Plan 1993/94,* and recent reports of the Water Board [1994a, 1994b] on its environmental management on the Sydney, Illawarra, Blue Mountains region).

## Achieving equity objectives

In addition to the inconvenience of roads being frequently dug up, another reason for the public takeover of the private water com-panies in London in the nineteenth century was that the companies found it unprofitable to supply low volume consumers, often those living in low income suburbs, especially in periods of short-age. For public suppliers, the provision of services to all consumers within their supply areas is an obligation that goes with their monopoly supplier privileges.[5] A classic example is the responsibil-ity of Telstra to supply telephone services to remote clients, even where the cost exceeds revenue. Where there are private suppliers it is necessary to spell out such obligations in the regulations under which they operate, and to monitor their performance to ensure that the same quality of supply is provided in rich and poor areas alike. These problems are not unknown with public supply, as high income users often succeed in lobbying for better services, but there are not the same financial incentives for public suppliers as for private suppliers to avoid the obligations of universal service at standard charges. For example, Eli Noam (1992) bases a theory explaining the pressures for privatisation of telephone networks on the advantages to high volume users in large urban centres of avoiding their share of the costs of extending the service to low volume users in more remote locations that are more expensive to serve. He assumes that third-party suppliers making use of the existing network will not have to meet their share of such equity costs.

Given that governments wish to achieve equity objectives through the provision of these services, it is sometimes argued that they should not be funded by cross-subsidisation from other consumers but from government funds. Community service obligations (CSOs) can be imposed on both public and private suppliers. In the latter case, no matter how they are funded, the supplier has to be regulated to ensure that the obligation is in fact met.[6]

One particular equity impact of the privatisation of public infrastructure authorities results from different amortisation periods. It is likely that private providers will amortise the capital cost of investment in the provision of infrastructure services over shorter periods than public providers. This is a disadvantage of private provision since, as pointed out in Chapter 8, it is both equitable and efficient for the capital cost of assets to be paid for by users over the whole of their productive lives. Private provision makes users, in the period immediately after new assets are provided, pay too high a proportion of their cost. This is a well recognised impact of the introduction of developer funding of the reticulation on services in new subdivisions.

A second, largely unintended, impact on equity objectives resulted from the requirement that developers provide reticulation of services within subdivisions and contribute to off-site costs. Since those costs are passed on to the buyers of developed property they are now borne by renters as they pay their rent and home buyers at the time of first purchase. When they were financed by loans amortised from revenue over a long period, the costs were spread over all users of the services and therefore spread more uniformly over the family life span.

## Evidence of the effects of privatisation

There are two ways in which the benefits of level 4 privatisation (see page 200) of a previously public supplier could be manifested. The first is that the governments that are selling the business or franchising the private operation could be made richer as a result of selling the assets and the operating rights to a more efficient private operator. This would be the expected short-term effect if it is assumed that the private supplier charged at the same level as the public owner. Such benefits would show up as a high sale price. A measure of such benefits is whether the saving in interest which would have resulted if all of the proceeds of the sale were used to reduce public debt was greater than the expected flow of earnings to the public sector (both dividends paid to the government and retained earnings) if the public authority had continued to operate. In a recent Australia Institute Discussion Paper, John Quiggin (1994) applied this measure to assess the results of a range of sales of Government Business Enterprises (GBEs) in different countries and concluded that in all cases the public wealth was reduced as a result of the sale: the saving in interest that would have resulted was smaller than the forgone income from continued operation.

Part, but only part, of the difference is a result of the interest rate on public debt being lower than the rate at which a private buyer discounts future returns when deciding how much to pay for an asset, or for a claim on income earned from assets, for example, by buying shares in a company. The difference between these two rates of discount is too large to be a result simply of the smaller risk of lending to the government. This is the 'equity premium puzzle' (Mehra & Prescott 1985), and opinions are divided on the reason for the large difference. As Quiggin points out, whether this is a genuine difference between the costs of private and public provision of infrastructure services depends on the explanation for the large difference. The conclusion still holds, however, that public wealth has been reduced by the sales of a wide range of infrastructure suppliers.

The second way in which the benefits could occur is that the greater efficiency of the private supplier results in lower prices to consumers. This would be expected to be a longer term effect. It is much more difficult to assess than the impact on public wealth because it requires assumptions about what the prices would have been if the supplier had remained in the public sector. Even if private buyers were able to operate at lower cost, they would do so only if required to under the terms of sale, or as the result of competition. Indeed the only way in which Quiggin's results could be consistent with efficiency benefits from privatisation would be if private bidders anticipated that the prices they could charge would be reduced following privatisation, either as a result of competition or of public regulation of prices.

Many of the important organisational and pricing reforms in the supply of infrastructure in Australia have been made by public authorities, for example, the introduction of pricing and investment reforms by the Hunter Water Board. Such reforms have been followed by almost all other suppliers. It is arguable indeed that all, or a very large proportion, of the benefits that can be gained from privatisation can also be gained from public provision: as the Industry Commission (1994b) found, efficiency of natural monopolies is not related to the type of ownership. Certainly there is no convincing argument for subsidising either the sale of public assets or private investment in new infrastructure assets. If such investment needs to be subsidised, or if assets can only be sold at a price that is less than their value to the public sector, as Quiggin's evidence shows has occurred in a number of cases in the past, that is prima facie evidence that private providers are not more efficient than public providers.

The one clearly evident 'benefit' from privatisation is that it has resulted in a reduction in the need for public borrowing. By itself, however, this is a dubious benefit, and it is one that results to a large extent from restrictions on borrowing by public authorities. Those restrictions are designed to limit the use of borrowed funds for public consumption, but if public funds are borrowed for investment in income-earning assets it has the same effect on the economy as private borrowing for the same purposes. One of the concerns about privatisation is that its major attraction to governments appears to be that it has permitted them to use the revenue from sale of infrastructure assets to reduce taxes or to increase current expenditure rather than to retire debt. Selling assets and using the proceeds for current consumption, like selling the family silver to pay for a holiday, is not a sustainable policy. Unfortunately, in the absence of balance sheets that show government assets and liabilities, it is not obvious to the public that their wealth is being eroded by such practices.

**Criteria for assessing the role for private ownership**

The above analysis provides some criteria for choosing the areas in which private ownership and operation of infrastructure is more likely to bring net benefits. The following criteria are among the most important.

*What are the opportunities for competition?*

Private operation gains most in terms of efficiency when there is competition in the various markets in which the supplier operates. First and most important is the market for the services provided, and this depends on the extent of natural monopoly in their supply. For example, it is feasible to have competition between producers of electricity and gas but inefficient to have competition between distributors of these services. Similarly competition, or at least contestability, between providers of bus services and even between providers of train services is feasible (but not in the provision of railway tracks). Competition is feasible also in the markets for long-distance telephone services but not in the provision of networks in residential and local business areas. For the same reason that competition between providers of electricity is feasible, it might be feasible between providers of bulk water, and indeed between providers of sewage treatment. These two activities, however, account for a much smaller part of the total cost of the relevant services than does the production of gas and electricity.

In summary, competition is more feasible for the headworks part of infrastructure services than for their networks. Contestability is feasible in the provision of services through some networks, and most services provided on the road network already are highly competitive. The provision and maintenance of the networks themselves, however, is a true natural monopoly where competition is not feasible except at high cost, and where any private provider would have to be as heavily regulated as a public provider. For reasons described above, it does not follow that competition is efficient wherever it is feasible. A good counter-example in at least some circumstances is competition between urban bus, tram and rail passenger services.

*How 'essential' are the services?*

Where households and businesses have a choice about whether or not to use the services, the government has less of a responsibility for ensuring that they are provided. As a result telephone and gas supply are more suitable for private provision than water supply or roads.

*How important are externalities?*

Where the services are provided in large part to safeguard public health or the environment, or where they produce significant impacts on people other than those purchasing the services, the government is necessarily involved in regulating standards of provision and the extent of the impacts. As a result there are inescapable risks for private investors that the standards required might change in ways that reduce profitability. As a result, full privatisation of infrastructure required for sewerage, drainage and garbage services is unlikely to be efficient. Of course, private involvement through contestable contracting is feasible and is common in individual parts of these services, for example garbage collection.

*How sensitive is profitability to other actions of government?*

If changes in policy and the ordinary actions of government have a large impact on profitability, private investors are likely to discount future returns very heavily. For this reason private operation of individual freeways is not likely to bring large gains to the public sector: almost any building or expansion of other roads or public transport in the vicinity is likely to have either positive or negative impacts on the volume of traffic using a particular road.

*To what extent is the provision of the service used to redistribute income?*

If equity considerations are important, the government is likely to want to impose conditions on a private provider that will limit the extent to which innovation is possible. The prime example in Australia is the provision of public transport.

**Conclusion**

Private ownership and operation of public infrastructure is used by governments primarily as a way of reducing their need to borrow for capital expenditure, or to increase taxes to pay for current expenditure. Private borrowing is almost always more expensive than government or public authority borrowing, and the difference seems to be greater than can be accounted for by the relative risks. Partly for this reason, the evidence suggests that if the returns from privatisation were used to pay off public debt it would commonly reduce the level of interest payments on the public debt by less than it reduces the public income from operation of the services. It appears also that many of the advantages of private involvement can be achieved, and in some cases have been achieved, by reform of public providers. One possible reason for these adverse conclusions is that private buyers have heavily discounted future returns because of the risks of government policy changes that might adversely affect those returns. Another is that the benefits are reduced by the need for considerable regulation of private providers in order to avoid exploitation of natural monopoly power and to achieve environmental and equity objectives. None of these arguments reduce the benefits that have long been obtained from contracting out construction and some other elements of the provision of infrastructure services, but they do suggest that the attractions of long-term ownership of infrastructure assets by the private sector have frequently been exaggerated.

There are, however, parts of a number of infrastructure services where competition or contestability provides the opportunity for greater gains from private ownership of assets. But the ownership and maintenance, and some aspects of the operation, of the networks through which most of these services are delivered are true natural monopolies, and competition is not efficient. In these circumstances, private ownership has almost no advantages and is likely to be more costly than public provision.

---

## CASE STUDY 1: BRITISH BUS DEREGULATION

Prior to their deregulation in 1986 local bus services in Britain had been highly regulated for more than fifty years. Entry had been restricted, with a single operator on any given route and fares and timetables controlled (Nash 1993). The services had been provided by local monopolies, either local authorities or private operators, though most of the private operators subsequently became part of the state-owned National Bus Company. Fare controls were generally lifted in 1980, but all of the other controls remained in place.

Three main changes occurred outside London from October 1986. First, route licensing was removed, allowing any operator who satisfied basic safety standards to provide any service after giving 42 days notice of the proposed timetable, and services could be changed after giving the same notice. Fares could be changed at any time without the requirement to give notice. Second, the power of local authorities to subsidise services was limited to what was necessary to ensure the provision of socially necessary services that could not be provided commercially, and these had to be franchised through competitive tendering. As a result the level of subsidies fell dramatically. Third, the National Bus Company was broken up and privatised, and the operators owned by local authorities had to be set up as 'arm's-length' authorities with company structures.

London was not deregulated with the rest of the country since London Regional Transport had recently been reorganised (Kennedy 1995). Competitive tendering was progressively introduced, however, and by 1993 just under half of the bus kilometres in London were on routes that had been subject to competitive tender. The contracts that resulted from tendering were typically for three years and specified the routes, the vehicle capacity and the minimum number of departures per time period. Unlike many of the competitively tendered contracts used for non-commercial services elsewhere, those offered in London were cost contracts, with all revenue from fares going to London Transport. Most of the contracts were allocated to tenderers offering the required service at the lowest cost. In terms of the typology used earlier in this chapter, London experienced level 2 privatisation while elsewhere it was mostly a mixture of level 3 and level 4 (see pages 198–200).

The British experience offers an opportunity to assess the effects of at least two different kinds of private sector involvement. At the time of its introduction academic opinion about the merits of the proposals were sharply divided, with Beesley and Glaister (1985) strongly supporting the fuller deregulation outside London and critical of the partial deregulation in London, while Gwilliam et al. (1985) were sharply critical of the whole process. Recently there have been a number of evaluations, including two which involved

Gwilliam's co-authors (Mackie et al. 1995; Nash 1993) and others by Evans (1990, 1991), White (1990) and Gomez-Ibanez and Meyer (1989). The more recent evaluations include information about effects over a longer period, and it is reassuring that there appears to be less disagreement among the authors than there was before the event.

Gwilliam et al. (1985) claimed that the case for deregulation could be reduced to four propositions: it would result in competition, substantially reduce costs, improve resource allocation, and not cause any significant undesirable side effects. It might also be expected that if these things occurred, fares would fall and the use of public transport would increase, though given that all demand studies show that its elasticity is relatively low, the increase in patronage would not be expected to be large. The fullest assessment of the results by Mackie et al. (1995) shows that some of these expectations have been borne out but other results have been surprising.

**Outside London**

First, the extent of on-road competition has been much less than expected. The generally accepted view has been that there are only minor economies of scale and few sunk costs in the provision of bus services. Therefore markets would be expected to be highly, perhaps even perfectly, contestable and it was likely that there would be on-road competition with more than one supplier serving the busier routes. In the event on-road competition, though it occurred in many places, affected only a small fraction of all routes and was almost never stable. Price competition was very rare; new incumbents generally tried to win patronage by providing a better service, and they competed for the market. Competitors usually tried to displace the incumbent rather than to set up in stable competition providing a differentiated service. The final result of almost all periods of competition was either a merger between competitors or a win for the incumbent. This suggests that stable competitive supply is rare, and that monopoly provision prior to 1986 was not simply a result of regulation. In other words, as Evans (1991) concludes, local bus services are indeed a natural monopoly. Though it was expected that faster minibuses and slower large buses would compete on the same route this did not occur. At a different scale, Mackie et al. show that while the reforms of 1986 resulted in a highly fragmented industry with over 130 operators outside London, there have since been a large number of mergers with six bus groups emerging, each with fleets totalling between 1000 and 5000 by 1993–94. This suggests that there are managerial and purchasing economies. The objective of a competitive industry has not been achieved.

This is not mainly a result of economies of scale in the conventional sense but results from the inconvenience to passengers of the haphazard headways and schedules that occurred during periods of competition, frequent changes in schedules resulting in a lack of information for passengers, and of the non-transferability of tickets between competitors. Evans (1991) points out also that there may have been disadvantages in having different routes provided by different operators due to a lack of coordination in the schedules of complementary services, the argument of Mees (1996) discussed earlier. The fact that Evans dismisses this as a weaker case may be because bus operators have never integrated their schedules on different routes.

The evidence from deregulation suggests also that the degree of contestability is far from perfect since it was very rare for an incumbent supplier to be displaced by a challenger. According to theory this implies that there are indeed some significant sunk costs. Mackie et al. point to staff recruitment and training costs, marketing costs, the length of the learning period for the public to get to know about and have confidence in a service, and local managerial knowledge gained from experience. Because of these sunk costs it is difficult for a challenge to be successful and the incumbent has a strong base from which to repel any challenge.

The second expectation, that costs would be reduced, was fulfilled. Mackie et al. report that the average operating cost per bus kilometre (excluding depreciation) fell by 42 per cent outside London between 1985–86 and 1993–94. Part of this reduction resulted from the replacement of large buses by minibuses, a trend which began before 1986, but the number grew from 500 to 5000 (20 per cent of the total) by 1993–94. Minibuses not only cost less to operate but reduce the cost per kilometre further because they achieve higher speeds. Another quite large part was due to increases in labour productivity, and a somewhat smaller part due to reduction in real wages. Smaller parts again were due to reductions in real fuel costs and to deferment of investment by using older buses. There seems little doubt that the threat of competition was responsible for significant cost reductions by operators who were fearful of being challenged by a lower-cost supplier.

Deregulation also resulted in an increase of 24 per cent in the number of bus kilometres run. Again, this was partly because of the increasing role of minibuses, but it was partly also because operators have an incentive to provide a high level of service on all routes in the area of their operation to prevent competitors finding niche markets. Despite the reduction in cost per bus kilometre, real fares increased on average by 17 per cent, and the increases were largest in those places where services had previously been highly subsidised. Part of the explanation is that the reductions in cost were necessary to cover the reduced subsidies, but another part is that price competition was rare. Operators have to reduce their costs and maintain service levels in order to be able to repel a challenger, because they cannot change either at short notice. But they do not need to reduce their fares because they can always match a challenger's lower price by reducing fares without notice. Fare reductions are not a powerful competitive weapon because fares account for only a minor part of the time-plus-money cost of a journey, and fare reductions are mutually destructive.

The increase in bus kilometres travelled implies that there has been an increase in frequency, an important dimension of quality of services. Such increases would be expected to result in increased patronage despite the increases in fares. But in fact patronage outside London declined by 27 per cent.

Part of that decline was a secular decline, and part was due to increased fares, but after these effects and the expected effects of increased services have been taken into account a reduction in patronage still seems to have accompanied deregulation. The direct explanation appears to be that large increases in bus kilometres run have had very little impact on patronage, which may be because of increased uncertainty resulting from route and network instability, and loss of information about services. For these reasons, increased services may not have resulted in a reduction in the total time-plus-money cost of bus trips.

Mackie et al. summarise their results by estimating the welfare effects of bus deregulation outside London. If the reduction in subsidy is considered as part of the deregulation package, the overall effect on providers, workers, other sectors of the economy and consumers has been a fall of £104 million. If, however, the reduced subsidies are regarded as an independent policy measure that was taken for revenue reasons, the overall result has been a gain of £144 million. This implies the possibility that deregulation may have been a good means of adjusting to the reduction in subsidy, even though it was more costly than the benefits to taxpayers of the reduction in public expenditure.

## London

The provision of bus services in London was not deregulated; rather contestability or competition for the right to operate routes was institutionalised through the tendering process and cost contracts for the supply of services. London Transport remained responsible for the provision of bus services and monitored the performance of both the tendered routes and the block grant routes—those routes operated by the operating companies of London Buses Limited, a company wholly owned by London Transport, and which had not been subject to tender. The tendering process introduced off-road competition rather than the on-road competition that was to occur elsewhere. In London, as elsewhere, there was a large reduction in subsidies; indeed a larger proportionate reduction than elsewhere.

The strength of the London system was that a limited form of competition was introduced without the uncertainty and instability that occurred elsewhere. Its main weakness was that once the contract was signed the revenue of operators was entirely determined by the terms of the contract.[7] Therefore they had no short-term incentive to innovate in ways that would increase demand. In the long term, however, they might expect that increased demand for their services would improve their chances of success in contract renewal or bidding for other services. A second weakness was that the body responsible for tendering was a division of London Transport, whose wholly owned companies were also tenderers. Other tenderers not unnaturally suspected that the tendering process favoured the wholly owned companies (Kennedy 1995). This problem was remedied in 1993.

The results were significantly different from those elsewhere in the country, though it is not clear how much of the difference was due to the different policies and how much to the differences in operation and in market conditions. First, there was a 16 per cent reduction in costs on the tendered routes as a result of tendering (Kennedy 1995, p. 255). This is less than the 35 per cent fall in cost per bus kilometre for London as a whole (Mackie et al. 1995, p. 238) because it excludes a number of influences, such as the fall in fuel prices, which were unrelated to tendering. Second, Kennedy reports that the explicit contractual terms and contract enforcement have resulted in service quality, as measured by the per cent of scheduled kilometres run that were actually run, being higher than on the block grant routes. It is notable, however, that the margin between the two had become very narrow by 1992, presumably because operators of block grant routes believed that poor performance would increase the probability that their routes would be subject to tendering.

Fourth, the number of bus kilometres run increased as much in London as it did elsewhere. This, together with the cost reductions in both parts of the London bus system, suggests that innovation can take place in a regulated market, though managers reported that those innovations were made in preparation for expected privatisation and deregulation (Kennedy 1995). Fifth, to cover the reduction in subsidies, fares increased more than they did on average elsewhere. But passenger journeys fell by only 3 per cent compared with 27 per cent elsewhere. This could be because information about services remained good and services remained stable in London, and also because of the progressive introduction of integrated ticketing for all modes in London from 1985.

The conclusion of Mackie et al. (1995) is that tendering for services has been more effective than deregulation in introducing contestability into the provision of local bus services. It has led to reduced costs not only in London but also in non-metropolitan areas outside London where many non-commercial services have been tendered. The proportion of services which have some tendered and some non-commercial elements is much higher than the 20 per cent of the route kilometres that are fully non-commercial. The tendered London market that has not suffered from the poor information and instability of services and fares that affected many commercial routes outside London experienced a much smaller fall in patronage. Mackie et al. judge that, even when the effects of the reduced subsidy are taken into account, the welfare effects of tendering in London are unambiguously favourable while the effects of deregulation elsewhere in the country are, as pointed out above, unfavourable.

## CASE STUDY 2: WATER AND SEWERAGE IN ENGLAND AND WALES [8]

During 1989 the public water authorities in England and Wales were privatised as ten water and sewerage businesses, each business consisting of a holding company and a number of operating companies. It was recognised from the outset that it would not be feasible for them to compete with one another in the market for their products, but it was believed that competition in the market for capital would help to make them more efficient than the public authorities that they replaced. Because of the lack of competition and the fact that the activities of the companies had important public health and environmental consequences, an elaborate regulatory apparatus was set up to ensure that they operated in the public interest. The National Rivers Authority was established to be responsible for safeguarding the quality of water in the environment, the Drinking Water Inspectorate to monitor the quality of drinking water and the Office of Water Services (OFWAT) to regulate charges.

Although the regulation of charging for these services is described as price control, the remarkable feature of these services is that 95 per cent of all domestic use of water, which is two-thirds of all water used, is not metered and is funded through a property tax. In addition almost all sewerage services are funded from a property tax. The British water companies must be among the few private companies able to levy a tax as a method of charging for their services. Even if all water was metered it would scarcely be desirable for the companies to have an incentive to sell as much water as possible in order to maximise their returns, given the environmental cost of using additional water.

OFWAT carries out its regulation primarily by determining the level at which the property tax and other charges are permitted to increase from one year to the next. The formula is RPI + K where RPI, the retail price index, measures the rate of inflation and K is the additional increase that was determined in the first instance by the government and in later years by OFWAT, primarily to permit the companies to meet the higher environmental standards imposed by the European Community. It was generally recognised also that the infrastructure assets of the authorities were aging and needed increased expenditure on renewals and maintenance. The primary criterion for setting K is to enable the companies to meet EC standards and to adequately maintain their assets. In this respect water differed from other privatised industries for which price increases were held at less than the increase in the RPI. Regulation was not primarily to prevent the companies from exploiting their monopoly position. K was set at 5 per cent for the first ten years but after five years was reviewed and reduced to 2 per cent.

As in many instances of privatisation the terms on which shares in the companies were offered to buyers were very generous. Prior to privatisation the water authorities had large debts and a substantial amount of their net revenue was used to pay interest. In order to increase the attractiveness of shares in the new companies, the government wrote off £5 billion of debts and injected approximately £1.8 billion in cash. If those and other smaller costs of privatisation are taken into account the net revenue received by the government falls from the official £3.6 billion to *minus* £1.6 billion (Ernst 1994, pp. 87–8). Given that the public water authorities generated some £636 million for the government in their last year before privatisation and only £134 million two years after privatisation, the sale represented a massive transfer of public wealth to private owners. It is not surprising that the water companies' profits increased by 137 per cent between 1988–89 and 1991–92, or that the average annual real rate of return for those who bought shares at privatisation and held them to March 1994 would have been between 25 and 34 per cent; in 1993–94 alone the rate of return on fixed assets valued at historic costs was 14 per cent (OFWAT 1994). In the first four years following privatisation the holding companies had taken out in dividends more than the total profits of the operating companies and also more than the original purchase price. Having paid out so much in dividends the companies are now having to borrow for new capital investment, recreating one of the problems of the previous authorities.

The generous terms of sale and the generous permitted price increases were designed to provide sufficient revenue for the companies to meet EC environment standards and to carry out maintenance and renewal expenditures needed to maintain the quality and reliability of service in the long term. Did the companies actually perform in those respects? Schofield and Shaoul (1996) examined a range of data on the level of proposed and actual expenditure on capital expansion, renewals and maintenance and on the quality and reliability of services that resulted. They found first, that the level of proposed expenditure on renewals was insufficient to maintain the assets given their expected life. Second, the companies had spent less than they proposed. Together these two results imply that the assets of the companies were being run down. Renewals expenditure had fallen from 3.3 per cent of the historic cost of assets to 1.5 per cent. The companies had maintained profits by running down their assets.

The companies had all been invited to set performance targets for quality of service, using indicators such as the frequency of supply breakdown, restrictions on water use and flooding from sewer overflows. It was found that the targets set required little improvement in performance in most cases and frequently even those modest targets had not been met. Those results are not surprising given the inadequate levels of expenditure on their capital assets.

In 1995 during a period of summer drought the public water supply system in Yorkshire failed and supplies were maintained only by means of massive transport by road tanker. The chairman publicly appealed for users to save water. During a cold spell over Christmas of the same year many consumers had no water because of damage to their pipes and to Northumbria's water mains. It is clear that regulation of water companies had not been able to prevent two major failures of supply. Rather than being reinvested in the assets of the water and sewerage systems, much of the high earnings of the water companies had been paid out as dividends or retained as earnings that were subsequently used to allow the companies to buy into growth industries outside the water sector.

The ownership of a business is generally believed to lie with whoever takes the risks from its operations. Since a high proportion of the revenue of the water companies is guaranteed by decisions of the regulator, it is not clear what risks they take. Schofield and Shaoul (1996) suggest that a continuation of rising charges to ensure adequate dividends will make the water companies 'a *de facto* nationalised industry. Except that all the costs, including the cost of dividends, will ultimately be met by consumers through prices instead of some mixture of prices and general taxation, and most of the benefits accrue to the shareholders'. They conclude that private ownership of essential services is no more successful at the end of the twentieth century than it was at the end of the nineteenth.

# 10 Urban planning and infrastructure funding

In previous chapters I have argued that costs frequently vary with the location at which infrastructure services are used, and charges for their use and decisions about investment in infrastructure need to take account of those cost differences. It is desirable that funding mechanisms provide incentives for location in places where services can be provided at lower cost. They should take into account not only internal financial costs but also external environmental costs.

One of the objectives of land-use planning is very similar: to ensure that differences in the public costs of providing infrastructure are taken into account in decisions about the location of activities within cities. Does this mean that there are two alternative means of achieving the same objective, and that with appropriate charges land-use planning would be unnecessary? This chapter will show that the charging mechanisms recommended earlier can support land-use planning but cannot replace it. Consideration of the cost of providing infrastructure is only one of the functions of urban planning, and even that function cannot be entirely replaced by appropriate charges.

The chapter reviews what kind of charging policy provides the correct locational signals and then examines the role of land-use planning in three areas: first, in coordinating and providing improved predictability to investors in urban development; second, in dealing with environmental impacts of development that cannot be reflected in optimal charges; and third, in taking into account the preferences of those who are unrepresented or under-represented by market processes, including future generations and people with low incomes.

## Locational variation in charges

It was argued in Chapter 7 that user charges should vary with location whenever the variations in cost are large, choice of location is relatively elastic with respect to relative prices, and it is relatively easy to estimate the costs in different places and to levy charges that reflect them. Such a criterion leaves much room for judgment but at least it sets out the rather obvious factors that need to be taken into account.

For some services, such as the use of roads, there appears to be a strong argument for charges that vary with location. The cost of providing roads and the level of congestion vary greatly between parts of an urban area, it is relatively easy to measure those variations and, with electronic road pricing, to levy charges that reflect them. For other services such as water, sewerage and drainage, where there are major intra-urban cost variations in some cities, and relatively small variations in others, it is not easy to measure differences in costs of delivering the service to different localities. For others such as electricity, gas and telephones it is unlikely that the cost variations are large enough to make differential charging worthwhile. Currently, apart from capital costs paid by developers and operating costs paid by local authorities, variations between different parts of a city in the level of charges are rare. Greater variation in levels of charges within cities would provide stronger support for urban planning.

The costs to developers of providing reticulation of services within a development vary across metropolitan areas, and sometimes the charges levied on developers for contributions to the cost of off-site infrastructure also vary. Since, for reasons explained in Chapter 5, both of these kinds of charges are generally passed on to home buyers, they encourage development in places where charges are lower. In Chapter 7 it was argued that requiring developers to reticulate infrastructure within subdivisions is desirable as the cost of doing so varies not only with location but also with other features of the development which are under the control of the developer. Some difficult issues arise in defining 'on-site' infrastructure in a consistent way because on-site reticulation is a higher proportion of total infrastructure costs for large than for small developments. These problems have, however, been dealt with in existing charging systems by defining responsibilities in terms of size of main and type of road.

For reasons pointed out in the earlier chapters, reticulation mains for at least water and sewerage services in established urban areas commonly have surplus capacity. This appears to imply that infill or higher density redevelopment which takes up some of that spare capacity should have to pay nothing towards infrastructure costs. This would give infill and redevelopment a cost advantage compared with green-fields development. An alternative point of view might be that the responsible authorities installed excess capacity as a speculative investment, hoping in the future to reap a return in those places where the volume of use increases. Rather than a free good, spare capacity should be regarded as a valuable asset. The latter view would argue that developers carrying out infill and redevelopment should pay a capital charge for being able to connect with existing mains as an alternative to having to provide their own as they would at the urban fringe. From an economic point of view, whether spare capacity should be regarded as free depends on whether there are other prospective users in the future. A very crude rule of thumb that is sometimes used is that spare capacity is regarded as free after the elapse of 20 or 30 years from when it was installed, on the grounds that investors would have anticipated growth in demand for only a limited period when they installed the initial capacity. In principle, however, the criterion should be forward rather than backward looking.

Chapter 7 argued that developers in urban fringe areas should be charged for off-site infrastructure only to the extent that its cost for the particular development is in excess of some basic level: the *differential* off-site cost of a particular development. The objective in making that proposition was to provide appropriate location incentives without requiring developers to pay all of the off-site costs for which their development is responsible. Developers should, in particular, be required to pay for the cost of connecting services to the established networks of the city in order to discourage developments which are non-contiguous and therefore costly to service.

Counter-arguments have been made (Kirwan 1991; Industry Commission 1993) that a developer should be responsible for all of the off-site costs of capital works which are required to cater for the demands of the new development, including arterial roads, public transport, water and sewer mains and headworks. They argue that if that does not occur, the new development is being subsidised by other users. The argument implies that user charges should cover only marginal variable costs and should not cover the marginal cost of capacity, a view that was firmly rejected in earlier chapters.

Where, as proposed in earlier chapters, it is accepted that user charges will cover the marginal cost of (off-site) capacity, there is no need to recover the same costs from developers. Since user charges provide desirable incentives to economise on the use of the service and developer requirements do not, the former are a better source of funds for this purpose.

One objective of the proponents of fully charging developers for off-site capital works is to discourage what is seen as excessive extension of suburban development. This argument would be particularly strong if there was spare capacity in established areas, not only in the reticulation mains and access roads within localities but also in the larger mains and off-site roads. However, the usual situation in established areas is that there is spare capacity in some kinds of infrastructure but not in others. For example, roads in inner urban areas are generally congested, especially at peak hours, and have no spare capacity, and it is commonly much more costly to increase capacity in established urban areas than to provide it in new areas. Whether the cost of the additional infrastructure needed to service infill and redevelopment is lower or higher than that required on green-field sites can be established only by detailed study of individual projects. As in green-field sites, if user charges include capacity costs, off-site costs should not be charged to developers in established areas. This means that there are no locational incentives to reflect these cost differences and decisions about whether to permit redevelopment in particular areas must be urban planning decisions.

Because it is difficult to estimate the cost of the additional capacity required off-site for particular new fringe developments, charges to developers are commonly levied at a flat rate per dwelling or per hectare. It is even more difficult to estimate those costs for redevelopment and infill projects in established areas. Frequently the bottlenecks in underground services that will arise as a result of redevelopment cannot even be anticipated, because there is no adequate model of the network's capacity and use. To complicate matters further, breaking into hydraulic mains and dramatically altering the flows in them often leads to breakdown of what until then was a stable system. There is no good reason for assuming, as is usual in arguments for urban consolidation, that there will be no off-site costs of providing adequate capacity to service infill and redevelopment.

## Coordination and predictability

Decisions about investment in urban development by individual private and public investors are greatly affected by their expectations about the location and timing of other investments. This is particularly true of decisions about investment in urban infrastructure, for reasons discussed in detail in earlier chapters. It applies also to private decisions: it is much easier to decide where and when to build a shop if the location and timing of development in its catchment area can be predicted with some confidence. One of the major objectives of land-use planning is to increase predictability of the location of development. This is a function which is essentially collective; except in very large private developments the market cannot perform it.

In recent years land release programs have been developed for Australian cities which increase the predictability of the timing, or at least the sequencing, of development (NCPA 1993a). Under these systems, only a limited area of land is released for development at any one time. When that land has been substantially committed to development, the next release is made. It is easier to ensure that developments occur within the release areas when each developer is required to pay the cost of linking its development with existing networks. Of course the rate of development for different purposes over any given period is determined primarily by the market, and in particular by the level of expected demand. Controls over the use of privately owned land can increase the predictability of location and timing (sequencing) only by prohibiting development on land which either has not yet been released for development or has not been designated for the type of development proposed.[1]

Such land-use controls result in two kinds of costs. The first is that some initiatives by innovative developers may be prevented because they are not in locations scheduled for development in the current period, even though they may be desirable. In using land-use controls, governments are sacrificing the flexibility that permits innovation in location and timing for the improvement in the efficiency of conventional development which results from greater predictability. It can be argued that innovation is seldom dependent on developing a particular site, and that developers frequently argue for early development of particular sites because they are cheaper than the designated sites for the proposed kind of development. If that is true, the costs of land-use controls are small. The second cost arises because land-use controls inevitably restrict the supply of land available for development in general, and for development for a particular use, which inevitably results in a higher price of land, an argument which I have dealt with in some detail elsewhere (Neutze 1978, Chs 8 and 9; 1996).

Of course land-use controls, like any other regulatory policy measure, can be used for purposes other than those for which they are designed. One example of their misuse is to reduce the rate of development which increases the price of land with development permission and the price of existing housing. Another is to use them to discriminate against low income housing and locally undesirable community facilities (the NIMBY—'not in my backyard'—problem) or to protect the environmental quality of existing residents by excluding other people who would like to live in an area (the drawbridge problem). In deciding how large a role to give to the private and the public sector in determining land use, such failures of government to use policy measures to achieve desirable outcomes need to be balanced against the failure of the market to allocate land for its best use.

Since the mid-1980s decisions about which areas of land should be released for development in Australian cities have been heavily influenced by the cost of providing infrastructure services in different localities, often to the exclusion of other considerations. Appropriate charging regimes for infrastructure services, by providing financial incentives for location that take account of service costs, can reduce the need for land-use planning to be preoccupied with this question, and allow more attention to be given to broader environmental, urban design and social issues.

## Environmental considerations

It has been argued in previous chapters that user charges provide incentives for environmentally responsible use of services. But by themselves user charges are only a component of an environmental policy for urban areas, and the environmental impacts of infrastructure services are only one of the impacts of urban development. If, for environmental or heritage reasons, the community wishes to protect a particular area from development, the most efficient as well as the most effective way to do so is to decide through an appropriate political process that it should not be developed or can be used only for certain purposes, and to signal those decisions in advance of proposals to change the use of the land through a land-use plan.

Much of the development of infrastructure services has been carried out to limit the level of external costs of living and working in urban areas. It is seldom possible, and often not even desirable, to eliminate those external costs. It is also very difficult to measure them, and certainly to measure their levels at different locations within an urban area so that they can be included in locationally differentiated charges. As a result, taking account of these costs in deciding whether to permit a proposed change in land use remains an important function for land-use planning.

## The social role of planning

Decisions about the location of infrastructure, including streets and hydraulic services, influence the layout of a suburb or a city for a very long time. Most Sydney streets laid out by Governor Phillip 200 years ago are still being used. Subdivision patterns also are very stable, though individual blocks may be amalgamated and others subdivided. One of the responsibilities of land-use planners is to take account of the interests of future generations; their interests will not be a matter of concern to private developers, or to most initial buyers of newly developed property, because of the rate at which they discount the future.

The long-term effects of planning for the future can be observed by comparing the central areas of Australian cities such as Melbourne and Adelaide, which were planned to be large cities, with the central areas of those such as Sydney and Brisbane, which were initially short-term convict settlements. The width of the streets and their layout and legibility and the more generous provision of open space contribute to the amenity and ease of using the central areas of the planned cities.

Most cities go through periods in which long-term planning, and the control of land use to implement long-term plans, is strongly supported by government, and other periods when time horizons are shorter and immediate profits from property development are a more powerful influence. For example, private development in Melbourne was permitted to intrude into the generous reservations for the major arterial routes during the boom in the 1880s. The results can be seen in the narrow sections of some of the main arterial roads. In many cities the suburbs that were built during the interwar years are very poorly provided with open space compared with areas developed before World War I and since World War II. The road reservations in the Sydney area that were set aside by Cumberland County Council during the renaissance of urban planning after World War II have since proved invaluable as routes for the freeways built since the 1970s.

Land-use plans have commonly been concerned with improving the quality of the environment and with keeping options open for the future, even if at some cost in the present. In retrospect many of those decisions have been of great value, even those such as the much maligned large suburban block, which has proved to be better able to satisfy diverse demands for additional living space as standards of living have increased.

Land-use patterns which are driven by the market, including by cost-determined user charges, will provide services and forms of development that suit best those with the highest purchasing power. One of the social objectives of land-use planning has been to try to ensure that acceptable standards of urban amenity are maintained for those who have fewer resources and therefore less influence in the market. In some part this may occur through government determined and funded community service obligations, which require that services be provided to low income groups at prices they can afford.

It should not be assumed that all government subsidies for infrastructure services benefit those with lower incomes. For example, the largest subsidies on suburban railways are for long commuter trips during peak periods, which are predominantly used by people with relatively high income white-collar jobs who live in the outer suburbs but work in the city centres. On the other hand, the use of taxis is effectively taxed by the state and territory governments auctioning restricted numbers of taxi licences. The Industry Commission (1994a) estimates that the average taxi ride in Australia costs two dollars more than it would if restrictions on the number of licences were lifted.

Land-use planning usually attempts to ensure that standards of public services are comparable in low and high income areas. This can be achieved only to a limited extent, for example by requiring the setting aside of adequate road space and the provision of sufficient open space in high and low income areas alike.

In the past land-use controls have been used to a much greater extent than differences in charges to ensure that both residential and non-residential location decisions take account of both the costs to service authorities and the environmental consequences of different location choices. Differential charging for services can complement land-use controls in achieving those objectives.

# *11* Innovations and institutions

The general objectives of this book are to explore ways in which physical infrastructure can be provided in urban areas efficiently (with minimum use of resources), equitably (with appropriate sharing of the costs) and in ways that enhance rather than damage the environment. Earlier chapters have examined how the method of funding and financing the provision of these services can help to achieve these objectives. They have, for the most part, assumed that the technologies available were given, though it has been noted on a number of occasions that appropriate charges would encourage the use of more efficient and less environmentally damaging technology and that changes in technology could change the appropriate method of funding. Earlier chapters have assumed also that the institutional arrangements for the provision of these services, at least as long as they remain in the public sector, would be unchanged.

This chapter looks more systematically at some of the alternative technologies and alternative ways of meeting the demand for these services. It does so by again examining what users want from these services and asking whether there are more efficient or less environmentally harmful ways of meeting those wants. Examining the purposes of the services takes somewhat further the 'characteristics' approach that was used in describing factors affecting costs in Chapter 3. The different ways in which these wants may be met includes different techniques, changes in the nature of the services and changes in the institutional arrangements for supplying them.

Urban water supplies provide clean, safe, plentiful, reliable and cheap water for consumption, irrigation and industrial and commercial use. Only a fraction of that water needs to be potable—pure enough for drinking—and a significant amount is used simply as a means of transporting waste products in sewers. Sewerage is a system of water-borne transport of noxious waste materials and treatment by separation of the waste from the water before discharging the water into the environment. It is important that it be safe from the point of view of health, and odourless. Drainage is used to remove surplus water during rainstorms and to dispose of it into natural watercourses or water bodies in a manner which avoids nuisance flooding. Preferably also it should not carry material that damages water quality. Roads permit the movement of people and goods within the urban area. We want them to permit rapid, safe movement and want to avoid the adverse effects of noise and air pollution that arise from their use. From public transport also we want rapid, safe, reliable and cheap movement without adverse effects on the environment. We want cheap, reliable energy in the form of electricity and gas, and want again to avoid the pollution that occurs during their production and consumption. Telephone and postal services are expected to be reliable, rapid and cheap and to provide for the movement of messages, data and graphics. Finally we expect garbage services to prevent littering, avoid odours and to provide for the removal and safe disposal of a range of waste material that cannot readily be re-used.

One of the features of many of the alternative ways of achieving the objectives set out in the previous paragraph is that they shift the focus from having the services supplied by large hierarchical organisations through capital intensive infrastructure services, to ways in which individuals and individual property owners can meet more of their own needs. Some of them require decisions by the suppliers about the ways the current infrastructure is being used, or by authorities responsible for regulating the way in which services are provided and used. Others require decisions at the level of suburbs or localities rather than individual properties at one extreme or metropolitan areas or states or nations at the other. Considered as a whole, the changes described below call into question whether large centralised institutions, whether public or private, are still the best way to provide these services in large urban areas.

Some innovations provide opportunities to reduce the level of use, especially in places and times when the costs are high or where environmental damage is likely to be high. Others offer different ways to meet the demands currently satisfied through the provision of these services. The new technologies offer opportunities to provide services at lower resource cost or with less impact on the environment, or both. As with all changes, equity impacts will need to be considered. Patrick Troy (1996, Ch. 3) describes many of the innovations which can reduce the stress that urban areas place on the environment.

Consistent with the emphasis on location throughout the book, this chapter will consider first those innovations that can be made on individual properties, second, those that can be made within parts of urban areas, and third, innovations that relate to whole urban areas or states or nations as a whole. Provision of infrastructure services through metropolitan wide networks is, by its nature, capital intensive. If more of the objectives we seek can be achieved within individual properties or within parts of urban areas, the cost is likely to be smaller.

## Innovations within individual properties

To the extent that the occupants of individual properties can provide for their own requirements there will be less demand for most of the infrastructure services described in this book. Three general limits apply to the prospects for innovations of this kind. First, without the adoption of quite different lifestyles and methods of production, they have only limited application to transport and communication infrastructure; second, it is relatively expensive to provide within a property for peaks in demand which may be brought about by unpredictable events such as property fires, rainstorms or droughts; and third, providing for one's own requirements often requires space: there are more opportunities for occupants of single family housing than of medium density housing or flats. Notwithstanding these limits to self-containment, the new technologies provide important opportunities. These will become relatively more attractive with the higher user charges proposed in Chapter 7 which better reflect cost conditions.

### Greater use of rainfall that falls on individual properties

The more demands for water can be satisfied locally, the lower will be the demand for costly dams, treatment facilities and mains. Currently most councils require that rain which falls on the roof of a building must be discharged into stormwater drains. Much of the rain which falls on other parts of a property, depending on the permeability and water-holding capacity of the surface, also finds its way into drains. The more that runs off and the more rapidly it runs off, the greater the requirement for drains to prevent flooding, the greater the carriage of soil nutrients, sediment and trash into creeks, rivers, lakes and coastal waters, and the greater the silting of dams, weirs, lakes and pipes.

Depending on soil type, geology and whether or not the soil has been polluted, there are a variety of ways in which much of this water can either be used on the property or filtered as it runs off more slowly or as it soaks into underground aquifers. Collection from roofs into rainwater tanks, which is common in rural areas and was once common in many urban areas, permits rainwater to be used either within the house or for irrigation. Surface mulching slows and reduces run-off and reduces erosion. Lawns with grass several centimetres high have similar effects.

Even if all of these measures are adopted, in heavy rainstorms tank storage and the capacity of the soil to absorb water will be exceeded. Diverting rainwater to gravel-filled trenches permits it to soak more quickly into the subsoil, and diverting it to deeper sumps permits it to soak into underground aquifers (National Capital Planning Authority 1993b). In suitable situations, rainfall from paved areas also can be diverted to be absorbed or filtered in similar ways. Paved areas can be replaced by areas of hard standing that permit the penetration of rainwater. The scope for adopting these measures is greater in areas of relatively low density development where there are larger areas suitable for mulching and absorption of rainfall. Apart from collection from roofs into tanks, few of these measures have much application in high density residential, commercial and industrial areas. Like a number of other innovations, they can be more efficiently incorporated at the planning stage of new development or redevelopment, when the rainwater tanks can be included in the building design and other measures in the initial landscaping.

The result would be not only a smaller demand on the drainage system for dealing with rainwater, but also a smaller demand for fresh water from water mains for both inside use and for garden irrigation. These measures are seldom used in many countries for several reasons. First, building regulations commonly require that downpipes be connected to stormwater drains to avoid water flowing onto neighbouring properties during storms. Second, on-site absorption does not work well in some clay soils. Third, rainwater tanks provide a relatively expensive source of water, which may be contaminated in heavily polluted areas. Nevertheless there are much greater opportunities for on-site use of rainwater in many cities.

*Water-efficient appliances*

Advances in the design of water-using appliances have reduced the amount of water they use while still performing their original functions. Examples are washing machines, dishwashers, shower heads and dual-flush toilets that use less water. For those kinds of advances to reduce water consumption buyers need to be informed about the water-use efficiency of different appliances and to have an incentive to save water. A water efficiency rating system similar to the energy rating system which informs buyers of the efficiency of different brands of electrical appliances has been developed but is not yet widely known or understood. The incentive may be provided by a charge that varies with the volume of water used, or it may come with consumers' response to appeals to save water on the grounds of environmental impacts.

*Re-use of grey water*

Water which has been used within the house for washing clothes or dishes or for baths and showers (sullage or grey water) can be used for garden watering (NCPA 1993b, pp. 45–48). This has the advantage of reducing both water use and discharge to sewers. Because grey water needs to be stored if a significant amount is to be reused, and commonly needs to be pumped, it is more costly than use of mains water at current prices. It may be also more costly than rainwater and its re-use is possible only where there is a garden or lawn. Also it is more likely to produce unpleasant odours if storage is not well designed and if spreading is not well managed. These problems could be greatly reduced if simple membrane technology were used to improve its quality. If all grey water is to be re-used, large storages are required in many areas because of the difficulty of using it in periods of high rainfall and low plant growth, especially in areas where there is a high clay content in the soil. Like the use of rainwater, re-use of grey water is more easily adopted at the time of initial development of the property. One of the great advantages flowing from its re-use is that the nitrates and phosphates it contains, which are difficult to remove during sewage treatment and which result in growth of algae in water bodies and streams into which effluent is discharged, are useful fertilisers on lawns and gardens.

The quality of grey water could be improved also by changing the composition of household detergents to eliminate phosphates.

## Re-use of bodily wastes

Aside from grey water, households flush bodily wastes from toilets into the sewers. What is needed here is a technology that provides a clean, hygienic and odourless way of disposing of these wastes. Current sewage systems require large volumes of water as a transport medium, but new technologies can reduce the use of water significantly while still avoiding unpleasant odours. Dual-flush toilets, which use less water, are only one step in this direction. If flushing toilets were to be replaced with composting toilets, and grey water re-used, households could eliminate their discharge to sewers and hence their need for sewerage connection. The main limits to the use of composting toilets relate to their capital cost, the space they require, their management and the soil conditions that permit composting.

It would be costly to replace flushing toilets with composting toilets in most existing houses and almost impossible in flats. Given that the connecting sewers are already in place and most have a long life, the cost savings would not be great, at least for many years. In newly developing areas, however, where the whole investment in a sewerage network could be avoided, the cost savings would be large, and the cost of installation would be much smaller. Developers of subdivisions which did not need to connect to sewers could be expected to pass on the savings to home purchasers, who would have the added advantage of having to pay lower annual charges for water and nothing for sewerage. Composting toilets have been installed in some non-urban situations and, with appropriate safeguards, might be expected to be permitted in urban areas in the foreseeable future.

## Composting of organic wastes

Organic wastes comprise about one-third of household garbage. Many people with gardens already compost food scraps with garden and other organic waste and thus reduce the volume of solid waste material that needs to be collected and disposed of as garbage. Composting improves soil fertility, soil structure and water-holding capacity. Since it is an aerobic process it results in the discharge of $CO_2$ rather than the much more potent greenhouse gas $CH_4$ (methane) which is produced during the anaerobic process which occurs in landfill garbage disposal sites. Composting is inexpensive but there is a risk of creating a nuisance if it is not well managed. In a partly rotted form compost can be used as a mulch to reduce evaporation from the soil surface and to reduce run-off during heavy rain. Like most kinds of recycling it requires some yard and garden space.

*Recycling*

The development of techniques for greater re-use of materials such as glass, steel, aluminium and paper provides opportunities for reducing the amount of garbage that has to be disposed of. Recyclable material accounts for another third of domestic garbage. Recycling requires that materials be separated into classes, either at the point where they are first used or later. Households and businesses are increasingly separating waste materials into what can and cannot be recycled, and either depositing material suitable for recycling at designated depots or leaving it for collection. Recycling in industry frequently results in the recovery of valuable materials and occurs within the plant that generated the waste material.

Most of the recycling of this component of household waste occurs away from the home, but it is more efficient for at least the initial separation to occur at the place where the waste is generated. The extent of recycling depends not only on how much reusable material can be collected but also on the demand for it. That demand would be greater if appropriate resource rents were charged for the natural resources such as forest products, minerals and energy which are used to make the new materials with which reusable materials must compete. In addition, much recycling requires the development of a capacity to convert the used material into a form suitable for re-use, for example, through the de-inking of newsprint. Only when the supply of material for recycling can be shown to be large enough and sufficiently reliable will it be worth developing and installing such equipment: demand expands to use the available supply.

*Home collection of energy*

The collection of energy on-site in urban areas is currently most easily achieved through solar water heating, though the technology for direct conversion of solar energy into electrical energy through solar cells is rapidly becoming more efficient. Wind power is always likely to be more efficient at larger exposed sites than at individual properties. Solar water heating and solar generation of electricity are unlikely to be sufficient to permit most houses in urban areas to dispense with mains electricity for some time, but they can certainly be used to significantly reduce the demand for electricity from the grid. In due course, with more efficient storage batteries which can be recharged during the hours of sunlight, it is likely that some urban houses will join those in remote areas in relying solely on locally collected solar energy. Perhaps further into the future is the development of efficient small fuel cells which could be used to supply energy at peak periods.

*Replacement of transport by communications*

Technical innovations in communication have permitted some reduction in the demand for personal transport. Some kinds of work lend themselves to being performed at home, especially those growing areas which rely heavily on information technology. The inputs and the outputs may consist largely of information which can now be moved very cheaply over considerable distances. For some people, especially those who are self-employed or on contracts, working at home is attractive and congenial. Others, however, value the social contacts made at the workplace. Journeys to work are only a small proportion of total trips and the opportunities to replace other kinds of journeys by communications are more limited. Urban planning measures that allow more people to satisfy their demands close to home may have a significant effect on the total volume of travel by reducing the length of trips.

Telephone and video conferencing has reduced travel for some business purposes, but the large number of trips for shopping, recreation and social purposes appear likely to be largely unaffected by improved telecommunication. Development of mobile phones and the decreasing cost of both the handsets and other parts of the technology might in the future result in the disappearance of copper or fibre-optic networks from low density parts of cities, though it will be necessary to have a physical network for cable television, data transmission and other communication purposes.

## Innovations within sections of urban areas

Traditionally, most physical infrastructure systems have operated at the level of complete urban areas. Although local roads and drains have been the responsibility of local councils, they have fed traffic and stormwater into larger-capacity metropolitan systems. Similarly, water, sewerage, electricity and gas have been provided for whole metropolitan areas and in some cases whole states or nations. Little attention has been paid to what can be done locally within sections of urban areas. Although local councils have some powers over land use within their borders, the emphasis has been on metropolitan plans, and the high level of interconnectedness between different parts of the metropolitan area has been assumed to be both necessary and desirable. In this section we consider what more could be done locally.

*Stormwater drainage and use of rainwater*

Individual property owners are limited in their ability to store and use rainwater by the space within their properties. Furthermore, a large proportion of the rainwater going into drains comes from public space, especially roads and parking areas but also some recreation areas. Many of the important decisions that affect the extent and speed of run-off are made at the time an area is subdivided and converted from rural to urban use. Some local authorities in North America require that the run-off characteristics of a newly developed urban site put no greater load on the drainage system after than before development. This can be achieved by the installation of storage basins which retard run-off and permit some of the stormwater to be used locally for irrigation of public areas and, if supplies are sufficient, reticulated for garden watering. This kind of use is more efficient if the water is stored locally because it requires little pumping and only short pipes to be used broadly in the same area where it falls. One model for this kind of system is of an urban area in which each sub-area collects its own rainwater which is used in an adjacent area at a slightly lower elevation. Doing the same thing for larger areas is more costly.

Pondage not only retards the discharge into local watercourses, but during the time it is stored, some of the nutrients, sediment and other pollutants carried in stormwater settle out. Smaller downstream drains are then sufficient to prevent flooding and there is less impact on streams and natural water bodies. Demand for potable water to be used in irrigation is reduced.

A somewhat different approach which has some of the advantages of local pondage is for stormwater drains to discharge on to local playing fields. Excess water then soaks into the ground and recharges groundwater. Sediment and nutrients carried in stormwater are generally beneficial for local parks, and gross pollutant traps can prevent the deposit of litter on the playing fields. This protects the quality of watercourses draining the urban area. The playing fields are, however, unusable for a longer time after heavy rain than they would be if the area was drained in the traditional way. Unlike local pondage, these arrangements do not provide additional water for irrigation of other public or private land.

The use of wide, shallow grassed drains slows run-off after rain and permits some of it to soak into the groundwater. Where insufficient space is available for such drains, small concrete drains that leak achieve some of the same advantages.

## Local re-use of treated effluent from sewerage

Recent developments in treatment of sewage permit efficient small scale recovery of water from sewers which is at least safe enough for use in lawn and garden watering. The more concentrated sewage that remains continues through the sewers to treatment in the normal way. As well as being small in scale the new treatment facilities can be placed underground and installed in many established urban areas. The advantages of the new technology are twofold. First, it reduces the need for additions to capacity of main sewers and treatment facilities downstream, and permits smaller sewers and lower capacity treatment facilities to be installed to service future urban developments. Second, it facilitates the re-use of treated effluent for irrigation and possibly in the future for general use. It does so by making the treated effluent available throughout the urban area where there is a demand for it rather than having to pump it back from a more remote treatment plant which is likely to be at a lower elevation. Re-use of treated effluent will have both financial and environmental advantages in reducing the demand for potable water. Removal of nutrients, a costly part of sewage treatment, is less important if the treated effluent is to be re-used, especially for irrigation, than if it is to be discharged into a stream.

## Local planning of land use and transport

The principle that is proposed for water, to deal with the matter locally as far as possible rather than relying solely on metropolitan solutions, can be applied to some extent in land-use and transport planning. Provision of a wide range of jobs, services and facilities within each sub-region of a large city encourages people to make more, shorter trips to local centres rather than longer trips to metropolitan centres. There will always be a demand for some travel throughout the metropolitan area, but placing more emphasis on local accessibility relative to metropolitan accessibility can encourage greater use of local workplaces and services. Similarly, policies that emphasise the provision of entertainment, recreation and cultural facilities in each of the sub-regions can reduce the demand for long-distance travel.

Efforts to establish a few major sub-regional centres in metropolitan regions that are large enough to be competitive with the central business district have not met with notable success. Nevertheless, the great majority, and an increasing proportion, of employment is outside the city centre and there are many thriving and active suburban centres in all of these cities. In Sydney and Melbourne, for example, some 35 per cent of workers work within the local government area where they live. Since these data refer to some 40 to 50 local government areas in each urban area, a significant proportion of journeys to work are relatively short. In many respects the larger metropolitan areas are better understood as a number of urban areas that are located adjacent to one another and therefore have a lot of interurban travel than as single, highly integrated urban areas.

## Innovations on a wider scale

Some of the innovations that facilitate more efficient provision of infrastructure services in general have been mentioned above. For example, the development of a means of electronic triggering of in-vehicle meters permits the introduction of road pricing with variable prices at different locations and times of day without the need for highly centralised information systems. This removes the invasion of privacy argument against road pricing by ensuring that no car identification system is required. The development of smart watering systems in which a soil moisture gauge can activate the sprinkler control system has the potential to greatly increase the efficiency of use of water for irrigation. Low pressure drip systems for lawn and garden watering make it easier to use water collected from roofs and grey water for irrigation.

It may be easier to gain public acceptance of the re-use of treated effluent as part of the potable water supply if the treated effluent is mixed with 'new' water. In that case the treatment is best carried out at a large treatment facility from which the effluent can be fed into the water supply prior to treatment of that water.

## Institutional implications

If more of what we want from infrastructure services can be supplied from within individual properties or be handled more effectively within sections of large urban areas, the large metropolitan and state authorities which have been responsible for them in the past may be less appropriate in the future. It has long been recognised that important aspects of the demand for some services such as roads and drainage are predominantly local, and these demands are met by local authorities. While local authorities deal with access roads and local drains, state and metropolitan authorities respectively deal with main roads and main drains. Land-use planning, which has some responsibility for integrating the provision of the range of infrastructure services, and for control over land use to ensure that such services can be provided efficiently and equitably, is also a function of both local and state authorities in most states: local authorities deal with land-use changes that have local implications while those that have wider implications are the responsibility of state planning authorities or departments. The suggestion that there be more local responsibility for provision of infrastructure services is a suggestion for a change in balance between local and metropolitan rather than for wholesale re-organisation. Many current local authorities are far from ideal for this purpose as their boundaries seldom coincide with either the local water catchments, which are the natural units for hydraulic services, or the market catchments of shopping and employment centres, which are the logical boundaries for transport services. Nevertheless, they are the closest governments available.

Metropolitan and state authorities are needed when an infrastructure system functions in an integrated manner over the whole urban area or the whole state, and where the most important decisions have to be taken for the system as a whole. Examples are decisions about the future sources of new water for the urban area or about the future scale and operation of large sewage treatment plants. It has been argued above that the most important future decisions about provision of the services will be about what happens on individual properties, suburbs or groups of suburbs, in drainage catchments or the catchments of suburban commercial centres. In these circumstances state and metropolitan authorities may not be the best institutions to be responsible.

Authorities which are responsible to state governments are likely to be responsive to the political powers that are dominant at the state level, rather than those in individual localities. In water and sewerage, for example, the history, expertise and assets of the metropolitan authorities commit them to solutions to problems that use the large infrastructure systems they have inherited. They are less likely to see the opportunities for managing demand or dealing with problems through local measures.

Rather than thinking about how to reduce or delay run-off from individual properties or about the installation of local retarding ponds, such institutions will think about building larger drains to handle the increasing flows of floodwater resulting from growth in urban areas. Rather than focusing on local use of water that falls on a property or a small subdivision, or about 'milking' local sewers using small-scale treatment facilities, such organisations will do what they know best and build new or higher dams, larger mains and upgraded treatment facilities. They will build new freeways to cater for the traffic that wants to travel long distances rather than improving access to sub-regional centres so that people will no longer want or need to travel so far. Properly pricing the use of roads in congested areas would, of course, encourage people to arrange their lives to avoid such roads as much as possible.

If the future provision of infrastructure services is increasingly to depend on local decisions being taken by individual property owners and by, or on behalf of, people living in a limited part of the metropolitan area, local governments or some other bodies representing sub-metropolitan areas seem likely to be more effective as the main 'retail' suppliers of infrastructure services than state or metropolitan suppliers.

It has been pointed out that many of the new technologies are more effectively introduced in new areas than in established areas where existing infrastructure capacity has a long life and relatively low operating costs. The way to deal with the institutional change, in the case of hydraulic services, may be to establish smaller special purpose authorities to operate in newly developing areas. In order to provide them with the correct incentives, they would be required to pay for water wholesale on a volume basis, for sewerage on the basis of the volume and strength of discharge and for drainage on the basis of peak volumes. Each would then have an incentive to encourage or require the adoption of the new technologies described above, and to adopt them themselves.

The above suggestions for increasing the responsibilities of sub-metropolitan governments for urban planning and for the provision of physical infrastructure services have the added potential advantage of empowering, and therefore strengthening, local communities. If such governments can take measures to improve the quality of their local environments, they will have more control over their futures in qualitative as well as economic terms. The danger with this kind of decentralisation of responsibility is that the richer areas will be able to afford to provide a higher level of services than the poorer areas. Fortunately many countries have developed ways of redistributing tax revenue to ameliorate these problems, but increasing the devolution of functions in the way recommended above would place increasing strains on these resources.

# Notes

## 1 Introduction: Why study urban physical infrastructure?

1 Some commentators, in particular John Pitchford (1993), take the view that there is no need to worry about balance of payments deficits, especially because most of them are caused by private rather than government borrowing. The value of the Australian dollar should be permitted to vary and we should be happy that foreigners are willing to lend to us. The more conventional view is that if Australia has to borrow overseas to cover a deficit in consumption goods it is living beyond its means and a policy response is required. The value of the Australian dollar is seen as an indicator of our international economic soundness.

2 This latter view is widely shared, but the appropriate policy response is to introduce pricing for the services rather than simply to starve the authorities of investment funds.

## 2 The nature of physical infrastructure services

1 Frequently governments have not been good at facilitating these connections either by co-locating terminals for different modes or different services or by coordinating schedules.

## 3 Costs of infrastructure services

1 It will occur in other services when responsibility for provision of networks such as railways, gas pipelines, electricity and telecommunications is separated from responsibility for provision of services through those networks.

2 Even this case depends on some further assumptions about the distribution of use of water within the site. If the higher density of demand

results from using more of the site for residential and commercial purposes rather than (unwatered) open space, for example, the average cost may not be lower.

3 Brisbane City Council's costs in 1993–94 give some idea of the relative importance of the two components. It spent $17.9m on the purchase of water wholesale from the South East Queensland Water Board and $29.0m treating that water. Some of the treated water was then supplied to other distributors. The pro-rata share of those costs for the water it distributed itself was $38.5m. It then spent $45.5m distributing that water to its customers. The above costs include current cost depreciation on treatment and distribution facilities but exclude $16.9m interest costs and $4.4m spent on overheads and administration. Thus distribution cost $1.18 for each dollar spent on storage, transmission to the city and treatment. If interest cost on the distribution system were to be included, the ratio would be $1.61 on distribution for each dollar spent on storage, transmission and treatment.

## 4 Demand characteristics

1 In North America it is not uncommon for sewerage to be charged as part of the water account in proportion to the volume of water used. In some places garbage services also are charged according to the amount of garbage produced. Fuel taxes are a proxy for a price for road services, but they are not closely related to the cost of the services provided.

2 Congestion in this sense begins when the speed of an individual vehicle is reduced by the presence of other vehicles on the road.

3 The relevant measure of the spatial frequency is the frequency of public transport services which are not fully loaded and therefore can be boarded.

4 Diurnal peaks can be met relatively cheaply from service reservoirs.

5 Nieswiadomy and Molina (1989), using cross-sectional analysis, found a long-term elasticity of demand for water of 0.25 with respect to area of lawn.

6 The demand for duration of calls in both the short and the long term was much more elastic than the demand for number of calls: −3.8 and −1.0 for shorter distance calls and −3.0 and −1.7 for longer distance calls.

## 5 Objectives in charging for infrastructure

1 The assumptions needed for this to be true are restrictive, for example, that the distribution of buying capacity is socially optimal and that the use of the services produces no externalities, i.e. neither advantages

nor disadvantages for non-users. The second but not the first of these assumptions is considered below.

2   Noosa Shire, Queensland, has recently implemented an impact type approach in establishing appropriate differential developer contributions for off-site roads. The approach could have applications to estimating marginal cost differences. It divides the shire into catchments around local activity centres and charges a higher contribution the greater the distance from the nearest activity centre on the assumption that people living further from their local activity centre will make more use of roads (Kinhill Cameron McNamara, 1994).

3   Sagoff argues that people act both as individuals within a market making consumption and production decisions and also as citizens within an ethical community making collective decisions following public debate.

## 6   Alternative charging mechanisms

1   Unfortunately marginal cost is commonly defined as marginal operating cost which excludes the marginal cost of capacity. For reasons discussed in Chapter 2, user charges set equal to correctly defined marginal cost usually cover all or nearly all costs.

2   The elasticity of demand for housing is composed of two parts: the demand for separate dwellings, which seems likely to be inelastic; and the demand for quantity and quality of housing per dwelling, which is likely to be more elastic.

3   Bourassa (1995) has shown that very few renters surveyed in the 1990 Income and Housing Costs and Amenities survey could have afforded the loans they would have needed to buy the dwellings in which they were living.

4   Kearney (1995) has demonstrated that public investment complements private investment rather than crowding it out.

5   An interesting exception is reported in Kinhill Cameron McNamara (1994).

6   The figure uses the percentage of total expenditure rather than of total income because it appears that incomes at the lower end of the distribution were understated, for example households in the lowest decile spent $2.60 for every dollar of income. While there were some sources of funds that were not included in the definition of income for the survey, they are unlikely to have been that large. In addition the lowest decile reported paying more income tax than they are estimated to have been liable for (see Figure 1), and more than the second lowest decile. Again this could have been partly because the tax reported was paid on the previous year's income and there is a good deal of

fluctuation of income from one year to the next. This seems unlikely to be the only explanation.

7 A very similar issue is raised in respect of social infrastructure services such as schools and health and welfare services. Because distributional issues are more important for these services, the appropriate policies are likely to be different.

8 Ways in which this can be achieved equitably are suggested by Peiser (1988).

9 The sizes of the lumps of capacity are not immutable. It may be that the lumps that have been built in the past have been larger than is desirable, ignoring the cost of investing in large amounts of surplus capacity, and saving only modestly on construction costs compared with a two or more stage construction project.

10 This prescription is developed and explained by Ng (1987). An example of the results of using this approach is to be found in Dixon and Norman (1989). Turvey (1969, 1976) has developed a modified version of the traditional approach, which takes account of the fact that the increase in consumption in any one year brings closer the time at which the next dam will be needed, but still results in a (less extreme) saw-tooth pattern of prices over time. OECD (1987, Annex 2) compares these alternatives.

11 It may be due to the omission of the opportunity value of land from the calculation of LRMC.

12 The Industry Commission (1993) has discussed the question of infrastructure pricing in the presence of excess capacity in similar terms.

# 7 Optimal funding arrangements

1 Sagoff (1988) argues persuasively that a purely economic, or individualistic, response to environmental problems is inappropriate.

2 A.C. Pigon (1932, pp. 183–96) was the first to point out that in situations where the marginal social cost exceeds the marginal private cost of an activity, one appropriate way to discourage the offending activity is to levy a tax per unit equal to the difference between the two.

3 It could be achieved at a moderate level by abolition of vehicle registration charges.

4 There is a strong argument for including the cost of accidents involving two or more vehicles, in a similar way to congestion, as a cost that additional users impose on other users as roads become more crowded. The contrary argument is that as roads become more congested speeds fall and as a result the severity and perhaps even the likelihood of a

collision falls. There is not at present enough information to know which effect dominates.

5  Cox (1994) summarises much of the evidence for under-investment in urban roads in Australia. His analysis is flawed to some extent by his failure to take account of the opportunity cost of land in his assessment of the cost of adding to urban road space. Nevertheless the data he provides suggests that even taking account of the opportunity cost of land there are be areas where the return on investment may be high.

## 8  Financial issues

1  Of course it does not follow that loans will necessarily be paid off as soon as possible from revenue. For example, revenue raised from the Sydney Harbour Bridge would have been enough to pay off the loans some time in the mid 1950s. The revenue has instead been used to finance other road construction.

2  In 1967 the Board's predecessor had substantial 'Depreciation (Capital Repayment etc) Reserves' amounting to nearly one-third of the value of its fixed assets, and over half of the reserves were held in the form of investments and fixed deposits. Such 'hollow logs' were later raided by state governments short of funds.

3  It is a matter of some argument whether straight-line depreciation is appropriate (Parmenter & Webb 1976) but this is not an important question in the present context.

4  The weighted average life expectancy of the system assets of Sydney Water (which account for 90 per cent of all assets, and exclude land and buildings and plant and equipment used for general purposes, and work in progress) is slightly more than 100 years.

5  When the institutional arrangements for the provision of these services change, the question of which government is the owner is sometimes a matter of dispute. Recently in New South Wales the state government took over responsibility for distribution of electricity from special purpose bodies established by groups of local governments. Ownership of the assets was disputed in a number of cases, especially where the equity involved was large. Corporatisation and privatisation both imply government ownership.

6  The basis for calculation of the dividend is not revealed in the Annual Reports. In successive years the amounts paid were $102m, $179m, $70m, $37m and $57m. Clearly they are unrelated to equity, seeming to be determined by a political process of assessing 'what the market will bear'.

7  In 1991–92 the state government required the Board to pay a special dividend as well as an ordinary dividend. The total payment of $179m was 13 per cent of the Board's revenue in that year.

## 9  Private sector involvement

1   An exception to this occurs in Britain, where the regional water authorities have been given the right to levy charges for their services, based on the occupation of property, which are in effect property taxes.

2   The need for relationships that cannot be specified precisely to be included in contracts is one of the criticisms of attempted public sector reforms spelled out in the various chapters of Alford and O'Neill (1994).

3   Queensland's urban development is sufficiently dispersed that it may be inefficient for the whole state to be a single market for electricity.

4   This statement does not take account of the situations in which one level of government in a federal system is responsible for environment policy while another controls infrastructure. Increasingly, however, all levels of government are being held responsible for the effects of their policies and actions on the environment.

5   These obligations are not unqualified. For example, sewerage authorities may decide not to connect a suburb until some proportion of the allotments have been developed, or an isolated settlement which would be costly to service, and Telstra may decide to not provide broadband services to all homes in remote areas.

6   It is not clear that it is better for governments to pay the cost of community service obligations to providers of infrastructure services rather than requiring the suppliers, whether public or private, to meet those costs themselves. One reason is that it is difficult to define exactly what constitutes a CSO, and what responsibilities derive from the privileges suppliers are accorded when awarded a franchise. For example, how is the cost of supplying small consumers, discussed in the previous paragraph, from profitable parts of the operations of suppliers, classified? Use of infrastructure services is a suitable tax base for raising funds to achieve public purposes in that their demand is commonly inelastic and, because of externalities, the social marginal cost of providing most of these services is greater than the private marginal cost. The widespread use of motor fuel taxes shows that one element of infrastructure use, the use of public roads, is widely accepted as a suitable tax base.

7   Tenderers could, along with a conforming bid, put in another bid which proposed other ways of providing the services concerned. Such bids could be aimed at increasing patronage or saving cost through a variation in services.

8   There is quite an extensive literature on privatisation of infrastructure services in Britain. This section draws heavily on Ernst (1994), Schofield and Shaoul (1996) and Shaoul (1995).

## 10 Urban planning and infrastructure funding

1 Alternative ways in which land use plans can be implemented, some of which require public ownership of land, are described by Neutze (1996).

# Bibliography

Alford, John and O'Neill, Deirdre, eds 1994, *The Contract State,* Centre for Applied Social Research, Deakin University, Geelong.

Aschauer, D. A. 1989, 'Is public expenditure productive', *Journal of Monetary Economics,* vol. 23, pp. 177–200.

Australian Bureau of Statistics 1988–89, *Household Expenditure Survey, Australia: The Effects of Government Benefits and Taxes on Household Income,* Canberra.

Australian Urban and Regional Development Review 1995, 'Financing the Fringe', Australian Urban and Regional Development Review, Discussion Paper No 5, Canberra.

Bailey, Elizabeth A. and Friedlander, Ann F. 1982, 'Market structure and multiproduct industries', *Journal of Economic Literature,* vol. 20, pp. 1024–48.

Baumol, William J. and Sidak, J. Gregory 1994, *Towards Competition in Local Telephony,* AEI Studies in Telecommunications Deregulation, MIT Press, Cambridge, Mass.

Beesley, M. E. and Glaister, S. 1985, 'Deregulating the bus industry in Britain—(C) a response', *Transport Reviews,* vol. 5, pp. 133–42.

Bewley, Ronald and Fiebig, Denzil G. 1988, 'Estimation of price elasticities for an international telephone demand model', *Journal of Industrial Economics,* vol. 36, pp. 393–409.

Bourassa, Steven C. 1995, 'The impacts of borrowing constraints on home ownership in Australia', *Urban Studies,* vol. 32, pp. 1163–74.

Bourassa, Steven C., Greig, Alastair and Troy, Patrick N. 1995, 'The limits of housing policy: home ownership in Australia', *Housing Studies,* vol. 10, pp. 83–104.

Briggs, Sharyn 1994, *Guidelines and Methodology for the Application of Developer Contributions for Social Infrastructure, With a Focus on Queensland (Including Two Case Studies),* Commonwealth Department of Health and Human Services, AGPS, Canberra.

BTCE (Bureau of Transport and Communication Economics) 1988, *Review of Road Costs,* Occasional Paper 90, AGPS, Canberra.

———1984, *Assessment of the Australian Road System,* Report No 56, AGPS, Canberra.

Bureau of Industry Economics 1993, *Waste Management and Landfill Pricing: A Scoping Study,* AGPS, Canberra.

Butlin, N. G., Barnard, A. and Pincus, J.J. 1982, *Government and Capitalism: Public and Private Choice in Twentieth Century Australia,* George Allen & Unwin, Sydney.

Cox, John B. 1994, *Refocussing Road Reform,* Business Council of Australia, Melbourne.

Dahl, Carol and Sterner, Thomas 1991, 'Analysing gasoline demand: a survey', *Energy Economics,* vol. 13, pp. 203–10.

Department of Energy 1989, 'The demand for energy', *The Market for Energy,* eds Dieter Helm, John A. Kay and David Thompson, Oxford University Press, Oxford.

Dixon, Peter B. and Norman, Phillip M. 1989, *A Model of Water Pricing for Melbourne, Sydney and Perth,* Research Report No 2, Urban Water Research Association of Australia, Melbourne.

Economic Planning and Advisory Council 1991, *Issues in the Pricing and Management of Natural Resources,* Background Paper No 16, AGPS, Canberra.

———1995, *Private Infrastructure Task Force Report,* AGPS, Canberra.

Ernst, John 1994, *Whose Utility? The Social Impact of Public Utility Privatisation and Regulation in Britain,* Open University Press, Buckingham.

Evans, Andrew 1990, 'Competition and the structure of local bus markets', *Journal of Transport Economics and Policy,* vol. 24, pp. 255–81.

———1991, 'Are urban bus services natural monopolies?', *Transportation,* vol. 18, pp. 131–50.

Foster, H. S. and Beattie, B.R. 1979, 'On the specification of price in studies of consumer demand under block price scheduling', *Land Economics,* vol. 57, pp. 624–9.

Gilligan, Kevin 1995, 'The investment process', *Investing in Infrastructure,* Australian Urban and Regional Development Review, Workshop Papers No 5, Canberra.

Gomez-Ibanez, J. A. and Meyer, J. R. 1993, *Going Private: The International Experience with Transport Privatization,* The Brooking Institution, Washington DC.

Goodwin, P. B. 1988, 'Circumstances in which people reduce car ownership: a comparative analysis of three panel data sets', *Journal of the International Association of Traffic and Safety Sciences,* vol. 12, no. 2.

———1992, 'A review of new demand elasticities with special reference to short and long run effects of price changes', *Journal of Transport Economics and Policy,* vol. 26, pp. 155–69.

Grant, Malcolm 1982, *Urban Planning Law,* Sweet and Maxwell, London.

Gunn, Hugh F. 1981, 'Travel budgets—a review of evidence and modelling implications', *Transportation Research*, vol. 15A, pp. 7–24.

Gwilliam, K. M., Nash, C. A. and Mackie, P. J. 1985, 'Deregulating the bus industry in Britain--(B) the case against', *Transport Reviews*, vol. 5, pp. 105–32.

Harrison, Bil 1986, 'Electronic road pricing in Hong Kong, 3. Estimating and evaluating the effects', *Traffic Engineering and Control*, vol. 27, (January) 13–8.

Hau, Timothy D. 1990, 'Electronic road pricing: developments in Hong Kong, 1983–1989', *Journal of Transport Economics and Policy*, vol. 24, pp. 203–14.

——1992, *Congestion Charging Mechanisms for Roads: An Evaluation of Current Practice*, Policy Research Working Paper WPS1071, Transport Division, Infrastructure and Urban Development Department, World Bank, Washington DC.

Hensher, David A. 1989, 'Behavioural and resource values of travel time savings: a bicentennial update', *Australian Road Research*, vol. 19, pp. 223–9.

Industries Assistance Commission 1989, *Government (Non-Tax) Charges*, Report No 422, AGPS, Canberra.

Industry Commission 1992, *Water Resources and Waste Water Disposal*, Report No 26, AGPS, Canberra.

——1993, *Taxation and Financial Policy Impacts on Urban Settlements*, Report No 30, AGPS, Canberra.

——1994a, *Urban Transport*, Report No 37, AGPS, Melbourne.

——1994b, *Improving the Efficiency of GBEs*, Information Paper, AGPS, Canberra.

Interstate Commission 1990, *Road Use Charges and Vehicle Registration: A National Scheme*, AGPS, Canberra.

Ironmonger, D. S. 1972, *New Commodities and Consumer Behaviour*, Cambridge University Press, Cambridge.

Katz, Bernard S. 1982, 'Infrastructure', *Encyclopedia of Economics*, ed D. Greenwald, McGraw-Hill, New York.

Kearney, Colm 1995, 'Public Infrastructure and Private Investment: Theory and Australian Evidence', *Investing in Infrastructure*, Australian Urban and Regional Development Review, Workshop Papers No 5, Canberra.

Keeler, Theodor E. and Small, Kenneth A. 1977, 'Optimal peak-load pricing, investment and service levels on urban expressways', *Journal of Political Economy*, vol. 85, pp. 1–25.

Kennedy, David 1995, 'London bus tendering: an overview', *Transport Reviews*, vol. 15, pp. 253–64.

King, Stephen 1994, 'Review of Baumol and Sidak 1994', *Economic Record*, vol. 70, pp. 462–5.

Kinhill Cameron McNamara 1994, 'Reducing dependence in development contributions: efficient and equitable charging for urban infrastructure', report prepared for the Australian Urban and Regional Development Review, Canberra.

Kirwan, Richard 1991, 'Financing urban infrastructure: equity and efficiency considerations', National Housing Strategy, Background Paper 4, AGPS, Canberra.

Kraus, Marvin 1981, 'Scale economies analysis for urban highway networks', *Journal of Urban Economics,* vol. 9, pp. 1–22.

Lago, Armando M., Mayworm, Patrick D. and McEnroe, J. Mathew 1981, 'Further evidence on aggregate and disaggregate transit fare elasticities', *Transportation Research Record,* no. 799, pp. 42–7.

Lancaster, K. J. 1966, 'A new approach to consumer theory', *Journal of Political Economy,* vol. 74, pp. 132–157.

Luck, D. P. and Martin, I.J. 1988, *Review of Road Cost Recovery,* Bureau of Transport and Communication Economics, Occasional Paper 90, AGPS, Canberra.

Lyman, R. Ashley 1992, 'Peak and off-peak residential demand', *Water Resources Research,* vol. 28, pp. 219–67.

Mackie, Peter, Preston, John and Nash, Chris 1995, 'Bus deregulation: ten years on', *Transport Reviews,* vol. 15, pp. 229–51.

Marchetti, C. 1992, *Anthropological Invariants in Travel Behaviour,* International Institute of Applied Systems Analysis, Laxenburg, Austria.

Martin, Randolph C. and Wilder, Ronald P. 1992, 'Residential demand for water and the pricing of municipal water services', *Public Finance Quarterly,* vol. 20, pp. 93–102.

Mathews, Russel 1967, *Public Investment in Australia,* F.W. Cheshire, Melbourne.

Mees, Paul 1996, *Do Public Choice and Public Transport Mix? An Australian–Canadian Comparison,* Working Paper No. 57, Urban Research Program, Australian National University, Canberra.

Mehra, R. and Prescott, E. C. 1985, 'The equity premium: a puzzle', *Journal of Monetary Economics,* vol. 15, pp. 145–61.

Metropolitan Water Sewerage and Drainage Board 1967, *Annual Report for the Year Ended 30 June, 1967,* Sydney.

Metropolitan Water Sewerage and Drainage Board 1985, *Annual Report for the Year Ended 30 June 1985,* Sydney.

Mills, Edwin C. 1972, *Studies in the Structure of the Urban Economy,* Johns Hopkins Press, Baltimore.

Mohring, H. 1972, 'Optimisation and scale economies in urban bus transportation', *American Economic Review,* vol. 62, pp. 591–604.

——1976, *Transportation Economics,* Ballinger, Cambridge, Mass.

Moncur, James E. T. 1987, 'Urban water pricing and drought management', *Water Resources Research,* vol. 23, no. 3, pp. 25–30.

Mountain, D. C. and Lawson, E. L. 1992, 'A disaggregated nonhomothetic modelling of responsiveness to residential time-of-use electricity rates', *International Economic Review*, vol. 33, pp. 181–207.

Muth, Richard F. 1969, *Cities and Housing*, University of Chicago Press, Chicago.

Nash, C.A. 1993, 'British bus deregulation', *Economic Journal*, vol. 103, pp. 1042–9.

National Capital Planning Authority 1993a, *Infrastructure Coordination and Land Release Systems*, Better Cities Program Occasional Paper Series 1, Paper 1, AGPS, Canberra.

——1993b, *Designing Subdivisions to Save and Manage Water*, Better Cities Program Occasional Paper Series 1, Paper 3, AGPS, Canberra.

Neutze, Max 1965, *Economic Policy and the Size of Cities*, Australian National University Press, Canberra.

——1978, *Australian Urban Policy*, George Allen & Unwin, Sydney.

——1993, 'Infrastructure funding techniques: an economic perspective, in *Infrastructure Funding Techniques*, Better Cities Program, Occasional Paper Series 1, Paper 7, AGPS, Canberra.

——1996, *Two Kinds of Land Use Planning*, Centre for Urban Planning and Environmental Management, University of Hong Kong, Working Paper No. 68.

Ng, Yew-Kwang 1987, 'Equity, efficiency and financial viability: public utility pricing with special reference to water supply', *Australian Economic Review*, 3rd Quarter 1987, pp. 21–35.

Nieswiadomy, Michael L. 1992, 'Residential water demand—price, conservation and education', *Water Resources Research*, vol. 28, pp. 609-15.

Nieswiadomy, Michael L. and Molina, David J. 1989, 'Comparing residential water demand under decreasing and increasing block rates using household data', *Land Economics*, vol. 65, pp. 280–9.

Noam, Eli 1992, 'A theory for the instability of public telecommunications systems', *The Economics of Information Networks*, ed C. Antonelli, Elsevier Science Publishers, Amsterdam.

New South Wales Auditor General 1994, *Private Participation in the Provision of Public Infrastructure: The Roads and Traffic Authority*, Sydney.

OECD 1987, *Pricing of Water Services*, Paris.

OFWAT 1994, *Future Charges for Water and Sewerage Services*, Report, Birmingham, July 1994.

Otto, G. and Voss, G. 1994, 'Public capital and private sector productivity', *Economic Record*, vol. 70, pp. 121–32.

Parmenter, B. R. and Webb, L. R. 1976, 'Amortization and public pricing policies', *Australian Economic Papers*, vol. 15, pp. 11–27.

Paterson, John 1971, 'Water utilities and water resources', *Issues in the Pricing and Management of Natural Resources*, Economic Planning and Advisory Council, AGPS, Canberra.

Peiser, Richard 1988, 'Calculating equity-neutral water and sewer impact fees', *American Planning Association Journal*, vol. 54, pp. 38–48.

*Penguin and Macquarie Dictionary of Economics and Finance* 1988, Penguin Books Australia, Ringwood.

Pigon, A.C. 1932, *The Economics of Welfare*, 4th edn, Macmillan, London.

Pitchford, John 1993, 'The exchange rate and international policy in Australia', *The Exchange Rate and Macroeconomic Policy in Australia*, ed A. Blundell-Wignall, Reserve Bank of Australia, Sydney.

Quiggin, John 1994, *Does Privatisation Pay?*, The Australia Institute, Discussion Paper No. 2, Canberra.

Ramsey, F. P. 1927, 'A contribution to the theory of taxation', *Economic Journal*, vol. 37, pp. 47–61.

Renzetti, Steven 1992, 'Evaluating the welfare effects of reforming municipal water prices', *Journal of Environmental Economics and Management*, vol. 22, pp. 147–63.

Richardson, Harry W. and Gordon, Peter 1989, 'Counting nonwork trips', *Urban Land*, (September), pp. 6–12.

Sagoff, Mark 1988, *The Economy of the Earth*, Cambridge University Press, Cambridge.

Schofield, Richard and Shaoul, Jean 1996, 'Regulating the Water Industry: Swimming Against the Tide or Going Through the Motions?,' Bolton Business School and Manchester University, unpublished.

Sexton, Richard J., Sexton, Terri A., Wann, Joyce Jong-Wen and Kling, Catherine L. 1989, 'The conservation and welfare effects of information in a time-of-day pricing experiment', *Land Economics,* vol. 65, pp. 272–79.

Skaburskis, Andrejs and Qadeer, Mohammad 1992, 'An empirical estimation of the price effects of development impact fees', *Urban Studies*, vol. 29, pp. 653–67.

Skinner, Rob 1995, 'The Resource Balance', *Investing in Infrastructure*, Australian Urban and Regional Development Review, Workshop Papers No 5, Canberra.

Small, Kenneth A. 1982, 'The scheduling of consumer activities: work trips', *American Economic Review*, vol. 72, pp. 467–79.

——1992, *Urban Transportation Economics*, Harwood, Chur, Switzerland.

Small, Kenneth A., Winston, Clifford and Evans, Carol A. 1989, *Road Work: A New Highway Pricing and Investment Policy*, Brooking Institution, Washington DC.

Snyder, T. P. and Stegman M.A. 1987, *Paying for Growth: Using Development Fees to Finance Infrastructure*, Urban Land Institute, Washington DC.

Thomas, J. and Syme, G. 1988, 'Estimating residential price elasticity of demand for water: a contingent valuation approach', *Water Resources Research*, vol. 24, pp. 1847–57.

Troy, Patrick N. 1996, *The Perils of Urban Consolidation,* Federation Press, Sydney.

Turvey, Ralph 1969, 'Marginal cost', *The Economic Journal*, vol. 79, pp. 282–9.

——1976, 'Analysing the marginal cost of water supply', *Land Economics*, vol. 52, pp. 159–68.

United States Department of Transport, Federal Highway Administration (US FHA) 1982, *Final Report on the Federal Highway Cost Allocation Study*, Washington DC.

Vickrey, William S. 1980, 'Optimal transit subsidy policy', *Transportation*, vol. 9, pp. 389–409.

——1985, 'The fallacy of using long-run cost for peak load pricing', *Quarterly Journal of Economics*, vol. 95, pp. 1331–4.

Viswanath, M. N. 1989, 'Effect of controls on water consumption in Newcastle', *Water*, August, 1989, pp. 18–21.

Voith, R. 1991, 'The long run elasticity of demand for commuter rail transportation', *Journal of Urban Economics*, vol. 30, pp. 360–72.

Walters, A. A. 1987, 'Congestion', *The New Palgrave: A Dictionary of Economics*, eds John Eatwell, Murray Milgate and Peter Newman, Macmillan, London.

Water Board 1994a, *Clean Waterways Report*, Sydney.

——1994b, *Special Environmental Levy Management Report*, Sydney.

White, P. R. 1990, 'Bus deregulation: a welfare balance sheet', *Journal of Transport Economics and Policy*, vol. 24, pp. 311–32.

# Index

community service obligations, 31,
130, 134–6, 148, 157, 171, 215,
260
competition, 201, 208–15, 218,
222–6
composting, 246–7; toilets, 86, 246
compulsory land acquisition, 30
congestion, 34–5, 42–3, 100–1, 103;
pricing *see* roads, funding of
contestability of markets, 211, 218,
222–7
contracting out, 198–200, 221
coordination, 236–7
costs, 33–62; effects of location on,
61, 73–4; historic, 104–5; long
and short run, 33–48, 136–45;
variable, 139 *see also* marginal
cost pricing
Cox, John B., 259
cross-elasticities of demand, 80, 85,
91–2
cross-subsidies, 134–6
Cumberland County Council, 239

Dahl, Carol, 71
deferral of expenditure, 11
demand, 63–95; for access, 65,
75–8, 82, 88; derived, 69–70; at
different locations, 72–8;
elasticity of, 63–4, 68–95,
115–16, 122;
in the short and the long run,
68–72, 84–5, 91, 93, 141–2;
non-price influences on, 64–6, 85;
for reliability, 78, 81, 86, 88–90,
92, 94;
time distribution of, 74; for
volume, 68–74 *see also* peak
demand
Department of Energy, 71
depreciation, 179, 183–7, 192–5
deregulation, 220–5
developer requirements/charges, 10,
75–8, 108–11, 117–25, 133–4,
150, 152–8, 181, 191, 198–9,
233–6; effects of house prices,

118–25; for on-site and off-site
costs, 117–18, 121–4
distributional considerations *see*
equity
dividend payments by suppliers,
179–82, 186–90
Dixon, Peter, B., 258
drainage *see* stormwater drainage
Drinking Water Inspectorate, 228
driving licences, 115
durability of infrastructure assets,
23–5, 59

Economic Planning and Advisory
Council, 200
economies of scale, 20–2, 25,
33–5, 37–48 *passim*, 101–2,
208–10, 222–3; in garbage
services, 21; multiproduct, 53–8;
in public transport, 171; in roads,
21–2; in water and sewerage
services, 20–1
economies of scope, 53–8
efficiency in resource use, 96–102,
112–13
electricity supply, 90–2, 173;
and the environment, 6, 67–8
energy, home collection of, 248–9
England and Wales, 227–30
environment, 3–6, 40–2, 87, 102–4,
148, 202, 214, 237;
costs of damage to, 60–1
equity, 30–2, 107–11, 113–14,
119–36, 143, 148, 203, 214–15,
219, 239–40
Ernst, John, 28, 229, 260
essential services, 28–9, 197, 202,
204, 218
Evans, Andrew, 222–3
externalities, 27–8, 30, 102–4, 131,
148–9, 157–8, 219

Fiebig, Denzil G., 93
fixed charges, 101–2
flood mitigation, 67
Foster, H.S., 64
franchising, 203–5

## PUBLIC POLICY IN AUSTRALIA

### Second edition

### G. Davis, J. Wanna, J. Warhurst and P. Weller

How do Australian governments make decisions? Are the problems facing decision-makers here unique? What impact do the federal system, an active state, the structure of government and the behaviour of parties and pressure groups have on the policy outcomes?

*Public Policy in Australia* addressed those questions and introduced students to the study of public policy. This second edition has been almost entirely re-written, drawing on recent experiences in Australia and on analyses of public policy here and overseas. By skilfully interweaving theories of government with the analysis of Australian institutions and actions, it provides a lively, stimulating and realistic account of the government of Australia. It emphasises the importance of values, interests and resources, working through institutions and mediated by that essential ingredient—politics.

Designed for undergraduate and masters courses, *Public Policy in Australia* is essential reading for students of public policy, political science, public administration and applied economics; indeed, for anyone with an interest in how and why governments make the choices they do.

**Glyn Davis** and **John Wanna** are Senior Lecturers in Politics and Public Policy in the Faculty of Commerce and Administration at Griffith University. **John Warhurst** is Professor of Politics at the University of New England. **Patrick Weller** is Professor of Politics and Public Policy and Director of the Centre for Australian Public Sector Management at Griffith University.

ISBN 1 86373 433 3

## THE GREAT EXPERIMENT

*Labour parties and public policy transformation in Australia and New Zealand*

Edited by

### FRANCIS G. CASTLES, ROLF GERRITSEN AND JACK VOWLES

*Labour parties came to power in Australia in 1983 and in New Zealand in 1984. In both countries, the new governments embarked on programs of economic and social transformation more comprehensive in scope and intensity than elsewhere in the Western World.*

The authors of this book seek to understand the causes, processes and consequences of these changes in both nations. A broad spectrum of policy areas is examined—economic, constitutional, industrial relations, social and environmental policies, foreign relations, women's policies and indigenous affairs. Each area is analysed jointly by specialists from both sides of the Tasman to ensure a truly comparative study.

*The Great Experiment* examines the ways in which public policies have been transformed in Australia and New Zealand, the contrasts between the two nations and the likely consequences for politics and future policy directions. It is a book for those who wish to understand politics and policy development over the past decade. It is, at the same time, a book which, for the very first time, makes it possible to add a meaningful component to courses in both Australian and New Zealand politics and public policy.

**Francis G. Castles** is Professor of Public Policy at the Australian National University. **Dr Rolf Gerritsen** is a leading figure in the fields of Australian politics and political economy who now teaches at the University of Canberra. **Dr Jack Vowles** of the University of Waikato is a prominent New Zealand political scientist and electoral specialist.

ISBN 1 86448 003 3

# HUMAN ECOLOGY, HUMAN ECONOMY

*Ideas for an ecologically sustainable future*

*Edited by*

MARK DIESENDORF AND CLIVE HAMILTON

'*A brilliant synthesis of ecology and economics that provides a sure guide to a sustainable future. It is a must for all environmentalists and economists.*'

CHARLES BIRCH

'*This book is such a useful guide to responsible decision-making that it should be supplied in bulk to senior government officials and managers in the private sector.*'

IAN LOWE

Human well-being is wholly dependent upon the continued good health of the Earth's ecosystems. Human behaviour as it interacts with the biophysical environment is enormously complex, as governments (and individuals) who must make decisions about resource use are becoming increasingly aware. *Human Ecology, Human Economy* provides the basic concepts and tools for understanding how to analyse that interaction.

*Human Ecology, Human Economy* is designed to be used as a text for undergraduate and graduate students in environmental studies, human and social ecology, ecological economics, futures studies and science and technology studies. It is also intended for interested members of the public and for policy-makers working on environmental issues—especially where these intersect with economic policy.

**Professor Mark Diesendorf** is Director of the Institute for Sustainable Futures at the University of Technology, Sydney and Vice President of the Sustainable Energy Industries Council of Australia.

**Dr Clive Hamilton** is Executive Director of the Australia Institute, Canberra and teaches in the Public Policy Program at the Australian National University.

ISBN 1 86448 288 5

# ACCOUNTABILITY AND CORRUPTION

## *Public sector ethics*

Edited by

### GORDON L. CLARK, ELIZABETH PRIOR JONSON AND WAYNE CALDOW

*'I have never regarded politics as the arena of morals. It is the arena of interests.'*

ANEURAN BEVIN

*'The Australians appear to a man to regard their politicians as time-serving crooks or simple-minded hirelings.'*

JIM CAMERON

Why have political institutions failed to live up to our expectations? Why do we need enquiries into the conduct of state and federal agencies such as the police and departments of education and elected officials, including state premiers and federal senators?

In *Accountability and Corruption*, politicians and political analysts draw on their first-hand experience to explore the tensions between political power and ethical ideas. Each is thoroughly conversant with the realities of political life and draws the reader into the world of political action to demonstrate the difficulties faced in sustaining ethical practice in public service. Their findings will inform and challenge citizens to understand better why the role of ethics in maintaining a workable political system is becoming increasingly an issue in our contemporary pluralist society.

Before becoming Halford Mackinder Professor of Geography at the University of Oxford, **Gordon L. Clark** was director of the Institute of Ethics and Public Policy at Monash University. **Dr Elizabeth Prior Jonson** is a program director at the Institute of Ethics and Public Policy. **Wayne Caldow** is a doctoral student in urban political economy at Monash University.

ISBN 1 86448 423 3

## PUBLIC VOICES, PRIVATE INTERESTS

### Australia's media policy

#### Edited by

#### JENNIFER CRAIK, JULIE JAMES BAILEY and ALBERT MORAN

*Public Voices, Private Interests* examines the social and policy context of Australian media and communications in the 1990s.

Dealing with both print and the broadcast media, it covers the key areas of debate: new communications technologies; deregulation; cable and pay television; major restructuring within the communications industries; and Australian content requirements. It also includes chapters on community radio, SBS and Aboriginal and Torres Strait Islander media.

This collection is essential reading for students in Media Studies and Politics, and anyone looking for a better understanding of our Fourth Estate.

**Jennifer Craik** is Deputy Director of the Institute for Cultural Policy Studies. **Julie James Bailey** is Professor in the School of Film and Media Studies. **Albert Moran** is an Australian Research Council Senior Research Fellow. All are at Griffith University, Brisbane.

ISBN 1 86373 628 X